ALSO BY WALTER LAQUEUR

Fascism: Past, Present, Future

Russia and Germany: A Century of Conflict

The Dream That Failed: Reflections on the Soviet Union

Breaking the Silence: The German Who Exposed the Final Solution

Europe in Our Time: A History, 1945–1992

Soviet Union 2000: Reform or Revolution

A History of Zionism

Young Germany: A History of the German Youth Movement

Looking Forward, Looking Backward

The Human Rights Reader

Stalin

The Age of Terrorism

Guerrilla: A Historical and Critical Study

Weimar: A Cultural History

The Road to War

Thursday's Child Has Far to Go

*The Israel-Arab Reader:
A Documentary History of the Middle East Conflict*

Fascism: A Readers' Guide

The Guerrilla Reader

The Terrorism Reader

The Missing Years

THE
TERRIBLE
SECRET

THE TERRIBLE SECRET

SUPPRESSION OF THE TRUTH ABOUT HITLER'S "FINAL SOLUTION"

With a new introduction by the author

WALTER LAQUEUR

Owl Books
Henry Holt and Company   New York

Henry Holt and Company, Inc.
Publishers since 1866
115 West 18th Street
New York, New York 10011

Henry Holt® is a registered trademark
of Henry Holt and Company, Inc.

Library of Congress Cataloging-in-Publication Data
Laqueur, Walter.
The terrible secret: suppression of the truth about Hitler's
"final solution": with a new introduction by the author / Walter
Laqueur.—1st Owl books ed.
        p.   cm.
Includes bibliographical references and index.
ISBN 0-8050-5984-9
1. Holocaust, Jewish (1939–1945)—Censorship.   I. Title.
D810.J4L278   1998   98-27001
940.53'18—dc21   CIP

Henry Holt books are available for special promotions and
premiums. For details contact: Director, Special Markets.

First published in Great Britain by
Weidenfeld and Nicolson in 1980

First published in the United States by
Little, Brown and Company in 1981

First Owl Books Edition 1998

Printed in the United States of America
All first editions are printed on acid-free paper.∞

1   3   5   7   9   10   8   6   4   2

CONTENTS

THE
TERRIBLE
SECRET

INTRODUCTION

THIS book first appeared in 1980; since then it has been
reprinted numerous times and translated into a dozen languages. Although several of the topics I covered had already
been touched on in a number of valuable monographs, my
book was the first, I believe, to bring together and examine
the many questions raised by the 'terrible secret': When did
the Jews in occupied Europe know about their destination
(and their destiny)? To what extent were the Germans in the
Reich informed? When and through what channels did the
information reach London, Washington, and the capitals of
the neutral states? When did it reach Palestine? And finally, if
so much was known so early, why was it so often disbelieved or,
at best, discounted as exaggeration? I did not specifically address one obvious question that flowed from the others: What
could have been done to help the victims? At the time, the
material available was simply not sufficient to allow for a comprehensive appraisal. I am all the more grateful, therefore,
for the new information that has surfaced, and for the revela-
tion it offers about what was and was not known in those crucial years.

These new books and articles, as well as the new material
discovered in formerly inaccessible archives, complement my
work to a substantial extent. Far from revising my earlier conclusions, the details that have come to light reinforce them,
with the result that one can now write with far greater certainty about the events of that time. Twenty years ago, for example, it was still widely argued that prior to the summer of
1944, no one in the West, and hardly anyone in occupied Europe, had heard anything but vague rumours of Auschwitz
and the other extermination camps. While it is of course
highly unlikely that everyone knew everything, it now seems
clear that much fuller information was available than was earlier thought and that it reached even people who were almost

totally isolated and had no access to privileged sources of information. I myself can attest to this: As I was writing this introduction I received from relatives of my late wife, Naomi, a number of letters I had written to my in-laws from a kibbutz in what was then Palestine. In these letters, written between 1942 and 1944, I found mention of Auschwitz and other extermination camps. I was certainly not privy to information unavailable to others.

It has taken a full fifty years for other similar documents to be unearthed. The diary of Viktor Klemperer, published only in 1995, is a case in point. A retired professor of Romance languages, Klemperer was living in Dresden with his Aryan wife in 1942. His marriage protected him from deportation, but he assumed that sooner or later his turn too would come. Totally cut off from the outside world, living in a 'Jew House', forbidden to have a radio or buy a newspaper, virtually unable to speak to anyone but his Jewish neighbours, Klemperer kept a journal that did not appear until more than thirty years after his death. A sensation in Germany, it is a unique document that describes in agonizing detail the daily suffering in those years of despair.

What is of interest in the present context is the fact that this man, living in a virtual vacuum, was well informed early on about the terrible secret. The first Jews were deported from Dresden in November 1941; within a few days Klemperer noted in his diary that those on the train had all been killed in Lithuania upon their arrival. Not only does he mention Theresienstadt (which is close to Dresden), but in 1942–43 he repeatedly refers to Auschwitz as one of the main killing sites. He knew in 1942 that Vienna and Berlin were about to become *Judenrein*, free of Jews, and that the Romanian Jews had been massacred. He knew within a few weeks about the Warsaw ghetto uprising; this news was confirmed by a variety of sources. He noted many times in his diary that those deported to Poland would never return and that other Jews shared his conviction. In fact, the Gestapo had told them as much. Well before the end of the war an acquaintance in Dresden gave him a more or less exact breakdown of the number of victims in Eastern Europe. The figure he cited was approximately the same as the one generally accepted today.

Klemperer's informant was not an intelligence officer with superior sources in many parts of the world but a Dresden Jewish butcher of no particular intellectual sophistication.

Early on, in Switzerland, too, there was more widespread knowledge about the 'final solution' than I was aware of when I wrote this book. The information came from a great variety of sources, including Swiss diplomatic representatives abroad. While the Swiss envoy in Berlin, Hans Froehlicher (and the political secretary Kappeler) tried to suppress all information unfavourable to the Nazi regime, dissidents like Franz Rudolf von Weiss, the consul general in Cologne, made no secret of what they knew. In November 1941 Weiss sent the Swiss legation in Berlin a detailed account of the deportation of Cologne's Jews; the deportees, he said, were certain that they faced death. His report provoked the ire of his superiors. Even more detailed reports about the fate of Jews in Romania were received from René de Weck, the Swiss envoy in Bucharest, who told of the Jassy pogrom in January 1941, perhaps the greatest spontaneous pogrom in Europe, as well as of events in Transniestria and Odessa and other parts of the Soviet Union. On his annual leave in Switzerland, de Weck met with the Swiss foreign minister, colleagues from the foreign ministry, and political commentators.

Swiss businessmen traveled widely in Eastern Europe during the war and while they were not as a rule permitted to enter concentration camps, they saw and reported a great deal; one of them, for instance, had been present when twenty thousand Jews were killed in Odessa in 1941. Other important Swiss sources previously unknown to me were the records of interrogations of German deserters, whose numbers were not insignificant in 1942–3. Swiss military intelligence had only limited interest in the fate of the Jews but some of the deserters had witnessed scenes of mass murder and their eyewitness accounts can be found in the Swiss archives. Yet other accounts came from sick and severely injured Polish soldiers (among them several Jews) who reached Switzerland when the Red Cross arranged an exchange of prisoners in the summer of 1942. Nor had I been fully aware of the role of the radical press in wartime Switzerland. Periodicals such as *Nation*, *La Sentinelle* and *Das Israelitische Wochenblatt*, the organ of the

Jewish community in Switzerland, were of course subject to censorship. Yet while they carried on a guerrilla war with the authorities, forever afraid that irresponsible journalists might provoke Goebbels, a great amount of information did manage to get through. Virtually every major extermination camp, including Auschwitz, Majdanek, Treblinka, and Sobibor, was mentioned in their pages as early as 1942, even though the dimensions of the mass murder were not fully known.

In the earlier edition of this book, I described in some detail how the International Red Cross (IRC), despite receiving a steady flow of information about the 'final solution' from its own representatives as well as from Jewish organizations and the Allied governments, decided in October 1942 not to make the facts public. Whether the Red Cross could have taken any action at the time is not clear (toward the end of the war, in any case, it did extend help to Jews, for instance in Hungary); our present concern is how much the Red Cross knew. This question is largely answered by the work of an independent Swiss historian, Jean Claude Favez, whom the International Red Cross, responding to criticism of its silence during the war, commissioned to examine its archives and to write a definitive study. Favez had considerably more sources at his disposal than I had, yet the conclusions he reached were not dissimilar to mine. He quotes the letter of a member of the IRC executive committee to a British Red Cross representative: 'It is a very tragic situation,' she writes, 'and we cannot do anything about it.' This could have been the motto of the IRC all along. Needless to say, however, Favez's conclusions did not please the IRC, which published an appendix to Favez's book taking issue with his references to Laqueur's *The Terrible Secret* (which the IRC thought was not sufficiently 'scientific') and, generally speaking, with his assessment of the measure of knowledge at the organization's disposal. Even now, decades after the holocaust, the Red Cross apologist argues, it is hardly possible to fathom this greatest defeat of civilization and humanity. But this is hardly a persuasive line, for no one expected a philosophical analysis of the holocaust in 1942. The trouble with the International Red Cross is not that it failed to understand the reasons, but that it refused, however diffidently and indirectly, to share its information

about the disaster. More recently there have been further revelations about unseemly practises of individual IRC agents during the war. It was a difficult period and it would have been
wiser for the organization to have admitted that mistakes
were committed than to attempt to paint its wartime actions
in the best possible light.

By far the most important source of information has of
course been Poland, where the greatest number of massacres
took place. The Polish underground reported to the Polish
Government-in-exile almost every day: shorter items were
sent by wireless, longer, more detailed ones by courier to London. It can now be established with certainty that the first report of massacres was dated 30 August 1941. Civilian and
military underground leaders sent further detailed information from Poland during September and October. The gist of
this information was published in the *Bulletin* of the Jewish
Telegraphic Agency and *Dziennik Polski*, the Polish daily newspaper in London, on 29 October and 31 October 1941 respectively. Subsequent reports were transmitted to the Jewish
members of the Polish National Council. What all these accounts portrayed was a picture of devastation: 10,000 Jews
had been killed in Wlodzimierz; 8,000 in Pinsk; 6,000 in
Brzesz; in Homsk, Motel, and Kobryn, every Jew had been
killed. As for the areas to the north and east of Poland, most
Lithuanian Jews had been murdered, with the exception of
40,000 who remained in Vilna. In Borislaw, Mohylev, and
other cities where there had been major Jewish communities,
not a single Jew was left.

We now know that during the first half of 1942 the systematic extermination of Polish Jewry was reported by the Polish
underground and Jewish sources such as the *Bund*, the Polish
Jewish Labour party. The *Bund* report that reached London
before the end of May estimated the number of people killed
as 700,000 and insisted that their murders were part of a general plan, not isolated 'pogroms' however massive in scale.
Even before the London *Daily Telegraph* published a front-
page story on the *Bund* report, the Polish Cabinet had sent a
report to the Allied government. Over the next few days the
British Broadcasting Corporation made the news available in
various languages. In a press conference sponsored by the

World Jewish Congress in June, one million Jews were reported to have already been murdered. Stanislaw Mikolajczyk, the Polish Minister of the Interior for the Government-in-exile, estimated that the number of Jewish victims was merely 200,000, but he nevertheless mentions the existence of major extermination camps such as Belzec, as well as the use of poison gas.

News of the liquidation of the Warsaw ghetto on 22 July 1942 reached London within four days. It was said that 6,000 Jews were being deported daily; the actual figure was considerably higher. The Polish underground in Warsaw complained after the war that while it had sent many reports about this event to London, both the BBC and the Polish Government-in-exile were reluctant to publish them. In fact, only three such reports have been found; others may have been lost: a third or even more of the dispatches from Warsaw were lost in transmission. It is also possible, as Dariusz Stola has recently pointed out, that more stringent Polish censorship in London prevented the publication of details and that the arrest of a group of Swedes in Warsaw who had acted as couriers hindered the transmission of information. Be that as it may, the essential information was available in June and July 1942 and the liquidation of the Warsaw ghetto with its 400,000 inhabitants only confirmed what was by then a near certainty, that it was Nazi policy to exterminate Polish and East European Jewry altogether.

More is now known than twenty years ago about the extent of knowledge among the Jews in Palestine. Zionist emissaries in Istanbul, Switzerland, and other places sent home a steady stream of information; couriers sent to Eastern Europe, the Balkans, and even Germany also brought back a great deal of information. The recently uncovered personal archive of Nathan Schwalb, an emissary stationed in Switzerland, is of particular interest. Schwalb conducted a one-man rescue operation, dispatching money, couriers, and reports; the workings of this network have been described in some detail by Gad Beck, who was then a Jewish youth movement activist in Berlin. But while much publicity was given in the Jewish press in Palestine to the reports about mass killings, it was only following the arrival in Haifa in November 1942 of a group of

Palestinian repatriates, who had been caught in Europe when the war broke out, that the Zionist leadership finally accepted the facts they had somewhat doubted earlier on.

Only within the last few years has it become clear how much the British knew through their celebrated decoding operations. Not only military historians but also the public at large is now aware that the British had broken the most secret German codes and were reading the messages exchanged by the Germans during much of the war. Not every fact was reported in these messages, for the simple reason that no one would have dreamed of using the wireless for reports over short distances. Moreover, decoding could take a long time, and whenever the Germans changed their codes there was bound to be a lag until the Allied decoders could catch up. But the amount of information obtained in London about the European theatre of war is indeed astounding and historians have speculated for a long time on how much information about the holocaust was received by the Allies in this way. Some historians doubted whether anything of significance percolated from this source prior to 1944; others, including myself, suspected that the British had decoded a tremendous amount of information even though they did not publicize this fact. This dispute was finally settled in 1996 when decrypts released in London revealed that British Intelligence knew virtually from the day Hitler launched the invasion of the Soviet Union that the *Einsatzgruppen*, the special unit that had been set up to kill Jews, had started their sinister operations. Almost daily, reports were intercepted detailing the number of Jews killed by what unit and where. On 12 September 1941, for instance, the following note was sent by the chief decrypter to Churchill and designated recipients: 'The fact that the Police are killing all Jews that fall into their hands should by now be sufficiently appreciated. It is not therefore proposed to continue reporting these butcheries specially, unless so requested.'

Senior intelligence officers knew, but did anyone else? Perhaps these officers kept this information to themselves because it was of no military use, as some historians have suggested? Since Churchill countersigned the reports sent to him, and since these reports included information about the mass murder, this debate too has been settled. We are not certain with whom Churchill shared this information, but precisely because it was not of great military or operational importance, he may well have talked about it to others. We know, for example, that Churchill in a public speech at the time mentioned that mass murder was being committed by police battalions, a fact that was as yet quite unknown.

In reviewing all this new information, I do not mean to suggest that no more work needs to be done. On the contrary, I can think of at least three major lacunae. One concerns, paradoxically, the situation inside Germany. The extermination of the Jews was considered a state secret in Nazi Germany. It could be discussed in a small circle but only indirectly, by way of hints and circumlocution, in the mass media and in public speeches. And yet, a massive amount of information was available to hundreds of thousands, perhaps millions, of Germans from an early date in the testimony of eyewitnesses, in the aesopian (and not so aesopian) language of bureaucratic memoranda, and in the personal letters and memoirs written at the time. These many sources have not yet been systematically explored, perhaps because the amount of material is so overwhelming. Just as my letters were returned to me after fifty years, there must be many thousands of such collections that survived, at least some of which, despite official censorship and self-censorship, must contain references to the persecution of the Jews.

Nor do we know the extent of the Vatican's knowledge. Through its international connections the Catholic Church was the first to hear of the mass murder but to date no outsiders and only a few trusted priests have had access to its archives. What publications there have been are selective and of an official character.

Glasnost has not yet reached the Vatican, but nor has it been practised in Russia. Though details about other aspects of recent Soviet history have come to light, the matter of Soviet knowledge of the murder of the Jews remains shrouded in secrecy. And yet the Kremlin must have known a great deal: Soviet intelligence had many informants behind the German lines. That the murder of the Jews did not figure high on the Soviet agenda goes without saying. But some of the information they received and relayed to Stalin and other Soviet leaders must have touched on it. With few exceptions, neither the files of military intelligence nor those of the NKVD have yet been opened. True, even if Moscow and Rome had had a full and accurate picture early on, they are not likely to have taken action. But still it is important to know.

Despite these lacunae, however, it is abundantly clear from the sources that have become available since my book was published that the murder of European Jewry was not a secret, even if the Nazi leadership tried to make it so. This is no surprise: the disappearance of millions of people could hardly be concealed. Yet how do we explain the claims of many Germans after the war that they had not known the destiny of the Jews, and how do we explain the corresponding unawareness of many Jews that their deportations could lead only to one end?

As for the Germans, except for those who directly or indirectly participated in the mass murders or who happened to witness them, few had a full picture of the 'final solution'. Nor did many of them know details, for instance about the gas chambers. But they did know that the Jews disappeared and they assumed that they would never return. When Goebbels and the Nazi security services spoke of the 'harsh measures' taken against the Jews, these could not possibly have been understood as referring merely to the fact that Jews were compelled to leave their homes or forced into hard labor, for millions of Germans also had to give up their homes and do all kinds of things that were dangerous or unpleasant or involved great physical effort. In wartime these are not 'harsh measures'. 'Harsh measures' could mean only one thing and since Hitler had spelled it out – destruction and extermination – even before the outbreak of war, the destiny of the Jews was not in doubt. But neither was it a very important issue for most Germans, who feared for their families and friends, and themselves suffered all manner of deprivations and dangers. The murder of the Jews was a minor affair that dominated the thinking of very few Germans. It was also an unpleasant affair, something no one felt particularly proud of – and therefore better suppressed. Those who later argued they hadn't known that between five and six million Jews had been killed, many of them in gas chambers, were not lying: neither the number of victims nor the manner of killing had ever appeared in the papers. And yet, people did know that the Jews had perished.

The extent of knowledge among Allied leaders and the public in Britain, America, and the neutral countries was also greater than commonly believed, and a similar mechanism was in operation: The fate of the Jews was not a secret, but it seemed a small matter in comparison with the truly decisive issue, namely the conduct of war. How much longer would the war last, how many more sacrifices would be required for victory, what kind of future awaited the neutrals? As far as the Allied leaders were concerned, any effort to save Jews would only distract from the general war effort; moreover, they reasoned, the Jews would be safe only when Nazi Germany was destroyed and full victory achieved. That the victory might come too late for the victims was bound to be a matter of little concern. Since, as it seemed to these leaders, nothing could and should be done to help these unfortunates, knowledge of their fate had to be relegated to a secondary place or temporarily forgotten. In time of war leaders had to concentrate on what was absolutely essential, and the fate of the Jews of Europe was certainly not among their high priorities.

As for the Jews, we have it from many sources that they knew that those deported to the camps were facing certain death. But there is also evidence that many of those arriving in the camps not only from distant countries like Holland and Greece but also from Germany and Austria were devastated when they understood that they were about to be killed. This they had not expected.

What had they expected? Deprivation, hard labour, inclement weather, difficult living conditions, but not immediate death for many and a slower death for those lucky enough to survive the first 'selections'. Many – probably most – of them had heard about the mass killings in the East; even if only one out of a hundred had listened to foreign radio stations, such information spread within days if not within hours. But they were not willing to accept the horrible truth, for the same reasons that many people even in normal circumstances are unwilling to accept certain death. They hoped that some of them would survive even if the worst came to pass, and perhaps they would be the lucky ones. This, at least, is true of those in the earlier mass transports to the extermination camps; among the later deportees there was little optimism left, for the news of the mass killings had filtered back through smuggled-out letters and other means.

These explanations are not, of course, new. Those today who did not live through that time, however, may have difficulty accepting them. Human beings know, more or less, how to cope with familiar situations. This seems to be true of both very sophisticated and very primitive people, of both leaders and followers. But the terrible secret was unprecedented, certainly in modern history. In such circumstances, how could confusion and apathy not be the natural response?

Walter Laqueur
Washington London Jerusalem, summer 1997

1

GERMANY: A WALL OF SILENCE?

WHEN did the news of the mass murder first reach Germany? According to an almost general consensus there was a 'wall of silence'. If it was possible in wartime to keep certain secrets even in the Western democracies (such as the 'Manhattan' project, or 'Ultra' or the preparations for the second front), it was, of course, much easier to do so in totalitarian countries with their far more effective means of control and repression. The Nazi authorities, moreover, made a determined effort to spread misleading information about the fate of the Jews.

All this is true, but it is not the whole truth. The comparisons with Manhattan and Ultra are hardly relevant because these projects concerned only a few hundred, at most a few thousand, people and the secret of the second front had to be kept only for a few weeks or months. While it is correct that only a handful of Germans knew all about the 'final solution', very few knew nothing. As Hans Frank, Hitler's viceroy in Poland, said at Nuremberg, one should not believe anyone claiming that he knew nothing, and he did not refer only to those on trial. Himmler in a famous wartime speech on the issue of secrecy surrounding the fate of the Jews solemnly announced: we shall never speak about it. There will be no record. But while he was talking the tape recorders were running and the speech can still be heard, loud and clear in most major sound archives. Millions of people cannot be killed without participants in the murder and without witnesses.

The party leaders, the SS, the security police and the other agencies involved used camouflage language even in their internal correspondence: Jews were not executed, let alone killed or murdered; they were only 'resettled', 'evacuated', 'removed', 'deported' or at worst given 'special treatment'. 'Special treatment' was, however, too outspoken for the sensitive Himmler; when Korherr, the chief statistician of the SS submitted to him an interim report about the progress of the 'final solution' – yet another of these euphemisms – Himmler ordered him not to use this term any more but simply to refer to the 'transport of Jews'. But even in a totalitarian system there is no consistency: the 'special units' (the *Einsatzgruppen*) did not use circumlocution in their daily, weekly or monthly reports. They were in a hurry and simply announced that so many thousands of Jews had been killed during a certain period. The same was true with regard to the war diaries of army units, big and small, which reported without any embellishment the massacres which had been witnessed. For, ironically, the SS could not tell them to use the special terms without also telling them why this was necessary, and this was thought inadvisable.

The issue became of importance in the post-war trials: some of the most senior SS leaders claimed that they had never heard about the 'final solution'. One of them was Karl Wolff: true, he had been Himmler's chief of staff and his rank had been that of an SS general, but Himmler had never mentioned mass murder to him; had he done so, he, Wolff, would have immediately committed suicide. How then could he explain that in a letter in July 1942 Wolff had expressed 'joy' that the 'chosen people' were transferred from Warsaw to Treblinka at the rate of several thousands a day? Well, the letter had been drafted by someone else, he had not been aware of any sinister meaning. . . .

The German experience shows that secrets cannot, in fact, be kept even in a totalitarian regime once they have percolated beyond a certain small group. Ten men or women may keep a secret, but thousands cannot. Even the walls of silence have their loose bricks and holes. To prepare and carry out the 'final solution' the active participation of thousands in many walks of life was needed. Who in 1942 was in a position to know in Germany? Above all, of course, the people who had ordered the mass murder and those who were directly instrumental in carrying it out. These were not many: Hitler, Goering, Himmler and then in descending order Heydrich, Eichmann and their immediate collaborators. Then the special units, the *Einsatzgruppen*, which were relatively small; they counted about three thousand members. Once the death camps had been established, those running the camps, serving and guarding them have to be added. Again, these were no more than a few thousand, and all of them, of course, under strict orders to keep silent. But in many cases these orders were not obeyed, guards talked, or at the very least dropped hints to relations or girlfriends. Neither the members of the *Einsatzgruppen* nor the camp guards belonged to élite units with a high degree of discipline. Once they had completed their mission they were reposted. Some of them talked more or less freely about their experience in the East to other soldiers or policemen.

If the number of those directly involved was fairly small, the 'final solution' could still not be carried out without the indirect help or knowledge of many others, and this especially applies to the very early period, the first months after the invasion of Russia. The special units, which killed some 500,000 Jews between late June and November 1941, entered occupied Soviet territory immediately after the *Wehrmacht*. They could, of course, act only in close co-operation with the German army. They had to announce their presence to the local commanders and they had to co-ordinate with them their forthcoming 'actions'. The daily or weekly bulletins of the special units frequently mention the state of relations with the army. Sometimes the army is praised for the help extended. Units from army group centre actually participated in some of the massacres and Field Marshall von Reichenau was warmly praised by the *Einsatzgruppen*. Elsewhere local army commanders actually requested the 'special units' to finish their work more quickly (Kremenchug, Dzankoi). This provoked protests on the part of the otherwise not oversensitive ss commanders: 'We are not the hangmen of the army. . . .'

At other times there were complaints about the lack of assistance or even the criticism voiced by army officers who failed to show understanding for the thankless work done by the 'specials'. Thus, many German army officers were bound to know, except those who were constantly in the front line or those in regions in which there were no Jews at all, of which there were not many. For every army officer who had to be taken into confidence by the ss there were several others who saw or heard about the killing by accident.* There are countless reports of

---

*Rudolf von Gersdorff, a major in the general staff, having been informed about the executions of several thousands of Jews in Borisov, wrote in the war diary of Heeresgruppe Mitte on 9 December 1941: 'In all longer conversations with officers I have been asked about the execution of Jews without having raised the issue myself. I gained the impression that the shooting of Jews is rejected by almost all officers.' (R.Ch.Freiherr von Gersdorff, *Soldat im Untergang* (Berlin, 1977), pp. 96–9). When

officers and soldiers who, having watched 'executions' inadvertently, had taken pictures. This seems to have been a fairly common practice even among the special units. There was a Heydrich order in November 1941 to stop this practice immediately – and a second order in early 1942 to collect all existing pictures. From now on all photographs were to be taken only by those authorized and this material was considered a state secret.

Some of those who witnessed the 'executions' talked or wrote about it with approval, others with horror, many just related the facts. This refers not only to officers and soldiers, but also to civilians (journalists, railway workers, technicians and others) who related what they had seen; many of them were not even bound by oath. This was, broadly speaking, how the news first reached large sections of the German people. Internal Nazi reports specifically mention soldiers on leave as the most important single source about the 'very hard measures' taken against the Jews. All this refers to the early phase, the stage of the *Einsatzgruppen*. Once the 'final solution' became institutionalized and more organized, with the installation of the death camps such as Chelmno, Sobibor, Treblinka and Auschwitz, army personnel were less likely to witness extermination.

The 'special units' continued their actions albeit on a smaller basis – not that many Jews were left in the occupied territories. On the other hand the number of civilians involved grew by leaps and bounds. Even in the very early planning meetings, such as the Wannsee Conference, representatives of the ministries of Foreign Affairs, Justice, the Interior and the Four-Year Plan, and the Reich Chancellery had participated and as the deportations from Germany and Central Europe came under way, officials of every rank from many other state offices had to be enlisted. For this was a major administrative operation which, given the intricacies of modern society, involved countless decisions, instructions, circular letters and correspondence. The mayor of a small or medium-sized town in Germany

---

General Busch, the commander of the 16th Army heard the executions from his hotel window in Kovno, he said that these things did not concern the officers and they must not do anything about it. (Peter Hoffmann, *Widerstand, Staatsstreich, Attentat* (Munich, 1970), p. 317.) But another highly decorated officer, Axel von dem Bussche, decided to join the conspiracy against Hitler precisely because he had accidentally been a witness to mass executions on Dubno airport in autumn 1942.

or Austria would get an order informing him that Jews were to be transported to the East and that he was to extend all possible help to those who would run the operation. The Jews had to be informed (for which the services of the post office were needed), the old and infirm had to be transported to the concentration point, physicians and nurses had to check whether all could be transported. The operation was frequently not even supervised by the SS, which was needed for more urgent commissions, but by the regular police. The offices of the railway services were needed; it was not at all easy to obtain special trains in wartime even if the deportations had the highest priority. The trains were accompanied by policemen from various branches, including the ordinary, regular police force. Reports had to be written about each transport and those in command would sometimes complain that station masters had shown lack of co-operation (of course they too had to be informed). Some had even gone out of their way to be friendly towards the deportees. Perhaps they had an inkling of what was in store for them.

But with the disappearance of the Jews the bureaucratic problems were by no means over. The neighbours of the Jews and the people in the factories where many of them had worked were, of course, aware that they had vanished. Many may have believed the official version of 'resettlement in the East'. But there is documentary evidence that at least some knew more; Jews working in Berlin factories were warned of impending razzias, and sometimes they were even told by well wishers among factory managers and foremen that the fate in store for them was not just 'resettlement'. The bureaucratic machinery continued to work. The property of the Jews was taken over by the state. Banks and insurance companies had to be informed that the Jews were legally dead, other offices had to be told that the Jews no longer needed food and clothing stamps. All kinds of legal complications concerning property arose and the law courts had to deal with problems of this kind.[1]

Then, at a later stage, the administration had to cope with new problems. Certain belongings of those who had been killed in the camps were shipped back to Germany. Money and other valuables, including gold fillings, were sent to the banks; blankets, glasses, children's dolls, handbags, linen, watches, pipes, umbrellas, fountain pens and sundry other belongings were sent to various agencies specializing in social work such as the *Winterhilfe* and to the families of wounded soldiers. The women were shaved before being subjected to 'special treatment' and their hair was sent to Alex Zink felt factory near Nuremberg to be used in the war effort. It is unlikely, to put it cautiously, that the recipients of these shipments had no idea whatsoever where these commodities came from.

As the transports from Germany and other countries were rolling towards the East – it has been said – the Jews disappeared without a trace. For as the extermination camps were located far away from the borders of Germany, no one but the few directly involved in the 'final solution' could possibly know about the fate of the Jews. This version is widely believed but it isn't quite true: two of the extermination camps, Chelmno, the first to become operative, and Auschwitz, the largest, were actually within the borders of *Grossdeutschland*. Though Auschwitz was in many ways a state within a state, this meant that various branches of the German civilian bureaucracy were involved in the establishment and running of the camps. It was not occupied territory where bureaucratic procedure could frequently be disregarded. A glance at the map shows that Auschwitz is located not in the middle of a desert but at the border of the Upper Silesian industrial area, near such major cities as Beuthen, Gleiwitz, Hindenburg (Zabrze) and Katowice.

Auschwitz, furthermore, was both a work and extermination camp, unlike places such as Treblinka and Sobibor which were factories of death, *tout court*. Auschwitz was a veritable archipelago with some forty branches (*Aussenstellen*). The list of these branches reads like a gazetteer of Silesia: Kosel, Blechhammer, Gleiwitz, Beuthen, Laurahuette, Bunzlau, Langenbielau, Ottmuth, Gogolin, Annaberg, Neukirch. The Auschwitz branches extended as far as Riesa, in Saxony, and Warsaw. Not every worker in every branch knew, but some did. Auschwitz workers were employed by AEG, the German electricity trust, and by IG Farben; they worked for the German railway system and other enterprises connected with the war effort. It is known from various sources, Polish and German, that the Polish population living in the neighbourhood of far more isolated camps than Auschwitz were well aware of what went on inside these camps. It is impossible to believe that no resident of

Gleiwitz, Beuthen or Katowitz had any idea of what went on within a distance of a few miles from their homes. Moreover, those Auschwitz inmates who had been fortunate enough to be selected for work rather than death were, in fact, dispersed all over Silesia, and since they met with thousands of people it is inconceivable that the news about Auschwitz did not reach many non-Jews. If Jews living in the nearby ghettos did know, others who had greater freedom of movement knew too.*

Charles Joseph Coward, a British prisoner of war, said in his evidence in the post-war trial against IG Farben:

The people in the city [Auschwitz], the s.s. men, the camp inmates, foreign workers, all the camp knew it. All the civilian population knew it, they complained about the stench of the burning bodies. Even the I.G. Farben employees to whom I spoke, a lot of them would admit it. It would be utterly impossible not to know.

A physician serving with the *Waffen* SS said during the interrogation: Question: 'Did these civilians living in the shadow of the crematoria know about the gassings?' Answer: 'Yes, that is the way I meant it, because in Katowitz one was able to smell the stench of the crematoria just as well as in Auschwitz.'[2] According to Pery Broad, a member of the SS, civilians from all parts of Germany had heard of Auschwitz, at least as a rumour, 'otherwise the great interest cannot be accounted for shown when the trains passed near the camp. The passengers usually rose from their seats and went to the windows. . . .'[3]

Adolf Bartelmas, a railway employee in Auschwitz, said in his testimony at the Auschwitz trial in Frankfurt many years later that the flames could be seen at a distance of fifteen–twenty kilometres and that it was known that human beings were burned there. Even more emphatic were Kaduk and Pery Broad

*Two examples should suffice: a Palestinian citizen, a resident of Sosnowice who was repatriated in November 1942, reported to the Jewish Agency about the chimneys of nearby Auschwitz – and what they were used for. Her evidence together with that of others – on which more below – was distributed by the Information Department of the Jewish Agency on 20 November 1942. She must have heard by August or September 1942 at the latest.

According to a Gestapo report dated 18 March 1942, Karl Golda, aged twenty-eight, a member of the Order of the Salesians, and resident of a monastery near Auschwitz, was arrested for having gathered material about the camp. He was sent to Auschwitz where he died on 14 May 1942. This happened even before the mass killings had started. To show excessive curiosity was dangerous, but as the mass transports began to roll those living nearby could not help but notice.

who appeared in the same trial: when the chimneys were operated there was a flame of five metres. The railway station, full of civilians and soldiers on leave, was covered with smoke and there was an all-pervasive sweet smell. According to Broad the pitch-black clouds of smoke could be seen and smelled for kilometres: 'The smell was simply intolerable. . . .'

Hundreds of civilian employees, Germans as well as Poles, worked at Auschwitz, arriving in the morning, leaving in the afternoon. The families of some of the higher officials lived there too. Many technicians and workers from various parts of Germany and the occupied countries came to Auschwitz for shorter and longer periods of time, and there is evidence that they discussed in public places what they had seen in the camp.[4] Workers from Krupp, such as Erich Lutat and Paul Ortmann, said in evidence at the Nuremberg trial that the workers used to discuss the events in the camp, and when they went home on leave to see their families in Essen they also told them, *ganz entsetzt* ('quite horrified').

If the workers knew, it stands to reason that at least some of the bosses knew too, which is not to say that every director of Krupp or IG Farben was aware of the systematic killing. But it seems to have been an open secret even in business circles not directly connected with either making deliveries to Auschwitz or having a branch in the camps. In 1961 Dr Guenther Prey, a German industrialist, made a deposition at the Dutch Government War Institute, according to which he had discovered, by chance in late 1941 or in 1942 in Danzig, that Jews were killed by gassing. Perhaps this was a mere accident, perhaps others were unlikely to learn the secret the same way. But Dr Prey also said that the matter was openly talked about in the German circles in which he moved in Holland, where it was generally known that the Jews in Auschwitz and other camps were murdered *en masse* (Dr Prey used the German term *Grossbetrieb*).[5]

Altogether 40,000 Auschwitz inmates were employed by various German industrial enterprises. IG Farben, which was the pioneer, alone had some 10,000 inmates – including British prisoners of war – working in the BUNA (synthetic rubber) and acetic acid plant. There was a fairly rapid turnover in this labour force: of the 35,000 who worked for BUNA at least 25,000 died.[6] The details of the IG Farben activities in Auschwitz came to light in a famous post-war trial. They are of relevance in this context only to answer two questions: how many non-Jewish personnel were needed to run the Auschwitz plant? And how many others in the IG Farben head offices from the directors of the production, planning, personnel and sales divisions down to the last construction worker and book-keeping clerk were bound to know about Auschwitz? Several hundred at the very least.

This list is, of course, far from complete. Physicians were engaged in medical experiments in the camps, and while there were no published reports, some of them, no doubt with the blessing of the authorities, made oral reports before various professional gatherings in the presence of dozens of colleagues. Journalists travelled in the General Government and were bound to hear, so were the diplomats in Berlin frequently confronted with queries concerning the fate of foreign nationals who had disappeared in the maelstrom of destruction. There was a special department in the Foreign Ministry (*Referat Deutschland*) dealing with these affairs, but diplomats stationed abroad were also bound to hear. If no one had told them under the veil of secrecy they were bound to read it in the Allied or neutral press. Such clippings were, in fact, found in the files of the Foreign Ministry and other offices. This was true also with regard to satellite capitals. Again one example should suffice. Dr Doertenbach who was councillor at the German Embassy in Rome in 1942 stated in a sworn affidavit after the war that in the summer of 1942 he had already read in the British and Swiss press that SS units were raging in a terrible manner in Russia:

I believed this news because I had my own experience in Poland. These incidents were discussed in a circle of German and Italian friends, German officials among them, and always an expression of indignation. . . . During my activity as councillor of the Embassy at Rome in the fall of 1942 I also heard of the killing of Jews in concentration camps in the Eastern territories. The first intimation I received from an official of the Italian Foreign Office. . . .[7]

Doertenbach also said that in the course of time he had discussed these events with some thirty colleagues at the Foreign Ministry. Doertenbach was not a top echelon Foreign Ministry official nor was he initiated in the 'secret' because he had to deal with

'Jewish affairs', directly or indirectly. If, nevertheless, he knew, his superiors knew *a fortiori* – and earlier at that. Beginning in October 1941 the reports of the *Einsatzgruppen* were circulated in the German Foreign Ministry, some in full, others in summary. Each report referred to many thousands of Jews who had been killed. Eventually it was next to impossible to know how many had been exterminated and how many were still alive. In December 1941 Fritz Gebhardt von Hahn, a junior official, was asked to provide a statistical summary. He calculated that about 7–80,000 Jews had been liquidated by each *Sonderkommando*. Since there were several such units in each of the four *Einsatzgruppen*, Hahn's figures were actually in excess of the gruesome reality.[8]

These reports were sent to various desks in the Political Division and were initialled by twenty-two different people. They were seen by more, and the number of those who were orally informed, fully or in part, could well have been in the hundreds. In January 1942 Foreign Ministry senior staff read in the seventh report covering December 1941 that the Jewish question in Ostland was solved. This announcement was repeated in the tenth report.

There are indications that even in remote embassies at least some people had known even earlier. Thus on 2 September 1941 the German Embassy in Uruguay had objected to the emigration of a Jewish teacher from Warsaw, because her experience of the 'newest developments' of the Jewish question in Eastern Europe would be grist to the mill of anti-German propaganda.[9] The killing of many thousands of Serbian and Romanian Jews featured in Foreign Ministry correspondence in October 1941, was widely circulated and did not even rate 'top secret'.

The question who knew what and when became a major bone of contention in the post-war trials against officials of the German Foreign Ministry. The defendants could claim that in its second, post-Wannsee stage, the 'final solution' became a top secret (*Geheime Reichssache*) and only a small number of people were officially initiated. Those who had initialled the *Einsatzgruppen* reports argued that they had not read them. If Secretary of War Henry Stimson had said in a famous aside that gentlemen do not read other gentlemen's letters, these gentlemen were arguing that they were not reading their own letters.

A careful study of the evidence shows that indeed only a few were informed officially and that requests for information about the fate of the Jews were directed to the Main State Security Office. But it also shows that information was passed on orally, inside the office and apparently even more often outside, through friends or members of the family, usually soldiers returning for leave from the eastern front.[10] But with all these precautions some items of information still slipped through and are found in the files. An over-eager employee (Paul Wurm) in a letter dated October 1941 had mentioned 'special measures' to 'exterminate the Jewish vermin'. The representative of the Ministry in the Netherlands cabled on 13 August 1942 that the Jews had found out the truth about the deportations and some were no longer reporting for the transports. German secret service reports in the Foreign Ministry files referred to 'special treatment' in contradistinction to work; another Foreign Ministry official (Bargen) reported rumours of 'butchery' from Belgium in November 1942. Hahn, whom we have already quoted, wrote in a reply to the legal department that the International Red Cross must not be allowed to transmit letters to and from deported Jews. For if such permission was given 'they would be able at any time to visualise approximately the number of deported Israelites as well as their fate at the place of deportation and on their way there'.[11] Quite frequently information was provided by the Foreign Ministry liaison officers with the *Wehrmacht*.[12]

Officials of the Ministry of Propaganda, and through them key journalists, were kept informed by Goebbels at conferences which took place almost daily. Goebbels' general policy was, as he said in his conference on 8 December 1942, that the treatment of the Jews was a 'delicate question' which had better not be touched at all. A few days later, on 12 December, he said that in view of British propaganda about alleged anti-Jewish atrocities in the East something had to be done after all; one should not, however, engage in polemics but instead give prominence to British atrocities in India and elsewhere. He elaborated on the subject in his conference on 16 December: the general idea was to create a general hullabaloo about atrocities

'as our best chance of getting away from the embarrassing
subject of the Jews'. All this was clear enough and the journalists
hardly had to wait for Goebbels' public speech in the *Sportpalast*
on 18 February 1943 in which he talked about the 'exter . . .',
correcting himself 'elimination of the Jews', in order to
understand why the subject was embarrassing.[13]

Listening to foreign broadcasting stations, whether enemy
or neutral was, of course, strictly forbidden in wartime Nazi
Germany and there was draconian punishment for transgressors
who were caught. But still many people in Germany and the
occupied countries did listen to foreign radio stations. Nazi top-
secret, internal bulletins such as *Meldungen aus dem Reich* (but also
the regional information sheets) repeated time and again
throughout the war that this was the main source of unofficial
and, of course, undesirable information as far as the population
was concerned. It was also stressed that the enemy radio news
spread very quickly and that it was very difficult to apprehend
the transgressors who, transmitting 'hostile information',
would, of course, not reveal their sources. If, in 1941, 720
German citizens were sentenced to long prison terms or the
death penalty for having listened to foreign stations (the figure
for 1942 was 985), the total number of listeners was, of course,
infinitely greater.* According to a semi-official German post-
war source, 'millions of Germans listened in all secrecy to the
forbidden information not seldom observing the rules of
conspiracy'. According to a BBC report of 1943 the number of its
German listeners was about one million at the time. According
to an American survey of 1945, 51 per cent of all Germans
claimed that they had heard 'enemy stations' at least once.[14]

These illegal listeners quite apart there were others who had
official permission to listen to foreign stations and to read enemy
newspapers. More than five hundred experts were employed in
the German monitoring service (*Seehaus*) which, according to its
historian, was a 'breeding ground of defeatism' rather than a
bulwark of the Nazi spirit. According to the same source most of
those serving in this institution were not willing to accept the
responsibility for the crimes of the regime of which they learned
from foreign radio stations. This referred specifically to 'the
extermination of another race'.[15] The *Seehaus* daily and weekly

---

*Not all sentences were, however, reported in the daily press.

reports originally went to some four hundred recipients. In January 1942 Hitler decided to cut this number drastically. But even after this the circle of recipients was much wider than Hitler and Goebbels intended and furthermore there were many other secret information services for leading Nazi dignitaries. At a ministerial meeting in February 1942 State Secretary Gutterer announced that there were some hundred such services all of them 'secret' or 'top secret' and some with a circulation of up to four thousand.*[16]

Little attention has been paid to the role of the railway in the 'final solution'.[17] The special deportation trains were commissioned directly by the SS, more specifically by Eichmann's section IV B4, in the Chief State Security Office (RSHA). The organization of the special trains in the middle of a war involved a major logistical effort. Not only the most senior officials knew about it but also regional directors. There were meetings and conferences in which railway staff and railway and political police took part. It could, of course, be argued that the special trains were needed for nothing worse than the transfer of Jews to the East. But most of the extermination camps were near main lines, the trains entering and leaving the camps could be seen (and were photographed) from passing or stationary passenger trains. Auschwitz railway station was little over a mile from the place where people were actually killed. The burning of the corpses was done, as a railway employee put it after the war, more or less in public.[18] But even those in the railway central offices who had never been near the camps were bound to reach the conclusion that Auschwitz had to be one of the biggest cities of Europe, if its inhabitants were still alive. Even the Allies, for reasons to be discussed later on, had to pay attention to this concentration of traffic in an unexpected direction.

The number of people in Nazi Germany who had a full picture was probably quite small, even by autumn of 1942. But hundreds of thousands, if not millions, had heard something from officers and soldiers on leave about the 'very hard measures' which figure in Bormann's circular letter of 9 October

---

*To provide but one illustration: DNB, the official German news agency, circulated a daily (restricted) bulletin which was read by hundreds of high officials. On 22 July 1942 the bulletin announced that there had been a mass demonstration of Jews in Madison Square Gardens, New York, in protest against the murder of one million Jews.

1942 ('for confidential information') to Nazi Party senior staff
members.[19] Even a year earlier, on 25 October 1941, in a
conversation between Hitler, Himmler and Heydrich, rumours
among the population about the destruction of the Jews had
already been mentioned. ('Public rumours attribute to us a plan
to exterminate the Jews.')[20] The fortnightly and monthly
reports of the SD (the Nazi party intelligence service), giving
unvarnished public opinion surveys in the Third Reich, do not
report any rumours at all about the ultimate fate of the Jews
throughout the year 1942. In 1943, on the other hand, it
published many such reports, mainly in connection with the
Allied bombings and the murder of thousands of Polish officers
by the Russians at Katyn. ('We should not complain, the SS has
done the same to the Jews' etc., etc.)[21] One does know, however,
from many sources that there were such rumours in great
numbers even in 1942 and it is unlikely that the efficient SD
could have missed them.

It is not difficult to explain this apparent paradox. The editor
of the SD review, Dr Otto Ohlendorf, certainly knew all there
was to know about the fate of the Jews: he had been commander
of one of the *Einsatzgruppen*. But he also knew that while his
reports went only to a limited number of key people in the Nazi
hierarchy, this list was by no means identical with the group
which knew all the details about the 'final solution'. While
Ohlendorf wanted to provide a candid review of public opinion,
he was aware of the fact that there had to be limits to his
candour. Just as he could not report a 'rumour' (especially if
true) about a forthcoming major military operation or a
scientific breakthrough of military importance, he would not
deal with a top secret of another kind. In 1943, on the other
hand, when the great majority of the Jews had already been
slaughtered, these restrictions apparently no longer applied.

Knowledge about the fate of the Jews, in any case, was
widespread even in early summer of 1942. Again one example
will have to suffice. Mr Haas, a teacher in Niedernhausen
(Odenwald), had forwarded to the *Stürmer* a letter written by
Private First Class Lothammer reporting in some detail the
killing of Jews in Jassy and in the southern Ukraine. But the
letter was not published. One of the editors informed Haas in
May 1942 that 'out of certain considerations' it was not always

possible now to publicize Jewish abominations.[22] The *Stürmer* had not been known for tact and delicacy of feeling prior to the outbreak of war. Why should it have shown such inhibitions in war time? *Sapienti sat.*

Private Lothammer should not have written about the massacres in the first place, but army instructions were frequently ignored: the reports circulated by army censors almost regularly mention such transgressions. Furthermore, letters written by German and foreign civilians from the East were not subject to such restrictions. A few letters were intercepted, most were not.

Of those who had heard that the Jews were killed most were not aware that gas was used. It was widely believed that the Jews were shot or burned or somehow killed by means of electrical shocks. Those who did know sometimes tried to mislead even the party élite and the higher state bureaucracy. Thus Dr Hans Frank, the head of the General Government, was not permitted to enter Belzec and Auschwitz. The language used even in the internal communications (except the progress reports of the *Einsatzgruppen*) hardly ever mentioned actual killings: hard measures were taken against the Jews, they were compelled to work hard, it was implied that many of them would probably die of disease and starvation. But the 'final solution' could mean after all a great many things other than violent death. In their conversations with neutral and satellite diplomatic representatives, leading Nazis never mentioned the murder of the Jews if a record was likely to be made of the conversation: the Jews were disappearing somehow, why discuss details which were neither particularly interesting nor important?

Such ambiguities had a certain effect, but only on those who had no particular wish to know. Those who had witnessed the murder of a thousand people or heard about it from an unimpeachable source could still persuade themselves that this had been an exceptional case. They might even forget it; after all, a great many people were killed in the war, human life was cheap. But information continued to arrive from more than one source. Each successive piece of evidence (as a pioneer of the detective story once wrote) would not just be proof added to proof, but proof multiplied by hundreds or thousands. Thus, by the end of 1942, millions in Germany knew that the Jewish question had been radically solved, and that this radical solution did not involve resettlement, in short, that most, or all of those who had been deported were no longer alive.* Details about their deaths were known to a much smaller number.

What was known in 1942 among Hitler's satellites? Government officials, diplomats, journalists, officers and soldiers returning from the eastern front knew a great deal. Slovak and Hungarian officers were among the main sources for the early phase of the 'final solution'. The internal correspondence of the SD shows that Italians visiting the eastern front had also inadvertently witnessed some of the massacres and that, as a result, there were 'unwholesome rumours' making the rounds in Rome.

The satellites had representatives in the German capital and they could not help listening to the Berlin gossip. They read in the German press speeches by Robert Ley and others which were anything but cagey: 'We have to fight the Jews to the very last consequence. It is not enough to isolate the Jewish enemy of mankind; the Jew must be destroyed.'[23] Or Goebbels in his organ, the weekly *Das Reich*: 'The Jews will pay with the extermination of their race in Europe and perhaps beyond.'[24]

These and other speeches were widely quoted in diplomatic circles in Berlin. The language was unmistakable: the Jew had been isolated, now he had to be destroyed. The term 'destroy' in this context had only one possible meaning, and it was neither resettlement nor productive work.

---

*This is not to dispute the evidence by Helmuth Count Moltke, one of the martyrs of the German resistance to Hitler, who wrote in a letter to a British friend that

> I believe that at least nine-tenths of the population do not know that we have killed hundreds of thousands of Jews. They go on believing they just have been segregated and lead an existence pretty much as they led (before) only farther to the East, where they came from. Perhaps with a little more squalor but without air raids. If you told these people what has really happened they will answer: You are just a victim of British propaganda, remember what ridiculous things they said about our behaviour in Belgium in 1914/18. . . .

(Moltke to Lionel Curtis, Stockholm, 25 March 1943, quoted in M. Balfour and J. Frisby, *Helmuth von Moltke* (London, 1972), p. 218.) Moltke, who was associated with the *Abwehr* as a cover, had known, albeit vaguely, about the mass murder even before the Wannsee Conference, as emerges from letters sent to his wife. It has already been noted that Allied propaganda about masses of Belgian babies allegedly bayonetted in 1914 was still widely remembered in Europe in 1942, not only among Germans, and dissuaded many from accepting the news about the mass murder of the Jews. But even if more than nine-tenths of the population did not know or did not believe, this leaves millions who had heard and did not doubt it.

The Finnish ambassador in Berlin was warned by Felix Kersten, Himmler's masseur, in June 1942.* Other ambassadors knew no less. Doene Sztojay, the Hungarian ambassador in Berlin, was a radical anti-semite who became Prime Minister after the German invasion in March 1944. He went to see the Germans from time to time with all kinds of mild protests about the fate of Hungarian Jews in Germany, but never forgot to add how distasteful these missions were for him personally. But he was fully informed at an early date. In the case of Hungary it is now possible to state with some accuracy when and in what circumstances the first information about the 'final solution' reached Budapest. The news was transmitted from Berlin by Andor Gellert who represented the (Hungarian) Revision League in the German capital. It was conveyed to the Political Department of the Hungarian Foreign Ministry which did not reject it outright but expressed doubts about its authenticity. ('Do not exaggerate,' Gellert was told by a leading official.) Gellert, a protégé of Prime Minister Pal Teleki, had been told in March 1942 by Ernst Neugeboren, an ethnic German from Transylvania, about the implications for Hungary of the Wannsee Conference. Neugeboren, an accountant by profession, had joined the SS and attained a position of some influence.† Gellert thought the news at first absurd and did not believe it, but similar information albeit more vague reached him from other people as well and he was sufficiently alarmed to go to Budapest to report. He still was not sure whether Neugeboren had wanted to warn him or whether it was an attempt to intimidate the Hungarians.[25] Thus Sztojay knew from Gellert, but he had also heard from other sources and on occasion he dropped broad hints to visitors from Budapest. One of them was György Ottlik, the editor of the *Pester Lloyd*, who was in Berlin in August–September 1942. After his return to the Hungarian capital he wrote a memorandum which he handed to the Foreign Ministry in which he said that Sztojay was all in favour of at least a 'token deportation' of Jews and that while he did not define the 'final solution' *expressis verbis*, he did not

*See p. 36
†According to his personal file in the Nazi Central Archives (Berlin Document Centre) Neugeboren was born in Brasov in 1905. In 1939 he joined the German Foreign Ministry. In 1942 he volunteered for the SS, but he spent the rest of the war doing staff work for the SS and the Foreign Ministry in Berlin and south-east Europe.

conceal (*titkolni* in Hungarian) its meaning either.[26] Sztojay's intention might well have been to induce the Hungarian Government to burn its bridges with the Western Allies which Kallai, the Prime Minister of the day, had no intention of doing.

The Ottlik report nevertheless leaves a number of questions open. It was not the habit of Sztojay to use precise language in such delicate matters as the extermination of Jews, nor was Gellert particularly close to him politically. Sztojay was a devotee of Gömbös, the protagonist of a pro-fascist orientation in Hungary in the 1930s, whereas Gellert was basically a 'Westerner' who resigned in 1935 as editor of the semi-official *Budapesti Hirlap* precisely because he resented the anti-Western line. True, *Pester Lloyd* too was a semi-official organ and Ottlik had compromised with the reluctant collaborationism of the Hungarian Government. But it still appears doubtful that he would have written his report unless he had received similar information from at least one other source. Such a source existed and it was none other than the Berlin correspondent of the *Pester Lloyd*, Ernst Lemmer.* Quite irrespective of the source of Ottlik's memorandum the mass extermination of Jews in 1941 had been witnessed by thousands of Hungarian officers and soldiers. In the words of a Hungarian historian: 'It is ridiculous and contemptible for anybody who served on the Russian front and passed through Poland and the occupied USSR, an area inhabited by six million Jews and by then devoid of Jews, to maintain that he did not know what was going to happen to the Jews when they were deported.'[27]

The Slovak and Italian ambassadors hardly knew any less and the same is true for the envoys of these countries in neutral capitals, for they were exposed to Allied newspapers and radio. The Slovaks insisted in their negotiations with the Germans that the Jews would never come back, but the equation 'resettlement = mass murder' appears in Slovak documents only in 1943. The Slovaks had close relations with the Vatican (and the Italians) and they had received warnings from these quarters as early as March 1942. Some of the evidence came out in the post-war trials of Dr Joseph Tiso, the President of the Republic, and Dr Anton Vasek. Even an ardent admirer of Dr Tiso admitted in later years that by July 1942 Tiso had been

*For Lemmer's role as a source on the mass extermination of the Jews, see Appendix 1.

informed by the Vatican that the Jews deported from Slovakia were killed (or had been killed) in the region of Lublin.[28]

Mussolini had been informed by Hitler about the true meaning of the 'final solution' in early 1942. Later that year Himmler had talked to him about it in some detail. How many other Fascist leaders knew cannot be established. Some did, this refers above all to the generals and diplomats dealing with East European affairs. The Italians in their occupied zone in France probably knew, they helped the Jews escape the deportation dragnet much to the annoyance of Eichmann and his aides. General Giuseppe Pieche, who represented the Italian *carabinieri* in northern Croatia and Slovenia, wrote in a note to his government that the Jews from the German zone of occupation were deported to the eastern territories and 'sono stati eliminati mediante l'impiego di gas tossico nel treno in cui erano rinchiusi'.* This message was dated 4 November 1942. It was seen by Ciano, the Foreign Minister, and General Roatta and eventually it was submitted to Mussolini. Mussolini read it, wrote with a blue pencil '*Visto dal Duce*', seen by the Duce – and there was no comment.[29]

But why should there have been reason for surprise? On 21 August 1942, four months earlier, there had been a memorandum from the Italian Foreign Ministry to Mussolini, according to which von Bismarck, the adviser of the German Embassy in Rome, had submitted a request by the German authorities that all Croatian Jews should be extradited so that they could be deported to the East. The memorandum made it clear that deportation meant '*in pratica – eliminazione* . . .' The Duce commented in his handwriting: '*Nulla osta*' – 'No objection'.

Notes of this kind were read by dozens of people and if such state secrets were not kept even in Germany, one can imagine how widely such information would be shared among Italians not bound by any solemn oath.

Mussolini was close to Hitler, the Finns were not. Their alliance with the Nazis was purely pragmatic, their aim the return of Karelia. But even they knew what the 'final solution' meant and when Himmler arrived in 1942 to claim the few Finnish Jews, the Finnish Government had already been

---

*'. . . are eliminated by the use of toxic gas in the train in which they are locked.'

warned by its ambassador in Berlin.* They had a good excuse: the Jews could be surrendered only after a debate and vote in parliament and Himmler, needless to say, was not at all eager to have publicity of this kind. But the Berlin embassy had not been the only source of information. Arno Anthoni, the head of the Finnish state police, was brought to trial in Abo in 1947 for having handed over to the Gestapo several Jews who did not have Finnish citizenship. He admitted having met Eichmann in Berlin in 1942 but claimed that he did not know about the mass murder 'because he had no time to read the newspapers'. But among his own files a report of a subordinate, Olavi Viherluoto, a state police officer, was found. It concerned a visit to Estonia, dated late 1941, and contained details about the extermination of Estonian Jewry, one of the very first authentic reports to get out of the Baltic countries. Anthoni claimed that though he initialled the report he had not read it. It is far more likely that he did read it, and that he reported to his superior, Toivo Horelli, the pro-German Minister of the Interior. Thus even in far away Finland there were people who knew the secret and there was no reason why they should have kept this knowledge to themselves. The consensus in Finland after the war was that Anthoni must have known, and that he did inform some members of the Government.[30]

But it is more than doubtful whether members of the Finnish Government or indeed anyone else in Finland even needed to be told. As the German ambassador in Helsinki, Bluecher, reported

---

*According to post-war Finnish literature 'nothing was known during the entire war about the methods used in German concentration camps'. (Mannerheim, *Memoirs*, Finnish ed., p. 388). This is true only if the stress is put on 'methods', i.e. the question of whether poison gas was used or some other means. Kiwimaeki, the ambassador in Berlin, wrote that he learned through Kersten that Hitler intended to demand that Finland hand over her 8,300 (*sic*) Jews (*Suomolaisen Politikon Muistelmat*, 'Memoirs of a Finnish Politician' (Helsinki, 1965), p. 243). A few pages later the author says that he had learned that the Finnish authorities on their own initiative had taken measures to deliver to Germany Jews who had reached Finland as refugees (p. 246). These Jews were handed over to the Germans on 6 November 1942 – one of them survived. A kibbutz in Israel is named in their memory. Lastly, Kiwimaeki mentions that though he had no certain knowledge of the details of the fate planned for the Jews he had enough information to know that the days of many of them were numbered. He also says that Swedish newspapers which carried information about the systematic extermination were widely read in Finland in 1942. For most Finns who had no access to classified information this was the main source of information, a fact which has been noted by recent authors (for instance Boris Gruenstein, writing in *Helsingin Sanomat*, 22 April 1979).

to Berlin in January 1943, Germany's Jewish policy was so unpopular in Finland that rumours in October 1942 about the forcible expulsion of a handful of Jews had seriously undermined the position of Horelli.* There was an even greater storm of indignation in December 1942 when it became known that Anthoni, the head of the political police (no doubt with the support of Horelli), had handed over to the Germans several 'Jewish criminals and Communists'. Their transport on the SS *Hohenhörn* was delayed because of an air raid; during this time the prisoners on board ship made their presence known to others in the harbour. The information reached the Swedish press and there was a confrontation within the Finnish Government with Väinö Tanner, the Social Democrat, at the head of those censuring Horelli and Anthoni. It is most unlikely that Tanner, Fagerholm, the ministers who supported them and Finnish public opinion would have protested so vehemently if it had just been a question of deporting some stateless Jewish Communists to German prisons or even an uncertain fate.† The point surely is that everyone knew that their fate was certain. As a result of the protests, the deportations were discontinued after this incident.

The Hungarians knew a great deal more than the Finns even though their leading statesmen later claimed that they heard about the mass murders only in 1943 – perhaps only in 1944. Eichmann's emissaries were in constant touch with their Hungarian opposite numbers and they explained to them the meaning of the 'final solution'. The Hungarian opposition, on the other hand, was kept informed by the Jewish rescue

*Wipert von Bluecher to Auswärtiges Amt, 29 January 1943. Witting, the Finnish Foreign Minister, was also generally blamed for having been only too willing to give in to the German demands. The Finnish press was quite outspoken in its criticism of the authorities. *Suomen Sosialdemokraati* (11 December) and *Hufvudstadsbladet* (12 December) stressed that this was a political issue, not one for the police to decide, and that the right of asylum should not have been violated. There were other such voices. Only relatively unimportant pro-Nazi newspapers such as *Ajan Suunta* and *Uusi Eurooppa* had editorials in the vein of *Much Ado About Nothing*.

†The Finnish Government had yet another important source of information: having broken the American code, from early 1942 the Finnish secret service systematically intercepted the signals between Washington and various European capitals. A post-war Finnish author notes that the Finnish Government was particularly well informed as the result of reading the cables sent out daily by the American legation in Bern. This was the place from which most of the information emerged about the 'final solution' in 1942. (Jukka Mäkelä, *Im Rücken des Feindes* (Frauenfeld, 1967), p. 159.)

committees. There cannot have been many people in positions of responsibility in Budapest in late 1942 who did not know. The Swiss ambassador in Budapest reported to his Government that the Germans wanted to transfer the Hungarian Jews to Eastern Europe. Those incapable of work 'would be made to disappear in a way which was not specified in detail'. In the same report the Swiss ambassador also said that the Slovaks had 'confidentially' told him that in their country the German demands had been fulfilled 'in conformance to Hitler's thesis that European Jewry has to be exterminated' (*ausgerottet*).[31] In a later report the Swiss ambassador referred to a long talk with Kallai, the Hungarian Prime Minister, who told him that Hungary could not possibly accept a solution of the Jewish question which was not in line with Hungary's Christian culture and its spiritual tradition, *Seelenverfassung*.[32] The German correspondents in Budapest kept repeating to anybody who cared to listen that although 'there might have been some place for the Jews in the "New Europe" there was none in "fortress Europe"'.[33] So much for latter-day claims that Slovak and Hungarian officials were kept in ignorance. Hitler's Croatian satellites did not pretend that they were not informed. They were in some ways the pioneers of a 'final solution' affecting Serbs and Jews alike. The Romanians did, of course, know about the activities of the *Einsatzgruppen* almost immediately; they collaborated, after all, with them in southern Russia. But once Eichmann and his cohorts appeared in 1942 with the demand that Romanian Jewry should be handed over, Marshal Ion Antonescu, the Romanian leader, pretended to be hard of hearing. Bucharest was no longer certain that Germany would win the war and furthermore their national pride forbade them to let others interfere in internal Romanian affairs.

Initially the Bulgarians knew less. They had *not* declared war on the Soviet Union and their troops were not stationed in Russia. But in June 1942 the Bulgarians were informed by Beckerle, the German ambassador in Sofia, that all European Jewry was to be deported to Poland. Beckerle's contact was Belev, the newly appointed Commissar for Jewish Affairs. Belev tended to accept the demand to hand over the Jews, others opposed it. The story of the tug-of-war has been told in detail. It culminated in a compromise: 11,000 Jews from Bulgarian

Thrace and Macedonia were deported in 1943 and killed, the rest permitted to stay in Bulgaria. German pressure continued as in Romania, but the Bulgarians, like the Romanians, pretended not to understand. The Führer had told them that at the end of the war the Jews would have to leave Europe. Very well then, ·why not wait for the end of the war? Most of the Bulgarian Jews were workers and they were needed for the time being. Stalingrad and El Alamein did not strengthen the Bulgarian belief in a German victory and they had no wish to compromise themselves unnecessarily.

Did the Bulgarian Government know anything more tangible about the 'final solution'? Not officially, but there were many channels of communications. The Russians had diplomatic representatives in the Bulgarian capital during the war. The Bulgarian ambassador in Switzerland was no other than Georgi Koseiwanow, the friend of the King, former prime minister and personal friend of many high officials. Like most ambassadors, Mr Koseiwanow was in the habit of reading newspapers. Istanbul was still nearer than Bern; Bulgarian officials and parliamentarians visited there and met fairly regularly neutral and Allied representatives. Members of a Bulgarian trade mission in Istanbul went out of their way in late 1942 to meet Bulgarian Jews who had temporarily settled in Turkey.[34] There was almost constant contact between Bulgaria and the outside world. In short, there were no secrets even in Sofia.

Lastly France, the occupied zone and Vichy. The arrests began in July 1942 with the great razzia in Paris (*Vel d'Hiv*) when some 13,000 stateless Jews were rounded up. Many more arrests followed and within a month the trains were beginning to roll to Auschwitz. According to the explanations provided by Vichy they were to be transported to southern Poland where they would be employed in various public work projects.[35] The use of this terminology (*Sprachregelung*) had been agreed upon from the beginning and was confirmed in a meeting between Pierre Laval, the Vichy vice-premier, and Knochen, the chief ss and police commander in France. Generally speaking, the Nazis tried harder in France than in any other country to draw a veil over the real meaning of the deportations; the term used by the authorities was in fact resettlement (*Umsiedlung*) rather than deportation.

There were protests from many quarters, the US, Catholic bishops and Protestant clergymen, and even Hungary. But Laval declared that he would not be deflected from his course of action. If the official explanations had been believed there would have been no protests, for at the time a great many Frenchmen went to work in Germany and this had not provoked any major outcry. But the fact that the transports included many small children (who were furthermore separated from their parents) as well as elderly and sick people showed that the Nazis had different intentions. As Donald Lowry, a Quaker representative reported to Tracy Strong, general secretary of the world committee of the YMCA on 10 August 1942: 'They [the deportees] have few illusions as to the fate awaiting them in Poland.' Valeri, the papal nuncio, told the Vatican the same on 7 August: people in France did not believe the official version since the deportees included sick and aged people.

The news about the mass murders was broadcast from London in French (*Les français parlent aux français*) beginning in early July 1942. Some of the resistance newspapers and pamphlets mentioned the use of gas in October–November; one notable exception was *L'Humanité* which did not comment on the extermination of the Jews up to the end of the war.* But Laval stuck to his story about the Jews building an agricultural colony when Pastor Boegner came to see him in early September 1942 to protest. As Boegner later wrote: 'Je lui parlais de massacres, il me repondait jardinage.'[36] ('I spoke to him of massacres, he replied with gardening.') But Laval and his collaborators, needless to say, did not believe in *jardinage*. If they did not know the details of the 'final solution', they certainly did know that the Jews would not return.

---

*Ignorance cannot have been the reason for another Communist underground newspaper with a more restricted circulation (for students and teachers in the universities) did mention Auschwitz and the fact that the Jews were singled out for destruction.

2

THE NEUTRALS: 'UNANIMOUS AND RELIABLE REPORTS'

FOUR neutral countries played an important role as far as the news about the fate of European Jewry was concerned: above all Switzerland, where most of the Jewish emissaries were concentrated, Turkey, Sweden and to a lesser degree Spain. This is true for rescue work but even more so with regard to the gathering of information. It has been shown in the previous chapter that citizens from neutral countries had many opportunities to travel in Germany and the occupied countries and some of them were very well informed. The neutral countries were also of vital importance for the Polish intelligence network which brought most of the news out of the country to London. Bern and Stockholm were central 'bases' (so were Budapest and Istanbul). While the emissaries would if possible proceed directly to London, couriers would frequently deliver their messages in Stockholm and Bern for transmission to London.* British and US intelligence, needless to say, also had their representatives in these capitals.

The position of Switzerland was pre-eminent both as a listening post and for staging aid operations. Ten years after the war, after much heart-searching and public debate, the Swiss Government asked a leading academic, Professor Ludwig, to prepare a report about Swiss policy towards refugees during the war. A copy of the report was shown before publication to Dr Rothmund who had been chief of the aliens department of the Swiss police during that critical period. The main question posed by Ludwig was: at what stage was the Nazi campaign of destruction known? It obviously made a great difference whether Swiss officials did know about the 'final solution' in 1942, when they sent refugees back. But in Rothmund's view the question was not really of decisive importance: 'Enough was

*Emissaries were always members of the Polish underground; couriers could also be nationals of another country who acted as mail carriers.

known by that summer,' he wrote in a letter of comment. The records bear him out. On 30 July 1942 a twenty-three-page memorandum was sent out by Dr Rothmund to the local chiefs of police which mentioned *expressis verbis* the horrible (*grässlich*) conditions in the Jewish ghettos in the East, referring to 'unanimous and reliable reports'.[1] It should be mentioned in parenthesis that this knowledge did not prevent Rothmund two weeks later from circulating instructions to turn back Jewish refugees. A term such as *grässlich* is not easily used in wartime. It refers quite obviously to something worse than starvation and disease.

These 'unanimous and reliable reports' came from accidental sources as well as through the ordinary channels of information. The case of the Swiss citizen, who by chance watched the *Einsatzgruppen* killing Jews at Kamenets-Kasirski in late 1941 and reported to the Swiss consul in Hamburg, will be mentioned. Professor Ludwig's report frequently quotes the reports from Jewish sources received by the World Jewish Congress and the Jewish Agency. But it is not certain whether the Swiss authorities believed these reports; it had, in any case, access to the same sources and also additional ones.

There was the case of a Zürich physician, Dr Rudolf Bucher, a specialist in blood transfusion, who visited Warsaw, Smolensk and other East European cities between November 1941 and January 1942. He was a member of the first Swiss medical delegation to the eastern front, headed by Dr Bircher, a high-ranking Swiss officer (and also a medical doctor) of pronounced pro-German sympathies.[2] In a book published after the war Bucher maintained that he was told in December 1941 or January 1942 about Auschwitz and mass gassings in special chambers.[3] This seems most unlikely because the gas chambers in Auschwitz began to operate only several months later except for the trial run in September 1941 when some 800 Soviet prisoners of war had been killed. But even if Dr Bucher's memory failed him as far as Auschwitz is concerned, he certainly did witness some massacres and did hear of others. Almost immediately after his return to Switzerland, Dr Bucher appeared at public meetings in which he spoke about the inhuman condition in which the Jews were kept, and that he had seen with his own eyes the murder of many of them in

Warsaw and Smolensk. Hundreds of people attended these lectures. The German authorities protested and Bucher was threatened with dire consequences by his superiors in the Swiss army.[4] Bucher later became a public figure; he was a member of the Swiss parliament in the post-war period for a number of years. Those who knew him describe him as a somewhat unreliable witness, a man given to excitement and exaggeration. But, and it is all that matters, on this occasion he certainly did not exaggerate and his excitement was not misplaced.

His evidence was furthermore corroborated by the account of Franz Blaettler, (apparently a *nom de plume*) a sergeant-driver who had accompanied the same mission. He also wrote a book in which he described the 'scene of mass dying' in a Warsaw ghetto which he called 'one great cemetery': 'I was ashamed to leave as a free man this site of horror.'[5] His diary was submitted to the Swiss authorities. It included entries such as 23 October: 'Yesterday 3,000 Jews killed because of sabotage.' Or 7 November: 'Women and children liquidated [*umgelegt*] because of shooting at German soldiers.'

There were three more Swiss medical missions to the eastern front, the last in 1943, but meanwhile censorship had imposed a blackout on what its members had seen in the East. Examining both their official (unpublished) reports and some of the personal diaries preserved in the archives I found many medical case histories on one hand and descriptions of the Polish and Ukrainian landscape and the inhabitants on the other. But there is no word about the Jews. Perhaps the members of these missions saw no evil, perhaps they had taken to heart the order not to reveal any sensitive information on which they may have stumbled: all of them had to sign an understanding to this effect as they entered German territory. Or perhaps most of the Jews were already dead and there was nothing to be seen and reported.

Information also came, of course, from official sources. Stucki, the Swiss ambassador in Vichy, reported a meeting with Laval from which it appears that Laval was in a truculent mood, that the protests against the deportations of French Jews were unlikely to deflect him – and that he also knew what fate the deported expected. There were reports on the subject from Swiss consuls from places such as Marseilles.[6] Swiss citizens from Nazi-

occupied Europe returned home for short or long periods of
leave and related their impressions. Swiss citizens listened to the
radio speeches by Adolf Hitler on one hand and to Thomas
Mann on the other. In his New Year message for 1942 Hitler
had stated: 'The Jew will not exterminate the people of Europe,
he will be the victim of his own evil design.' And on 30
September 1942 in the *Sportpalast*:

I have said in my Reichstag speech on 1 September 1939 that if the
Jews unleash an international world war, not the Aryan people will be
exterminated by Jewry. . . . Once upon a time the Jews in Germany
were laughing about my prophecies, I don't know whether they still
laugh or whether they no longer feel like laughing. I can only assure
them they will stop laughing everywhere and I shall be right also with
these prophecies.

A Swiss newspaper, the *Thurgauer Zeitung*, commented after this
speech:

There is no room for doubt any more: Hitler's word can be interpreted
only in the sense that the extermination of the Jews remains one of the
points which will be carried out irrespective of the outcome of the war.
Hitler had destroyed all illusions which still existed on the fate of the
Jews. . . .[7]

Thomas Mann, broadcasting over the BBC in London,
mentioned in November 1941 the 'unspeakable' done to Jews
and Poles.[8] In the preface to the collection of these radio
addresses Thomas Mann wrote that: 'More people listened to
me than could have been expected, not only in Switzerland and
Sweden.' In his later broadcasts he was more specific: in
September 1942 he spoke about the total extermination of
European Jewry, about the gassing of thousands near Warsaw,
about the stories of the German engine drivers who had taken
the trains to the death centres.

The Swiss press was kept well informed. Charles Schuerch,
the secretary of the Swiss trade-union organization, published
an eyewitness account datelined Paris, 21 July 1942, entitled
'We cannot keep silent',[9] in which he described the big razzias in
France which were the prelude to the first large deportation.
Many Swiss newspapers wrote at the time that it was ridiculous
to argue that refugees turned back at the Swiss border were in no
real danger; in fact they faced certain death.[10]

The reports about the scenes in France on the eve of the deportation were bad enough. But there still was the question of what happened to the Jews from France, Belgium and the Netherlands after they had been deported. The Swiss press had few illusions: *Volksrecht* (Zürich) wrote on 15 August that most of them would die on the transport. The *Volk* (Olten) commented on 18 August that all these thousands would die a horrible death in a Polish or Ukrainian ghetto. The *Schweizerische Kirchenzeitung* wrote on 27 August 1942 that the scenes witnessed were reminiscent of the killing of the children of Bethlehem as reported in the Bible: there was only one aim behind all this – the extermination of the Jews.

From time to time Swiss censorship would intervene and punish those who had been 'too one-sided' in their reports. Thus the organ of the Swiss Jewish community was told that 'the cleverly selected quotations about the persecution of Jews was propagandistic in character and therefore inadmissible'. What [the censor asked] if someone were to publish a collection of anti-semitic quotations with the intention of engaging in anti-Jewish propaganda? Surely the discussion about the anti-Jewish persecution would have to proceed in a quiet and objective (*sachlich*) manner.[11] The measures taken by the Nazis, alas, were not quiet and objective. On the whole, however, Swiss censorship did not suppress the news about systematic mass murder in 1942; given the political situation and the constant German pressure this involved a certain courage. In the following year, 1943, Swiss censorship became more stringent. The Swiss newspapers were given a public warning because they had reprinted reports from the British press about the Babi Yar massacre two years earlier.[12] Some newspapers such as *Nation* were given constant warnings for having featured detailed descriptions about the death camps in which on certain days some 7–10,000 Jews were killed. Such reports were, in the words of the censor, 'atrocity stories of the worst kind' (*krasseste Greuelmeldungen*) which had come from the British press and which were scheduled to serve the propaganda of one of the belligerent sides.[13]

For the military censor it was quite immaterial whether the news was true or false. All that mattered was that the position of Switzerland in the second half of 1943 after the German seizure of northern Italy was even more tenuous than the year before. In the circumstances Germany was not to be provoked. But in 1942, the period under review in this study, even moderate papers, never given to hyperbole, were outspoken. Thus the *Neue Zürcher Zeitung* on 13 September 1942:

... these reports on measures whose incredible cruelty has no parallel even in this global war induce a feeling of horror. The present accounts do not yet give a final picture. But we do have moving testimonies of undeniable character, which leave no room for any embellishment.

Most of these comments concerned the circumstances of deportation, of uprooting people and dividing families. These were tragic events but few had as yet openly stated the equation deportation = murder. On the other hand would so much horror have been expressed about the deportations if there had not been suspicions (and more than suspicions) about the fate of those deported? Thus the *Tribune de Genève* wrote on 16 September 1942: 'Où vont-ils, tous ces malheureux? Ils ne le savent pas, mais ils le devinent . . .'* The *Schaffhauser Zeitung* on the same day wrote about the 'most hair-raising rumours' in connection with the transports. A small town newspaper, the *Volksfreund* of Flawil (10 October 1942), went even further and asked bluntly: 'Are the deported Jews killed?' The paper added:

The question may appear incautious. Some will say that whether the Jews deported to the East are actually killed, whether they are shot, whether they starve to death or die in some other way does not really concern us. But as Christian people in Christian Europe we have to be concerned whether mass murder of innocent people of another race does indeed take place.

Flawil is a little town in the canton of St Gallen. It had at the time some six thousand inhabitants. What was known in Flawil, was surely known in Bern, Zürich, Basel and Geneva. The Swiss press widely published a United Press report from Stockholm (11 October 1942) which said that it was an 'open secret in Berlin' that no preparations were made to resettle the Jews. Some of the 'death transports' were carrying the Jews to the overpopulated ghettos, others directly to the place of execution.

*Where are these unfortunate people going? They don't know, but they can guess. . . .'

The *Evangelische Flüchtlingshilfe* published a leaflet in October 1942 which said, 'The Jews, the people of God, are dying. All over Europe reverberate the shouts of those who are shot or killed by poison gas.' The question posed by the *Volksfreund* was answered by the *Basler Nationalzeitung*, one of the leading newspapers in the land:

The German authorities are not content with depriving the Jews of elementary human rights. They now carry out their frequently announced threat to destroy the Jewish race in Europe. Jews from all occupied territories are deported in horrible conditions. In Poland they are systematically exterminated. One has not heard a word from any of those who have been deported.[14]

Similar information appeared in other organs of the press.

Thus, seen in retrospect, Dr Rothmund was right when he said that 'enough' was known in 1942. Rothmund's superior, on the other hand, von Steiger, head of the Department of the Interior, wrote to Professor Ludwig in 1955 that he and his colleagues in the Swiss Government had come to believe only in 1944–5 that the rumours of the horrors were indeed true.[15] Rothmund, who with von Steiger's full support had given the order to turn the Jews back, was widely criticized and demoted after the war. Von Steiger, an accomplished timeserver, emerged with hardly a stain on his character. There is little justice in politics.

Von Steiger could have pleaded that since the Allied leaders were in no particular hurry to confirm that the news about the mass murder in the East was authentic, there was no reason why he, a minister in a neutral country, should have given more credence to these rumours. There was the official Allied declaration of December 1942 but it had not been a particularly strong one in the first place and it was further watered down by the American Government. All this may be quite true, but hardly constitutes a moral excuse. For the Swiss minister did, of course, know, just as the British and American ministers knew, unless he never read newspapers, did not listen to the radio and, generally speaking, refused to discuss politics. For anyone reading the Swiss press in late summer and autumn of 1942 there could be no reasonable doubt that mass murder was perpetrated in Eastern Europe, not isolated pogroms, but systematic extermination. Considering Switzerland's exposed position,

Swiss newspapers were as outspoken, if not more so, as those in England and America and even Palestine.

The 'rumours' came not only from Swiss newspapermen in occupied Europe but also from many other sources. They came through Swiss diplomatic channels and from Swiss citizens living in Germany or Eastern Europe or returning from visits to Germany or German-occupied territory. They originated with the refugees who succeeded in illegally crossing the Swiss border in 1942; some of the stories are mentioned elsewhere in this book. They came from the governments-in-exile such as the Polish and the Dutch, who had their representatives in Switzerland, from foreign intelligence agents, and from the International Red Cross and the Oecumenical Committee for Assistance to Refugees (Dr Visser't Hooft and the Reverend Dr Freudenberg). They even emanated from visiting German diplomats who dropped occasional hints. In short the news came from every possible direction. Von Steiger, and through him the Swiss Government, were kept informed by Dr Alphons Koechlin, president of the Swiss Protestant Association.

Sweden was in a less central position as a listening post, but the Swedish Government was still kept informed from a variety of sources. There was the presence of Swedish diplomats, journalists and businessmen in Germany and the occupied territories. Kurt Gerstein, the chief 'disinfection' officer of the SS back from his inspection tour of Belzec, had made his revelations to a Swedish diplomat, Baron von Otter, in a famous encounter on the Warsaw–Berlin express.

The question of what became of this report has been a matter of much speculation and it can now be answered with some assurance. Von Otter at first composed a written account of his dramatic meeting, but then decided not to send it with the diplomatic mail since he was to return to Stockholm within a week of the event. Interviewed many years after the war von Otter said that it was a 'totally unique situation'. He was the first diplomat to find out. What if his superiors had passed on the information to the Allies and if they had made the facts known? Von Otter thinks that the German people would not have believed them as they were in an 'iron grip'.[16]

Soederblom, the head of the political department in the

Swedish Foreign Ministry to whom von Otter reported, said 'We judged it too risky to pass information from one belligerent country to another'; he also said that there were a great many rumours at the time. Gösta Engzell, the Foreign Ministry spokesman at the time, had only hazy recollections: von Otter received some sort of information which was talked about in the Foreign Ministry. Eric Boheman, spokesman of the Government, also believed that there were some documents referring to this incident in the archives.

Following a request made by the present writer access was first given to the von Otter file in February 1980. But the only document found was a letter by von Otter to Viscount Lagerfelt at the Swedish legation in London.[17]* It relates the story of the meeting with Kurt Gerstein in late August 1942 and the report about the 'corpse factory' of Belzec (a literal translation from the Swedish). There are details about transport conditions, technical procedure, the reactions of the ss guards and the Jewish victims, the collection of jewellery, gold teeth and other valuables. Gerstein also showed von Otter various documents referring to the purchase of cyanide gas. Gerstein's objective was, as he himself said, to draw the attention of a neutral state to the events. He expressed his belief that the German people would not support the Nazi regime for a single moment if knowledge of the extermination was disseminated and confirmed by impartial foreign sources.

Gerstein visited von Otter again half a year after their first meeting in order to enquire what use the Swedes had made of his information. His looks, according to von Otter, indicated that he was in deep despair, ready to commit suicide at any moment, in view of the horrors that were taking place in Germany. Meanwhile von Otter had received independent confirmation from Bishop Dibelius about Gerstein's reliability as a witness. According to Dibelius he had volunteered for the ss in order to find out whether it was true that a large number of mental patients were killed upon Hitler's orders. Gerstein felt that as a sanitation expert he had a good chance to get at the truth.

*Another Swedish diplomat who heard about the mass murders in 1942 was Per Anger, stationed at the time in Budapest. His informant was the Hungarian journalist Kalman Konkoly. (Communications from Ambassador Anger, 28 January 1980.)

According to von Otter, Dibelius had received exactly the same report about the fate of the Jews from Gerstein.* What emerges from all this is that there was only an oral report by von Otter in 1942 which did not result in a written memorandum or note. The argument that the Swedish Government 'found it too risky' (Soederblom) to pass the information to the Allies can hardly be taken seriously for there were, of course, ways and means to transmit it without directly implicating the Swedish Government. If so, why was the report not leaked at least to the press? Because, to put it in the shortest possible way, it was August 1942.

The Swedish Embassy in Berlin was besieged by unfortunate Jews and 'Christian Jews' fearing deportation and death for whom a Swedish visa was the last lifeline. Those in the embassy dealing with these requests were, of course, familiar with the mortal dangers facing applicants.† The embassy parson had close contact with oppositionist circles in the German Protestant Church and was kept informed through them. According to a cable from Uxkuell, an Associated Press correspondent in Stockholm, on 11 October 1942 the 'death transports' continued despite the lack of rolling stock in wartime Germany and the Jews had become totally apathetic as the last hope to evade deportation, and thus execution, had disappeared, the only exceptions being a few highly qualified workers and doctors. Such information could have come from Swedish channels, but equally some of the refugees could have been the source. Not many refugees arrived in Sweden except from Norway and Denmark, but a few did throughout the war, and almost everyone had an extraordinary story to tell. Among the most outspoken newspapers was the *Göteborgs Handelsoch Sjöfartstidning*, edited by a courageous journalist, Torgny

---

*Gerstein had also tried to alert the papal nuncio in Berlin, not aware of the fact that of all the envoys of the Vatican, Orsenigo was the most reluctant to offend Hitler and the Nazis. Not surprisingly, Gerstein was shown the door. He then got in touch with Dr Winter, the coadjutor of the Archbishop of Berlin. If his message reached the Vatican 'it did no more than confirm facts of which the Vatican was amply apprised'. (S. Friedlaender, *Counterfeit Nazi* (London, 1969), p. 158.)

†The Swedish authorities were also kept informed by the Swedish Israeli Mission in Warsaw headed at the time by Birger Pernow. Some of their reports that three million Jews had been killed in Poland found their way into the press. (*Aftontidningen*, 7 October 1943.) But such publications only came later on.

Segerstedt. This paper, as well as the weeklies *NU*, *Trots Allt* and some others, contained information on the fate of the Jews. Sweden furthermore represented the Dutch Government in Berlin, and the Dutch mobilized the Swedes even in 1941 when the first news about the execution of young Dutch Jews in Mauthausen was reported. The Swedes approached the German authorities in Berlin and were told that this was an interference in inner German affairs and the subject could not be discussed. But the Swedes again approached Berlin later in 1942 when the mass deportations got under way; they also acted on behalf of the Norwegian Jews who were deported. The result of their efforts is of no relevance in this context. All that matters is that through these interventions Ambassador Richert and his assistants came to know about the mechanics of the 'final solution'.

The Swedish press was more reticent about the 'final solution' than the Swiss although there was no censorship. It was only in December 1942, after the tide in the fortune of the war had changed, that outspoken and detailed reports and comments were occasionally published in Swedish newspapers. This is true even with regard to a liberal, pro-Western newspaper such as *Dagens Nyheter*. During the critical summer months of 1942 there were reports about anti-semitic decrees in Vichy (4 June) and Norway (19 June), about the deportation of Jewish 'criminal' elements from the Netherlands to the East and about even more stringent anti-Jewish laws in Germany (24 July). But massacres were mentioned only indirectly, as with Churchill's message to a Jewish meeting of protest and mourning in Madison Square Garden, New York (23 July 1942).

There were some exceptions but these were few and far between. Thus *Dagens Nyheter* reported on 13 September 1942 that the technique of persecution (of the Jews) had become harder and more ruthless. But this could mean a great many things short of murder. Perhaps the first outspoken editorial comment appeared on 21 October 1942 in the *Eskilstuna Kuriren*. It spoke about indescribable barbarity and a 'war of extermination' against the Jews and said that this was 'the responsibility of all of us' and asked whether Swedish Christians were not their brothers' keepers. Eskilstuna is a provincial town west of Stockholm. What was known there, was known, of course, in the capital. If the Stockholm newspapers refrained from such comment, the reason was not lack of information.

Exact information was difficult to obtain but this was true *a fortiori* with regard to partisan warfare in Yugoslavia about which the papers had a great deal to report during this period. Since the Swedish Government had first-hand, detailed information about events in Poland from leading members of the Swedish colony in Warsaw up to their arrest in July 1942, as well as from other sources, and as British and American newspapers were available in Sweden, the question has to be asked why the information was suppressed at least in part. The answer is, very briefly, that although there was no censorship the Government had the right to confiscate a newspaper without taking the matter to a court of law if the paper had published information or comment 'likely to cause misunderstanding with a foreign country'. The Swedish Board of Information sent 'grey slips' to the editorial offices drawing attention to subjects unsuitable for publication. Among these topics were 'atrocities committed by the belligerents'. Swedish cabinet ministers, in particular Foreign Minister Guenther, were apprehensive during this critical period about newspapers showing a deplorable lack of national responsibility: a New Order had come into being in Europe, the balance of power had changed and it was exceedingly dangerous to provoke the Germans, the strongest power in Europe.

The turning point came when the Quisling Government in neighbouring Norway had all Jews arrested and deported in November 1942, except those who succeeded in making their way to Sweden in time. In November 1942, it should also be recalled, the German Sixth Army was encircled at Stalingrad, Rommel was decisively defeated and the Allied landing took place in North Africa.

There was great commotion in Sweden: special services were held in Swedish churches, the bishops published appeals against the anti-Jewish measures and there were sermons on subjects such as 'the voice of thy brothers' blood crieth unto me from the ground'.[18] Speakers in public meetings said that the treatment of the Jews in Norway defied description. According to a Gallup poll 25 per cent of all Swedes said that they would remember longer (and with greater horror) the deportation of Jews from

Norway than any other event which had occurred in 1942 (*Dagens Nyheter*, 31 December 1942).

The Swedish press, including newspapers which had not previously taken a particularly sympathetic line towards the Jews, expressed indignation. *Svenska Dagbladet* said that platonic declarations were no longer sufficient, action was needed, all Jews from Norway should be given asylum in Sweden. Quite frequently reference was made to 'death ships' and the extermination of the Jews.[19] Some papers stressed both the 'sadistic character' and the 'mechanic precision' of the 'final solution' which was regarded as a terrible stain on European civilization. While some editorial writers decried the fate of the Jews without specifically mentioning that they were killed, others – and again surprisingly many provincial newspapers among them – said *expressis verbis* that this was a case of 'mass murder', that a whole people was killed with inhuman brutality.[20] But the focus was on Norway most of the time. Only rarely mention was made of the fact that the two thousand Jews of Norway were not Hitler's only victims and that the Allies had published a common declaration against the mass murder.[21] On 20 December 1942, *Dagens Nyheter* wrote that the silence of the Swedish newspapers regarding the persecution of the Jews in Norway was due to the desire to help the unhappy victims, at a time when the Swedish Government was believed to be doing everything it could in this direction: 'It is impossible at this moment to reveal details of the negotiations but when they have been concluded the public must be informed, and silence will no longer be necessary.' But once the gates of Auschwitz had closed behind the Jews from Norway, the issue disappeared for a long time from the columns of the Swedish press.

Among the neutrals, Spain was the country least interested in the Jews: Spanish newspapermen and intelligence agents certainly did not go out of their way to establish what happened to the Jews.* But even the Spanish could not help hearing the

---

*The same is true, of course, with regard to Turkey. Istanbul was of great importance in 1943 and the years after as a centre from which rescue operations were directed. But the various rescue committees were represented there only after January 1943, which is to say that during the most critical period, 1941–2, relatively little information about the fate of the Jews reached the West through Turkey. (About individual attempts to gather information, by Meleh Neustadt and others in 1942, see chapter 6.) The Turkish

'rumours'; they had ambassadors and journalists in the Axis countries and also in the neutral and Allied capitals. They had a volunteer division fighting on the eastern front; Jewish refugees succeeded in reaching Spain, which given the European situation was a secure haven. Spanish consuls in German-occupied territories were implored to give citizenship papers or visas to individuals about to be deported, however tenuous their relationship to Spain. The Spanish Government did extend such protection to some Jews of Spanish origin in Greece and other countries. It was, in fact, more helpful than other more democratic but also more fearful countries, and it even risked some German ill will in the process. Officially Spain knew nothing about the 'final solution' but from both Nazi and Allied sources it emerged that at least some people in Madrid were certainly in the know. Thus von Thadden, the German Foreign Ministry specialist for 'final solution' international complications, reported to Eichmann that a member of the Spanish Embassy in Berlin had informed a representative of the German Foreign Ministry orally that they would not mind handing over the Spanish Jews from Greece to Germany 'if only they could be certain that they would not be liquidated'.[22] One month later the British Embassy in Madrid reported that the Spanish Government would welcome the idea of permitting Jews with Spanish passports to come to Spain as an alternative to being sent to Poland where they would presumably die in concentration camps and be made into soap.[23] The Spanish archives have not yet been explored; but it is obvious quite irrespective of whether a search would result in startling new discoveries that Madrid, like everyone else in Europe, had heard about the fate of the Jews.

The role of the Vatican has been endlessly debated – whether Pope Pius had to keep silent, and whether by doing so he violated his elementary Christian duties. The Vatican did intervene in Slovakia and Romania, and, albeit not very forcefully, in France and Croatia. Would Hitler have arrested the Pope and executed the cardinals, if they had spoken out

---

Government and the press were not interested in the topic. There were few foreign correspondents in Istanbul in 1942. Neither they nor the more strongly represented intelligence services reported on Jewish affairs except on rare occasions. One such exception was the report made by Francis Ofner to Basil Davidson, representing British intelligence, in June 1942. The subsequent fate of the report is unknown.

loudly and clearly? Hardly; he was only too anxious to prevent an open conflict in wartime. Probably it was a case of pusillanimity rather than anti-semitism. If the Vatican did not dare to come to the help of hundreds of Polish priests who also died in Auschwitz, it was unrealistic to expect that it would show more courage and initiative on behalf of the Jews.

But the central question in this study is not what the Vatican did, but what it knew. While there can be legitimate differences of opinion on its activities (or lack of them) there is no shadow of doubt with regard to its knowledge. It has been argued (by M. Wladimir d'Ormesson) that the Pope and those around him had no idea what went on in the outside world in view of the 'total isolation' imposed by Nazi Germany and Fascist Italy, the fact that the telegraph was in the hands of the Italians, that there was interference with foreign broadcasts etc.[24] But M. d'Ormesson, who represented France in the Vatican up to October 1940, was not a disinterested party and his apologia is hardly convincing. There was a great deal of coming and going throughout the war between the Vatican and the outside world. It was kept informed by the Jewish representatives in Geneva who handed long memoranda to the nuncio in Switzerland, Bernardini (17 March 1942), as well as to Angelo Roncalli, the future Pope John XXIII, at the time papal nuncio in Turkey; it was bombarded with notes by Myron Taylor and Harold Tittmann, US envoys at the Vatican, Sir Ronald Campbell, the British ambassador, the Brazilian envoy and countless others. All these notes contained information about the mass murder committed by the Nazis. But for the tragic character of the subject, it would have been a subject for a comedy, for the Vatican did not, of course, need Myron Taylor, Sir Ronald Campbell and the Brazilians for information about events in Germany and Eastern Europe. It was better informed than anyone else in Europe. There were tens of thousands of Catholic priests all over Poland, Slovakia and the other countries. They were part of the community, if anyone knew what happened there, it was these men. There were many millions of practising Catholics in Germany, and again tens of thousands of priests – not a few of them serving with the German army in the East. If a Catholic priest learned about the conspiracy against Hitler's life, it is difficult to believe that they did not hear about the activities of the *Einsatzgruppen* and the death camps. A Catholic official of the Foreign Ministry talked to his bishop about the 'final solution' looking for spiritual guidance which he apparently did not get. But this became known by mere accident; there may have been many more such cases. The Vatican, furthermore, had direct or indirect channels of communication with every European country but Russia.* If some Catholic priests in Germany sympathized with the Nazis, many did not, and there were no Nazi sympathizers among the clergy in Poland and few in France.

From the little evidence that has become accessible it emerges that the Vatican was either the first, or among the first, to learn about the fate of the deported Jews. According to Hans Gmelin, counsellor at the German embassy in Bratislava, Burzio, the local nuncio, wrote in a letter to Prime Minister Tuka in February 1942 that it was an error to think that the Jews would be sent to work in Poland, they would be exterminated there. This is confirmed in a dispatch by Burzio to the Vatican dated 9 March 1942 which deserves to be quoted again in view of its importance: 'The deportation of 80,000 persons to Poland at the mercy of the Germans means to condemn a great part of them to certain death.'[25] Yet the official line of the Vatican throughout 1942 remained that it could not confirm the news about the 'final solution' and that, in any case, the information about massacres seemed to be exaggerated. True, Orsenigo, the representative of the Vatican in Berlin, had reported on 28 July, '. . . piu macabre supposizioni sulle sorte dei non-ariani.'[26]† But

---

*The Polish bishops had to report to Rome through Nuncio Orsenigo in Berlin, whom with some justification they distrusted. For Orsenigo's behaviour in his dealings with the Nazis certainly went well beyond the necessary caution. It is difficult to judge whether he thought he acted in the best interests of the Church or whether his own career was foremost in his mind; Orsenigo very much wanted to be a cardinal. His performance in Berlin did not make him very popular in Rome after the war and he did not attain his ambition. What has just been said about the Polish bishops refers, of course, only to official channels. There were various other ways to communicate with the Holy See – for instance through couriers to Bernadini the nuncio in Switzerland, or via Budapest. Above all, the Polish clergy was in contact with the Holy See through the London Government-in-exile which had throughout the war an ambassador at the Vatican, Casimir Papée. From the documents published by Papée as well as the reports of the Polish Home Army it appears that the Vatican was kept fully informed about events in Poland. (C. Papée, *Papiez Pius XIIa Polska-Przemowienia i listy papieskie 1939–46*. 2nd ed., 1946. See also Carlo Falconi, *The Silence of Pius XII* (Boston, 1970), pp. 109–244.)

†'. . . the most gruesome speculation on the fate of the non-Aryans.'

supposizioni were not facts on which a government (or the head of the Catholic Church) could base its policy. Both Catholic and Protestant church leaders (such as the German Bishop Dibelius) have claimed after the war that until the very end they were not aware of the full implications of the final solution. This may well be true if the stress is put on the 'full implications'. There was no evidence which would have stood up in a court of law; no cardinal or bishop was ever permitted to visit Auschwitz, Sobibor or Treblinka. Their knowledge was based on hearsay, but it is unlikely that they had any doubts as to the authoritative character of this information.

The Vatican was in a better position to know than the Protestants, simply in view of its superior organization and more extensive international connections. The Vatican archives are not accessible at the present time. I have been assured by Cardinal Casaroli, Prefect of the Council for the Public Affairs of the Church (and Secretary of State), that while the Holy See cannot depart from its principle of no access to the archives, the eleven volumes of 'The Holy See During the Second World War' have not omitted anything relative to the object of the present book.[27] If so, it must be assumed that the great majority of the notes, reports, letters, memoranda etc. exchanged between the Holy See and its own representatives on one hand and foreign governments on the other have been lost; one can only hope and pray that the loss is not permanent.*

Much of the information reached the Vatican, furthermore, not through diplomatic channels but through personal contacts between priests, high and low, and this will not be found in the archives at all. It can be argued that even the most energetic actions on behalf of the Vatican would not have saved a single Jew. But it cannot possibly be maintained that the Vatican had no information. As Carlo Falconi says: no one was better

---

*Such attempts to keep Vatican knowledge of events secret are politically and psychologically understandable, but not very far-sighted, for sooner or later at least some of the facts will become known. Even if the Vatican archives remain closed indefinitely, there are other sources. The Vatican representatives in the various capitals used an antiquated code for their communications which was undoubtedly intercepted and, in all probability, also broken by most (if not all) European secret services. It is quite likely that the Vatican emissaries did not trust their own code and that very secret or sensitive material was passed on only by word of mouth. But even so there are likely to be at least some revelations in the not-too-distant future.

informed than the Pope about the situation in Poland, with the exception, perhaps, of the Polish Government-in-exile.

Of all the unofficial international bodies no one was in a better position to know about the fate of the Jews in Europe than the International Red Cross. As the report of the IRC of its activities during the Second World War states:

Since the year 1863, when a committee of five citizens of Geneva, with Henry Dunant as their leading spirit and General Dufour at their head, gave the first impulse to the world-wide movement of the Red Cross, based on the formation of National Societies, and to the first Geneva Convention of 1864, the Red Cross, both as a humanitarian and a social institution, has attained far wider scope than its founder ever contemplated.[28]

The IRC stood for a particular idea, namely the protection of wounded and sick members of armed forces and succour for the defenceless victims of hostilities, respect for the human being, and the provision of effective aid on the basis of the principle of absolute impartiality.

During the First and Second World Wars, as on many occasions before and after, the IRC has done an enormous deal of good and its selfless work deserves the highest praise. During the Second World War it paid thousands of visits to prisoner-of-war camps and provided humanitarian help such as food and medical supplies and parcels to the civilian population: 36 million parcels were shipped and 120 million messages transmitted. It arranged the exchange of permanently wounded or sick prisoners of war and certain categories of civilians; it organized the exchange of short messages between civilians of belligerent nations.

Nevertheless much criticism has been levelled against the IRC for not having extended help to Jews, both to prisoners of war and the civilian population, except during the last phase of the war in Slovakia and Hungary. The line taken by the IRC was (as expressed by Professor Max Huber, its then president) that the civilian population in territory occupied by the enemy had little protection, merely the 'obsolete and incomplete provisions' of the Hague Regulations of 1870, and that furthermore for practical reasons stirring up a scandal would have endangered everyone without saving a single Jew. It is true that the IRC could not operate in former Russian territory since the Soviet

Union had not signed the Conventions and that the Germans put many obstacles into the way of the IRC. The national committee of German Red Cross, with which the IRC had to deal, was headed by several major war criminals such as Dr Grawitz and Professor Gebhardt, leading members of the SS, inventors of the gas chambers and initiators of 'experimental medicine' in the death camps. (The poison gas Zyklon B was transported in vans with the Red Cross insignia.) Lastly, Swiss neutrality imposed strict limits on IRC activities; all the leading members of the IRC were Swiss citizens. Swiss neutrality up to 1943 prevented any action that could have been construed as unfriendly by Germany and the Axis powers. But again the problem in this study is not whether the Red Cross did as much as it could have done, but at what stage it knew about the mass murder and what use it made of this information.

The structure of the IRC at the time was briefly as follows: the leading body was the Central (Co-ordination) Commission which had been established in November 1940. Its members were Professors Huber and Burckhardt and Messrs Chenevière and Barbey. Huber was a distinguished expert in the field of international law. Burckhardt was equally well known as a diplomat, historian and student of literature. They supervised committees dealing with prisoners of war, relief, legal questions etc. The IRC staff in Switzerland in 1942 was almost 3,000 and there were some 70 permanent employees abroad. By the end of the war the IRC had some 76 delegations with 179 members paying visits to POW camps and civilian internee centres; there were about one thousand such visits in 1942 alone. The emissaries and delegates covered enormous distances, they visited the German Foreign Ministry, they talked to countless civilians and army personnel on both sides and while they could not, of course, move about freely in German territory, they certainly could reach places which other foreigners (and many Germans) could not. Several POW camps were located in Poland. The IRC was bound to learn early on that Jewish soldiers and officers of the Polish army had been taken from the POW camps for 'an unknown destination'. The IRC had delegates not only in Germany but also in Croatia and Romania, the countries in which the first major massacres of Jews took place. Furthermore the IRC in Geneva was constantly approached by the local Jewish representatives with various requests for information about the fate of various individuals in Nazi-occupied countries. The IRC did try to find out until it was told by the German Red Cross that no information would be forwarded about 'non-Aryan prisoners'. What could the IRC have done in these circumstances? To protest was pointless, Professor Huber argued; the Red Cross was not an international tribunal. Had the committee adopted the method of public protest, it would inevitably have been forced more and more into taking a definite stand with regard to all kinds of acts of war, and even of political matters and this, of course, was quite impossible. It was the considered view of the IRC, on the grounds of past experience, that 'public protests are not only ineffectual but are apt to produce a stiffening of the indicted country's attitude with regard to Committee, even the rupture of relations with it.'[29]

'Germany had put the Jews into a new category, that of second-class human beings,' the IRC post-war report said. Just as the general laws did not pertain to dogs, cats and sheep, so they did not pertain to Jews. But what use would it have been to bang on the table and to protest – 'what protests and threats have ever changed criminal methods?'[30]

These and many other post-war writings ('Did we not fail in the fulfilment of certain duties?') shows that the IRC was aware that it had faced a grave dilemma, and that it might not have done all it could even within the difficult conditions facing it. For it was also true that keeping silent in these circumstances was tantamount to abetting the 'final solution'.

But what did the IRC know and through what channels did it get its information? It was not permitted to open a permanent delegation in Poland and only in late 1942 was it allowed to establish delegations in Slovakia, Hungary and Romania. But its emissaries did travel in Eastern Europe and from these missions and through other means the news about the fate of the Jews filtered through. On at least one occasion in late August 1942 Dr von Wyss, an IRC delegate, inspected the food distribution centre for the Polish ghettos. Some further examples will suffice.[31] There were frequent exchanges between Miss Warner and Miss Campion of the British Red Cross and Madame Ferrière in Geneva: what had become of the German and Czech Jews who were deported? Was it true that they were sent to Poland and Russia? There was no reliable information, Madame Ferrière replied, but it actually happened all over Europe. It was a tragic situation and 'we cannot do anything about it'. On another occasion she mentioned the 'tragic consequences of the situation'. Later, in August 1942, Miss Campion reported to Geneva 'enormous numbers of inquiries' about deportations. Meanwhile individual IRC officials had talked to Jewish doctors about the deportations from Berlin (Dr Exchaquet, 20 November 1941).

René de Weck, the Swiss minister in Bucharest, wrote in a private letter to Jacques Chenevière of the IRC about the systematic persecutions to which the Romanian Jews were exposed and said that 'the Armenian massacres which had shaken the European conscience at the beginning of the century were a mere child's play in comparison' (29 November 1941). In a postscript he stated that the basic tendency was the 'physical destruction of the Jews'. Following de Weck's initiative and urgings from other quarters W. Rohner visited Hungary and Romania in March 1942. In a long memorandum to Burckhardt he mentioned 'les massacres les plus atroces'* of Kamenets Podolsk as well as the fact that in the Ukraine some 100,000 Jews had been killed (report dated 10 April 1942). He also wrote that the Slovak Jews had been deported. According to one report he received the younger Jewish women thought they would be working in factories in Poland but this was probably mere self-delusion, they would be put 'à la disposition des soldats allemands'.† In Hungary he heard a report on the deportation to Auschwitz of eight thousand Jews and in Romania about the murder of twenty thousand in Odessa. Rohner was president of the *Commission mixte de secours*; his word carried weight.

Auschwitz, among other places, was also mentioned in a report by the head of the Slovak Red Cross, Skotnicky, (9 June 1942) and by the representative of the French Red Cross, Colonel Garteiser, who misspelled it 'Hauswitz'. He noted that those deported were never heard of; they were not permitted to write or receive letters (2 June 1942). Dr Marti, who represented

---

*'the most atrocious massacres'.
†'at the disposal of German soldiers'.

the IRC in Berlin, was another important source. He went to see Dr Sethe of the German Red Cross and intervened with him but was told that those deported from France were considered criminals; no help could be rendered (20 May 1942). He tried again in September: was it possible at least to correspond with those who had been sent to the East? Again there was a negative answer, except for some thirty individual replies to many thousand queries.

Dr Marti was permitted to travel to the General Government in August 1942 but seems not to have seen much. True, he reported horrible scenes at Rawa Russka where French prisoners of war from Stalag 325 had seen the execution of 150 Jews by Ukrainians. Several months before, Marti had reported that special SS units were exterminating civilians in the occupied Russian territories. When he told Sethe that people outside Germany were saying that conditions in the camps were worse than anything the Inquisition had invented, Sethe simply replied 'Let them talk' (28 January 1942). Later Marti reported that French Jews had been seen in Riga and that sixty thousand Jews were believed to have been killed there (14 November 1942).

So far the information had been sporadic but in late autumn the news came in from all quarters. Even the IRC delegate in Washington reported that the State Department had been informed that Jews were killed in great numbers in Poland (13 October 1942). Thus the question arose whether the IRC should make public what it knew. Discussions among members of the IRC executive went on throughout August 1942. By mid-September Professor Huber and his assistants had prepared a draft which, while mentioning no names and condemning no one in particular, simply said that civilians should be humanely treated. This was not sufficiently outspoken for Madame Odier (head of the subcommittee for civilian affairs) and Madame Bordier, a member of the relief commission. They thought that stronger language was needed in the face of an unprecedented catastrophe. However, the majority in the executive did not believe in appeals which it thought emotional and futile, but they were willing to support the Huber draft.

The decisive meeting took place on 14 October 1942. Huber was ill and the chair was taken on this occasion by Chenevière.

Philip Etter made one of his rare appearances on this occasion. He had been Swiss Foreign Minister in the 1930s and represented the Swiss Government. His orientation was if anything rather pro-Axis and he opposed even the anodyne Huber draft, arguing that it could be interpreted as a violation of neutrality. His opinion prevailed and as a result no IRC statement at all was issued concerning the murder of the Jews. If leading members of the IRC did not believe in the value of public appeals they were willing to pass on what they knew in their capacity as private citizens.

In October 1942, Carl Burckhardt began to talk.* He informed first an old Jewish friend and colleague from the Geneva Centre of Advanced Studies, Professor Paul Guggenheim, and then on 7 November he saw Paul C. Squire, American consul in Geneva. He told Squire that while he had not actually seen the order, he could confirm privately and not for publication that Hitler had signed an order in 1941 that before the end of 1942 Germany must be freed of all Jews. He had received this information independently from two very well informed Germans, one a German Foreign Ministry official (probably Albrecht von Kessel), the other a War Ministry official. Squire asked him whether the word extermination was used, whereupon Burckhardt said that the actual text was *judenrein* – empty of Jews. But since there was no place to send the Jews, and since the territory must be cleared, it was obvious what the result would be. Burckhardt also said that the IRC had considered directing a public appeal throughout the world on the question of the Jews but it had been voted down; it was thought that such an appeal would render the situation even more difficult and jeopardize the work undertaken for the

---

*He was not the only one to transmit information privately. Dr Riegner, writing in June 1942, mentions the fact that he was told by a leading personality of the IRC that the Jewish representatives in Geneva actually underestimated the number of Jews killed in the German-occupied territories of Russia. According to the same source the only way to stop the slaughter was to threaten the Germans with retaliation in kind. (Riegner to Goldmann, 17 June 1942.)

The official in question was, in all probability, André de Pilar, a Baltic baron who also had Swiss nationality. He was a member of the *Commission mixte de secours* of the IRC, a special agency for relief dispatches. De Pilar was in constant touch with the German Red Cross. Riegner recalls that he was very open in conversation 'and gave me from time to time extremely valuable information' (Riegner to author, 13 December 1979).

prisoners of war and civil internees which was the real task of the Red Cross.*

In a covering note to Leland Harrison, US minister in Bern, Squire wrote that he had always observed that the Nazis sought to cloak their documents in legality – the use of the term 'extermination' was too bloody for historical record, but it was clear that 'for the unfortunates only one solution remained, namely death'.[32]

Later in November Riegner went to see Burckhardt and was told that the Red Cross did not want to lodge a protest for the time being. It was feared that the information which the IRC still received about the deportations would cease altogether in case of a protest. Furthermore, it seemed advisable to protest only when there was no hope whatsoever of helping any other way. Meanwhile the IRC would continue to press the Germans constantly for information, to ask for permission to send delegates to the General Government, to Theresienstadt and Transniestria. A German Red Cross official named Kundt had, in fact, told him that such pressure was desirable (!), even though he could not promise that it would lead to any result.[33]

The Burckhardt revelations were not sensational. By October 1942 about two million Jews had been killed and the information had been received from many sources. But the very fact that he was willing to speak about a Führer *order*, even though unofficially and off the record was, of course, a breach of neutrality as his colleagues, such as Professor Huber, understood it. Burckhardt's conversation with Squire certainly influenced the American diplomats who had been reluctant to believe Polish and Jewish sources. The information was still considered inconvenient in Washington, but it could no longer be ignored.

---

*Burckhardt was a cautious man. There is an American record of this conversation, written by Consul Squire. I have been assured by a director of the IRC that a search made in IRC offices in Geneva showed that Burckhardt did not leave a report of this talk.

3

THE ALLIES: 'WILD RUMOURS INSPIRED BY JEWISH FEARS'

SHORTLY after the end of the war Abbé Glasberg, a courageous churchman of Russian-Jewish origin who had done much to save French Jews, wrote that he found it difficult to explain how during all these years the Allied intelligence services should have not known (or ignored) the truth about the Hitlerite extermination camps which extended over many square kilometres and in which millions of people had been incarcerated.[1]

It is a legitimate question. True, no intelligence service is omniscient, but in this specific instance there was no need for brilliant analytical skills and great penetration: letters and postcards told the story and sometimes it was even reported in the press. The critical period for this study is July 1941 to the end of 1942. American intelligence was then only starting its operations while the British services were already in top gear. While everything that happened in Nazi-occupied Europe was of interest to these services, there were, of course, priorities, and the fate of an ethnic or religious minority did not figure high on their agenda. But on the other hand no intelligence service in Europe could possibly not help hearing about the 'final solution' in 1942 for the simple reason that it was common knowledge on the continent. Details were perhaps shrouded in mystery, but the picture in general was not: as Hitler had predicted, the Jews were disappearing.

The Allied governments heard about this from a variety of sources. In Britain there was the SIS, Special Intelligence Service (military intelligence) which was, in principle, in charge of all news gathering operations. But the Special Operations Executive (SOE), which had been founded to engage abroad under the control of the Ministry of Economic Warfare (MEW), did in fact also collect news in France, in Denmark and in other countries. All intelligence from Poland was passed to the SIS automatically from the Polish Second Bureau except that concerning purely domestic affairs. Similar agreements existed between Britain and Dutch, French, Czech and Norwegian intelligence. But the SOE was also active in Poland. MI5, the security service, obtained interesting information from the interrogation centres it ran, so did MI9 (CSDIC) and MII9, dealing with British soldiers and civilians escaping from the continent respectively. Decoding and deciphering came from GC&CS (the government code and cypher school), whereas aerial reconnaissance was in the hands of the Air Ministry. The bureaucratic complications were manifold but whatever the source, important news should always have reached the Prime Minister, the War Cabinet and the chiefs of staff.[2]

But what is important news? Intelligence quite often consists of small and perhaps insignificant items, which taken in isolation appear to be of no consequence. A certain pattern emerges only if they are interpreted in a broader context. There is, furthermore, an unlimited number of ways of getting things wrong and only one right answer. Intelligence, like writing history, is a matter of selection and the fact that a certain event was duly observed does not *per se* mean that it was correctly understood. It certainly does not mean that such information always reached the higher ranks of the intelligence services, such as the Joint Intelligence Committee which acted as a liaison between the various agencies, and certainly not the War Cabinet whose capacity for absorbing information was, of necessity, limited.

Thus for the purpose of this study, it is not sufficient to establish that members of one branch of the Polish or British intelligence knew. It is important to know how widely the information was distributed and whether it was read and accepted, and this, of course, is usually more difficult to document.*

---

*But sometimes it can be documented. Emissaries from Poland arriving in Britain were interrogated and debriefed by the British services before they could contact the Poles. One of the wartime emissaries describes his arrival in Britain as follows: 'After my arrival on a Scottish airport I was first interrogated by Major Malcolm Scott, probably on behalf of counter-intelligence; his family owned a factory in Lwow and he spoke Polish as well as I did. I was then debriefed in the "Patriotic School" in south London by representatives of various other intelligence services; in greatest detail by MI9 who were interested in the fate of the British prisoners of war. I was also interviewed by McLaren and Osborn of the Foreign Office (Polish Intelligence). Depositions were made; I saw some of them recently among the papers in the Public Record Office. There was no

During the critical period London was the focal point for news from occupied Europe. Not all information received in the West came from intelligence sources. America, it will be recalled, had an embassy in Berlin until December 1941, in Budapest and Bucharest until January 1942, in Vichy up to late 1942. Jewish organizations received most of their information from their representatives in Geneva, and news was, furthermore, received through dozens of different channels, such as visitors to or from neutral countries, the press, soldiers who had escaped, civilians who had been exchanged and others.

Much information could be found in the daily press. Thus a report in a London, German-language newspaper in October 1941 entitled *The Apocalypse* said that the Jews deported from Germany were to be killed in one way or another. It was based on a report originally published in the Swedish *Social Democraten* on 22 October and stated *expressis verbis* that 'there was no doubt that this was a case of premeditated mass murder'. The account also mentioned Adolf Eichmann as the head of the operation.[3]

We must first turn to Russia, because it was in the areas occupied by the Nazis after their rapid advance between June and October 1941 that the systematic murder of European Jewry began. This was the task of the *Einsatzgruppen*; by November 1941 they had killed about half a million Jews. At first, little was known about this to the general public, for these areas were virtually cut off from the outside world. American Jewish newspapers carried reports about the killing of Jews in certain border towns but this was probably no more than guesswork based on the behaviour of the Nazis in Poland and elsewhere. A little later Swedish papers reported that ghettos had been installed in Vilna, Kaunas and Bialystok. According to a broadcast from Moscow radio in August some forty-five Jews had been machine-gunned near Minsk.[4] On 5 September the London Polish Government-in-exile knew about Riga ghetto, and on the 18th of that month the news reached Zürich from Poland that Bialystok ghetto had been destroyed – which

---

interest in what I had to report on the fate of the Jews; there was one exception, and this was on a personal rather than official basis.' To these three who were informed about the sytematic extermination of Jews, Majors (subsequently Colonels) Colin Gubbins and Perkins should be added, who were dealing with Poland on behalf of the SOE. Gubbins later became operational head of the whole SOE. Neither of them was apparently expected to, or did take an interest in the subject.

was quite untrue for it was one of the last to be liquidated, in 1943. On 22 October 1941 the Jewish Telegraphic Agency (JTA) correspondent in Zürich quoted a Ukrainian newspaper (*Krakovskie Vesti*) that the German forces had expelled the Jews to an unknown destination and that in Zhitomir out of 50,000 Jews only 6,000 remained. On 29 October a report, again from Polish circles in London, said that 6,000 Jews had been killed in Lomza, and in early November the Swedish press announced that Riga Jews were on half rations. More and more information was received, but perhaps not enough as yet to realize the magnitude of the disaster.

Then on 25 November 1941 JTA carried a sensational and remarkably accurate report which it said had originated 'on the German frontier' but had been delayed. According to an unimpeachable source, 52,000 men, women and children had been put to death in Kiev. The victims (it was said) did not lose their lives as a result of a mob pogrom but by 'merciless, systematic extermination'. It was one of the most 'shocking massacres in Jewish history' and similar such events had taken place elsewhere in other Soviet towns. We do not know where this report originated; it certainly did not come from a Soviet source. Most likely it emanated from Polish circles. Confirmation from Soviet sources came, however, in early January 1942 when it was made known that 52,000 people had been killed in Kiev. The US Embassy in Moscow tried to establish whether all (or most) of these had been Jews and on 16 March 1942 it received an affirmative answer. But on the next day the Jewish press announced on the authority of the *Soviet War Bulletin* in London that there had been a misunderstanding and that only one thousand Jews had been killed. This 'correction' was, of course, quite misleading, but it is impossible now to establish whose fault it was.

Meanwhile there was more alarming news. On 2 January 1942 the London *Jewish Chronicle* reported, on the authority of Soviet partisans operating behind the German lines, that the Germans had killed hundreds of Jews in Rostov-on-Don. Polish sources reported in March the destruction of Lithuanian Jewry. By 15 May 1942 this news was quite detailed: 7,000 had been killed in Shavli, 30,000 were left out of 70,000 in Vilna. The Stockholm newspaper *Social Democraten* reported that the Jews in

Riga ghetto were selling their last belongings; this was based on a report in the Nazi *Deutsche Zeitung in Ostland*. From Soviet sources there was very little information. A detailed report from Borisov was an exception: 15,000 Jews had been killed there (25 March 1942). There was a shorter and less specific account of the mass murder of Jews in Mariupol.

Meanwhile on 6 January 1942 the Soviet Union in a note signed by Molotov and addressed to all governments with which it maintained diplomatic relations dealt with the 'monstrous villainies, atrocities and outrages committed by German authorities in the invaded Soviet territories'.[5] This note extended over many pages and there were three references to Jews. Once they were mentioned together with Russians, Ukrainians, Letts, Armenians, Uzbeks and others who had also suffered; the second time there was a short reference that on 30 June when the Germans had entered Lwow they had staged an orgy of murder under the slogan 'kill the Jews and the Poles'. And lastly there was the reference to the murder of the 52,000 in Kiev. It stated that many mass murders were also committed by the German occupiers in other Ukrainian towns and then continued:

These bloody executions were especially directed against unarmed and defenceless Jewish working people. According to incomplete figures, no less than 6,000 persons were shot in Lwow, over 8,000 in Odessa, nearly 8,500 were shot or hanged in Kamenets Podolsk, more then 10,500 shot down with machine guns in Dnepropetrovsk and over 3,000 local inhabitants shot in Mariupol. . . . According to preliminary figures about 7,000 persons were killed by the German Fascist butchers in Kerch.

Altogether Molotov accounted for some 90,000 victims – less than one-fifth the figure of those who had actually been killed.*

On 27 April 1942 a second Soviet note was published, also signed by Molotov. It extended over twenty-seven pages, dealt with looting, the institution of a regime of slavery, the destruction of the national culture of various peoples, the

---

*The fact that Soviet reports about categories of victims were selective was noticed in Washington. The OSS Department of Research and Analysis published a nine-page memorandum in 1943 entitled 'Gaps in the Moscow Statement of Atrocities' which stressed that 'non-Aryans' were not mentioned. (OSS – Washington DC R&A – 1626, 12 December 1943)

desecration of churches, the torturing and killing of workers and peasants, the raping of women and the extermination of prisoners of war. But it did not mention that while indeed a great many people of various nationalities had been robbed, injured and even killed, the Jews, unlike the others, were singled out for wholesale destruction. In this document the Jews were mentioned just once – together with Russians, Moldavians, Ukrainians and other victims. There was a third Molotov note (14 October 1942) on the responsibility of the Hitlerite invaders and their accomplices for atrocities perpetrated in which the Jews were not mentioned at all. But as an addendum (or postscript) an unsigned statement was distributed on 19 December 1942 by the Soviet Foreign Ministry Information Bureau dealing specifically with the 'execution by Hitlerite authorities of the plan to exterminate the Jewish population in the occupied territory of Europe'. This was a relatively short document but it presented more facts and figures than published in the preceding year-and-a-half taken together. It also mentioned the plan to concentrate millions of Jews from all parts of Europe 'for the purpose of murdering them'.[6]

Why did it take the Soviet Government eighteen months to publish these facts and what were the reasons inducing it to play down the number of Jews among the victims or even pass over it in silence? The first six months of the war were the most difficult from the Soviet point of view: millions of soldiers were taken prisoner, a large part of the country lost. The population frequently gave a warm welcome to the invaders. There were few if any partisans during these early months of the war. But, on the other hand, not everyone in the occupied areas became a collaborator with the Germans, and many Soviet intelligence agents were left behind. In addition early in the war parachutists were dropped behind German lines, some to commit acts of sabotage, others to collect information. There was radio contact between the occupied territories and 'Bolshaia Zemlia' from the very beginning, and although there is no reason to assume that the secret police, the NKVD as it was then called, and the Red Army staff received daily bulletins from every occupied village, there is every reason to assume that the Soviet authorities were from the beginning well informed about all important events in the occupied territories. Although

Russian archives have not been opened to curious Western (or Soviet) researchers, Soviet authors proudly mention how well their authorities were informed about all that happened on the other side.

One of the most famous cases was that of N. I. Kusnetsov who, in the guise of a German officer (under the name of Paul Siebert), became part of the establishment of Erich Koch, one of Hitler's three satraps in Eastern Europe. Koch had established his headquarters in Rovno. Up to 1941 every second inhabitant of that city had been a Jew, so their disappearance (they had all been executed in the town or its vicinity) could not possibly have escaped the attention of this Soviet master agent. The fate of the Jews, and how much was known about it at the time, occurs infrequently in Soviet post-war writings. Thus a discussion between two KGB (NKVD) agents in Kiev in late 1941: 'You know, of course, what happened in Babi Yar?' 'Yes, and the same happened in Vinnitsa ...'[7] There is always the reluctance to mention the fact that these victims were Jews. For the Soviet authorities, the agents left behind in Kiev, Odessa, Minsk and many other places, were by no means the only source of information; in the winter offensive of 1941–2 as Soviet troops retook some of the regions previously seized by the Germans they saw what had happened under German occupation.

Thus with a few exceptions, such as the note of 13 December 1942, the Soviet line was that the Hitlerite invaders behaved generally speaking like barbarians. But there was no mention of the fact that the Jews were singled out for 'special treatment'. What was the reason for this silence? The Soviet authorities could argue that even though the Nazis singled out the Jews in their campaign of murder, little would be gained if the Soviet Union publicized this fact. For the murder of the Jews may well have been quite popular in some sections of the population: Ukrainians, Lithuanians and Latvians had played a prominent part in the massacres. If the German invaders, nevertheless, rapidly became unpopular in the occupied areas, it was not because of their behaviour towards the Jews. For this reason, and perhaps also for some other considerations, the Soviet authorities played down the 'final solution'. Like the Vatican the Russians certainly knew much more than they decided to publish. The news about the *Einsatzgruppen* came mainly from neutral journalists, Polish intelligence, and from Hungarian and Italian soldiers fighting on the eastern front. It did not come from those who knew most about it.*

By 1 July 1942 more than one million Jews had been killed in Eastern Europe. What was known about this in the West?

The German offensive in Russia was in full swing; the German armies were advancing in the direction of Stalingrad, Rostov and the Caucasus. The *Einsatzgruppen* had finished their second sweep in Russia. In Poland the destruction of the ghettos had begun in March with the removal of the Jews from Lublin district, the very region in which, according to the Nazi propaganda, a Jewish autonomous region should have come into existence. The gas chambers of Chelmno, Belzec and Auschwitz were working. The Wannsee Conference had taken place six months earlier, the deportations from Slovakia had begun in March and trainloads of Jews were beginning to arrive in Poland from Central and Western Europe.

From Russia there was little information. Correspondents in Switzerland picked up random items from Nazi newspapers in the occupied areas. Thus, the *Grenzbote* of Bratislava announced in April that the 'deportations' from Slovakia had taken place, and the Belgrade *Donauzeitung* wrote in June that no Jews were left in Kishinev. Also in April 1942 the correspondent in Turkey of the London *Sunday Times* reported that 120,000 Romanian Jews had been killed, a figure which was remarkably accurate. All these were minor items as far as the world press was concerned, overshadowed by the news of the great battles on the war fronts, and they did not attract much attention. In May and June 1942 with great delay some more information became available about events in the Baltic countries. On 15 May, Polish sources in London provided figures on Vilna – the murder of 40,000.[8]

The following day a correspondent of the London *Evening*

---

*Towards the end of 1942 some more material became known from Soviet sources, but more often than not it was scheduled for publication outside the Soviet Union. Thus a quotation from a diary written by Private 'Christian' in February 1942: 'Since we have been in this town we have already shot more than 13,000 Jews. We are south of Kiev.' Or the interrogation of POW Karl Brenner, Crimean front 20 June 1942: 'None of the Jews were ever seen again. It is said that they were shot 15 miles from Simferopol along the Feodosia road.' *New Soviet Documents on Nazi Atrocities*, Soviet Embassy, London 1942, passim.

Standard in Stockholm reported that the number was even higher: 60,000 Jews had been killed in this city alone. The news was published on the authority of a man who had escaped from Vilna and just arrived after a dramatic escape via Warsaw and the port of Gdynia. The report was quite specific, it mentioned Ponary, the railway station outside Vilna where most of the killing had taken place. The item was picked up by some American and Jewish newspapers. Two months later on 21 July the US ambassador reported it to Washington. Then there was silence for another two weeks but towards the end of May 1942 information, which had reached London through Polish couriers and radio messages, found its way into the press. On 2 June the BBC broadcast excerpts from various reports received from Eastern Europe: 700,000 Jews had been killed so far. This figure was based on a report sent out by the Jewish Labour *Bund* from Warsaw, and, in fact, considerably understated the number of victims. But the Polish Jews had no full picture of the situation in the Soviet Union and the Baltic countries. Unlike Himmler they had no professional statisticians at their disposal reviewing the progress of the 'final solution'.

The reports from Warsaw which are discussed elsewhere in this study caused a flurry of activity in Polish circles: General Sikorski notified the Allied governments in a dispatch ('Extermination of the Jewish population is taking place to an unbelievable extent'), on 10 June. The Polish National Council, the parliament-in-exile, addressed an appeal to the free parliaments. On 9 June Sikorski said in a broadcast on the BBC:

The Jewish population in Poland is doomed to annihilation in accordance with the maxim 'Slaughter all the Jews regardless of how the war will end.' This year veritable massacres of tens of thousands of Jews have been carried out in Lublin, Wilno, Lwow, Stanislawow, Rzeszow and Miechow.

At first the newspapers did not take much notice. After all, news about Nazi persecutions came from many parts of Europe and they were probably exaggerated. The fact that Jews were not persecuted but exterminated had not yet registered. The first to stress the difference was the London *Daily Telegraph* in two reports on 25 and 30 June 1942. These publications were a first turning point because the authors and editors had realized that from the various news items from Eastern Europe a sinister new pattern emerged: these were no longer pogroms in the traditional sense. The first dispatch began as follows: 'More than 700,000 Polish Jews have been slaughtered by the Germans in the greatest massacres in the world's history.' It then announced that 'the most gruesome details of mass killings even to the use of poison gas' were revealed in a report sent secretly to Shmuel Zygielbojm, Jewish representative on the Polish National Council, by an active group in Poland (the *Bund*, which was not, however, mentioned by name). The *Daily Telegraph* report reviewed the mass exterminations in East Galicia and Lithuania, the use of gas vans and the Chelmno camp, as well as other facts and figures. The correspondent ended: 'I understand that the Polish Government intends to make the facts in the report known to the British and Allied governments' (which had already happened).

The second report five days later said in its headline 'More than 1,000,000 Jews killed in Europe'. It was based on further investigations, not just the *Bund* report, and made one important point which had not been clearly spelled out previously: that it was the aim of the Nazis 'To wipe the race from the European continent'. The extermination of the Jews was also to cover the West. In France, Holland and Belgium there had been many executions, and mass deportations to Eastern Europe were now taking place. In Romania 120,000 Jews had been killed; two trainloads of Jews were leaving Prague every week for Poland: 'It is estimated that the casualties suffered by the Jewish people in Axis-controlled countries already far exceed those of any other race in the war.'

The *Daily Telegraph* stories attracted much attention. They were followed by radio broadcasts in June by Arthur Greenwood, leader of the Parliamentary Labour Party, by Cardinal Hinsley, by the Dutch Prime Minister, by Zygielbojm (speaking in Yiddish!) and a few others. The *New York Times* picked up the *Daily Telegraph* reports on 30 June and 2 July and published them somewhere in the middle of the paper. The editors quite obviously did not know what to make of them. If it was true that a million people had been killed this clearly should have been front page news; it did not, after all, happen every day. If it was not true, the story should not have been published at all. Since they were not certain they opted for a compromise:

to publish it, but not in a conspicuous place. Thus it was implied that the paper had reservations about the report: quite likely the stories contained some truth, but probably it was exaggerated. Such attitudes were by no means limited to the American press. From the moment Hitler had come to power in Germany, the *Manchester Guardian* had shown much sympathy for the persecuted Jews. Yet on 31 August 1942, more than two months after the news about mass extermination of Jews in Europe and after additional information had been received, an editorial in the *Guardian* stated 'that the deportation of Jews to Poland means that Jewish muscles are needed for the German war effort'. It was, in brief, a matter of slave labour rather than murder. But why single out the *Guardian*? President Roosevelt was saying exactly the same thing. The failure to understand was by no means limited to newspapers in Britain and the United States. Hebrew papers in Palestine were equally unhappy about the 'unproven and exaggerated rumours', the fact that news agencies and correspondents were competing in transmitting atrocity stories in gruesome detail.[9]

Zygielbojm, the *Bund* representative on the Polish National Council, had provided the material for the *Daily Telegraph* stories. His colleague on the Council, Dr I. Schwarzbart, was also active. He appeared on 29 June at a press conference sponsored by the World Jewish Congress in London together with S. S. Silverman, the Labour Member of Parliament, and E. Frischer, a member of the Czechoslovak State Council. Ignacy Schwarzbart (1888–1961) had been a member of the pre-war Polish parliament; unlike Zygielbojm he was not a socialist. His statement dealt with the murder of Jews in Wilno, Pinsk, Bialystok, Slonim, Rovno, Lwow, Stanislawow, Lomza and two dozen other places. He announced that in Lublin part of the Jewish population had been slaughtered and the rest disappeared and he also gave figures about the Chelmno gassings.* This press conference was reported the next day in

---

*But Schwarzbart took a more cautious line than Zygielbojm. In a letter to the editor of the London *Jewish Chronicle* (dated 29 June 1942, unpublished, Schwarzbart archives) he wrote that 'every exaggeration in rounding up figures is not only needless but also harmful and irresponsible'. He regretted that 'my colleague in the National Council' had taken it upon himself to refer to 700,000 Jews who had been murdered, whereas one should have said 'exterminated'. Schwarzbart followed the lead given by the Polish

most British newspapers under headlines such as 'Over 1,000,000 Dead since the War began' (*The Times*), '1,000,000 Jews Die' (*Evening Standard*). 'Million Jews Die' (*News Chronicle*), 'Bondage in Eastern Europe. A vast slaughterhouse of Jews' (*Scotsman*). But most of these reports were rather short, they were not conspicuously displayed and they contained few details. Few Western newspaper readers had ever heard about Lomza and Stanislawow, and while by now it seemed fairly certain that something sinister was happening in Eastern Europe, there were still doubts about the extent and the real meaning of these unhappy events.

The general attitude in July and August among Jews was a mixture of concern and confusion. On one hand there were mass meetings in New York (Madison Square Garden, 21 July), protest demonstrations in various other cities, and on 23 July the chaplain of the House of Representatives read a special prayer for the Jewish victims as the session of the house opened. In London there were resolutions by the National Executive Committee of the Labour Party (22 July) and the trade unions; a Labour delegation went to see Anthony Eden, the Foreign Secretary (24 August) and John Winant, the US ambassador. On 2 September there was a big protest rally in Caxton Hall in which Herbert Morrison and Jan Masaryk were among the speakers. Zygielbojm in a passionate speech reiterated that crimes had been committed that had no precedent in human history, crimes so monstrous, in the face of which the most barbaric acts of the past ages appeared as mere trivialities: 'In Poland a whole people is being exterminated in cold blood . . . it is estimated that the total number of Jews murdered by the Germans in Poland up to May this year was 700,000.' Zygielbojm seemed overexcited and overwrought to many of those present, yet, by the time he made his speech the number of

---

Minister of Information, Professor Stronski, who had said in a press conference on 9 July, sponsored by the British Ministry of Information, that the figure of 700,000 which had appeared in the press 'included both those murdered directly and those who died as a result of the German extermination policy'. It is not readily obvious why Schwarzbart should have attributed so much importance to the difference between being murdered and being exterminated, unless he doubted the veracity of the reports from Poland. The *Bund* report, in any case, was quite unambiguous: 700,000 Jews had been murdered (*Niemcy wymordowali* . . .).

Jews killed was at least a million and a half and Warsaw ghetto had been all but emptied.*

The question of the number of victims quite apart, a clear general pattern had emerged. Obviously, there had been a decision at the highest level to kill all Jews. When had it been taken? This information could not possibly come from Warsaw or Riga and we have now to turn to an episode which has been told before but which is still far from clear: the first news that Hitler had actually ordered the extermination of European Jewry by gassing was received by Dr Riegner, the representative of the World Jewish Congress in Switzerland, from a German industrialist in July 1942. Riegner sent the following cable to London and Washington:

Received alarming report that in Führer's headquarters plan discussed and under consideration according to which all Jews in countries occupied or controlled Germany numbering 3½–4 millions should after deportation and concentration in East be exterminated at one blow to resolve once for all the Jewish Question in Europe stop the action reported planned for autumn methods under discussion including prussic acid stop we transmit information with all reservation as exactitude cannot be confirmed stop informant stated to have close connections with highest German authorities and his reports generally speaking reliable.

Some of this was already known and some was incorrect: the plan was not 'under consideration' but had been adopted many months earlier. Nor was it intended to kill all the Jews at one blow, which would have presented insurmountable technical difficulties. But with all this it was, of course, true that Hitler had made a decision and now a German source had made it clear that this did not refer to widespread pogroms but to a 'final solution'. Riegner transmitted the information 'with all necessary reservation'. One could hardly blame him for such caution.

Gerhard Riegner was just thirty years of age at the time. He was a native of Berlin and a doctor in law. He and Richard Lichtheim, his senior by thirty years who represented the Jewish

---

*Zygielbojm committed suicide in March 1943 in protest against the general indifference shown with regard to the fate of the Jews in Poland. On the circumstances, see chapter 4.

Agency in Geneva, were the two chief Jewish representatives in
continental Europe. But who was the mysterious industrialist?
Various speculations have been published about his identity.*
He arrived in Switzerland in July 1942. It was not his first visit in
wartime. He had been in contact through a common friend with
Dr Benjamin Sagalowitz (1901–70), the press officer of the Swiss
Jewish community. The industrialist was in charge of a factory
employing some 30,000 workers; he was a passionate enemy of
the Nazi system. Driven by his conscience, he wanted to warn
the world so that something could be done in time to counteract
Hitler's designs. The industrialist asked the common friend to
convey the news to Sagalowitz, who was not, however, in Zürich
at the time. After his return he transmitted the information to
Riegner assuming that Riegner could reach Rabbi Wise in New
York and through Wise, President Roosevelt. Leland Harrison,
the US ambassador, insisted on knowing the name of the
informant and since there was no other quick and certain
channel to transmit to America, Sagalowitz gave the name (and
indicated the position) of the industrialist to Harrison, in a
closed envelope. Sagalowitz concludes his account as follows:
'Dr Riegner did not get the name from me, I brought the two
gentlemen together only in February 1945. To relieve my
conscience I told the industrialist after the war that I had given
his name to the American minister and he understood. . . .'[10]

Neither the archives of the late Dr Sagalowitz nor the files of
the National Archives in Washington nor the personal files of
Ambassador Harrison provide a clue. The files of the Berlin
Swiss legation, in which applications for entry visas in wartime
were preserved, have been destroyed and I have been assured
that the records of the Swiss border police no longer exist.

Why should the industrialist who, as these lines are written, is
no longer alive have insisted on anonymity even after the end of
the war? There are two possible explanations. Could he have
been a Swiss diplomat or an official of the International Red
Cross or the World Council of Churches? This, for a variety of
reasons, is unlikely. The second possibility is more probable and

---

*According to the introduction to the Hebrew edition of Arthur Morse's *While Six
Millions Died* it was Artur Sommer. About Sommer see Appendix 1 'The *Abwehr*
connection', and my article in *Commentary*, March 1980. The first letter of the name of
the mysterious messenger was 'S' – but it was not Artur Sommer.

more intriguing. When Riegner tried to establish in 1942 whether his informant could be trusted he was given to understand by Sagalowitz that the industrialist had on previous occasions given information on impending changes in the German army high command (the deposition of von Bock in winter 1941), and, even more important, the date of 'Barbarossa', the invasion of the Soviet Union. The official history of British intelligence in the Second World War mentions among other warnings that the SIS representative in Geneva had heard in late March or early April 1941 from a well-placed source in German official sources that Hitler would attack Russia in May.[11] The British authorities will not disclose the identity for another twenty-five years (if ever) and, in any case, it is not certain that the industrialist was indeed the source. But is it at all likely that Riegner, trying to find out in July 1942 whether his informant could be trusted, would have been told about this ultra-secret information provided by a most valuable source? There may be an answer to this question; a great deal of circumstantial evidence exists, but no absolute proof.[12]

The reaction to the Riegner cable in London and Washington can be summarized briefly. On 10 August 1942 the Foreign Office received the cable; four days later Frank Roberts of the Central Department wrote that the message could not be held up much longer although he feared that it could have embarrassing consequences: 'Naturally we have no information bearing on this story.' This was certainly true in the sense that there had been no report about a decision taken by Hitler. But then Roberts had heard from a colleague many months earlier about the disappearance of one-and-a-half million Jews; there had been other such stories from Polish sources as Allen (also from the Central Department) noted. But Allen still thought it was a rather 'wild story'.

The cable was handed by the Foreign Office to a Labour Member of Parliament, Sidney Silverman, who was subsequently seen at the Foreign Office by Sir Brograve Beauchamp and Colonel Ponsonby. He wanted to telephone Stephen Wise in New York but was told that this was out of the question; the Germans always listened in to such conversations. Furthermore, he should consider whether any action taken by the Jewish institutions might not 'annoy the Germans and make any action they were proposing to take even more unpleasant than it might otherwise have been'. Lastly he was told that HM Government had no information confirming Riegner's story.

The general view in the Foreign Office was that the Germans were indeed treating the Jews very cruelly, starving them and even massacring considerable numbers of those who were of no use to them in their growing labour difficulties. The Polish reports that the Germans had more far-reaching designs were apparently not believed. If the Jewish Congress wanted to publish Riegner's story there was no objection, even though there was the possibility that the Jews would be victimized as a result and that Dr Riegner's source would be compromised. The British Government on its part had no intention of giving publicity to the report or using it in propaganda to Germany without further confirmation.[13] In short, the Foreign Office was not very helpful but with all its reservations it did deliver the message.

The State Department did not. Howard Elting, the US vice-consul in Geneva, requested that the message be delivered to Rabbi Stephen Wise, but the State Department's Division in European Affairs opposed this. Paul Culbertson, the assistant chief, did not like the idea of sending the dispatch on to Wise. Elbridge Durbrow regarded the nature of the allegations as 'fantastic'. On 17 August Harrison in Bern was informed that the cable had not been delivered in view of the apparently unsubstantiated nature of the information.* But on 28 August a copy of the Riegner cable reached Wise via the British Foreign Office, which despite grave doubts (on which more below) had not suppressed it. Wise got in touch with Undersecretary of State Sumner Welles who advised him to refrain from any public announcement of Hitler's extermination order until confirmation could be obtained.

During August and September 1942 additional evidence reached Washington. Some came from Geneva; this refers to the confirmation of Hitler's decision by Carl Burckhardt, the 'foreign minister' of the Red Cross, which is mentioned elsewhere

---

*Harrison asked Elting to send the cable directly to the State Department. But his own comment in a cable to Washington on the same date was more than sceptical; he regarded it as a 'wild rumour inspired by Jewish fears'. A summary of his cable was passed on to the OSS. (RG 226, Bern, Folder 2, Box 2, Entry 4.)

in this study. On 3 October Riegner forwarded the evidence of two young Jews who had crossed the Swiss border. One of them was Gabriel Zivian who had been a witness to the massacre of the Jews in Riga and had arrived on 22 September.[14] The other new arrival had been from France to Stalingrad and back, and knew many details about the murder in Poland and Russia. Neither could possibly shed any new light on the Führer's order, nor could the postcards from Warsaw which had been received by Sternbuch, the representative of orthodox Jewry, which announced the liquidation of the Warsaw ghetto. But all these items fitted only too well into the general picture. So did a report from the US Embassy in Stockholm, and another very long and detailed one from Anthony J. Drexel Biddle Jr, US ambassador to the Allied governments-in-exile in London. This was based on a memorandum by Ernst Frischer, a Czech parliamentarian, who had appeared at the press conference in London in late June together with Schwarzbart and Silverman. His report stated that there was no precedent for such organized wholesale killing in all Jewish history, nor indeed in the whole history of mankind. A copy of Biddle's report was sent directly to the White House.

US diplomats abroad were asked by the State Department to find out whether they had heard anything which could shed light on the Riegner report. Finally on 22 October Harrison met Riegner and Lichtheim (the Jewish Agency representative), collected various sworn affidavits from them and forwarded the whole evidence to Washington. Eleven weeks had now passed since the original Riegner cable, eleven months since the news about mass murder in Russia had first been received in the West. Further reports from Jewish and non-Jewish circles continued to arrive: an account from a Vatican source said that the mass execution of Jews in Poland went on. The number of Jews killed in each of the major centres was counted in tens of thousands. The victims were said to have been killed by poison gas in chambers especially prepared for the purpose.[15]

The British Foreign Office forwarded the Riegner cable to the United States despite the fact that it feared 'embarrassing repercussions'. Even by late November officials in London still thought that there was no actual proof of these atrocities. But the probability was sufficiently great to justify some Allied 'action', which in practical terms meant the publication of a declaration.*

Not all the additional information emanating from Geneva was helpful and some was quite wrong. Thus, according to another cable sent by the Jewish representatives the order for extermination had been proposed by Herbert Backe, the Nazi commissar for food supply, who wanted in this drastic way to alleviate the existing shortages, whereas Frank and Himmler (*sic*) had been opposing the 'final solution' because Jewish labour and (particularly) Jewish specialists were needed for the war effort. This, needless to say, was pure speculation; Hitler's decision had nothing to do with Germany's food situation.†

There were certain discrepancies between the reports: some alleged that the Jews were killed by poison gas, others mentioned some form of electrocution. There was one account claiming that the corpses of the victims were used for the manufacture of soap and artificial fertilizers. This apparently came from Sternbuch in Montreux, the representative of orthodox Jewry, who had heard it from a Polish source. Riegner reported a similar story on the authority of an 'anti-Nazi officer attached to German army headquarters': there were two factories processing Jewish corpses for the manufacture of soap, glue and lubricants. These unlikely stories reinforced the scepticism in London and Washington. As Frank Roberts wrote: 'The facts are quite bad enough without the addition of such an old story as the use of bodies for the manufacture of soap.'[16] It emerged after the war that the story was in fact untrue. But the hair of female victims was used for the war effort, and the rumours about the production of soap from Jewish corpses had gained wide currency, in any case, among non-Jews in Poland, Slovakia and Germany. It appeared in various confidential German reports and even in exchanges between Nazi leaders.[17] But the repetition of rumours of this kind made all information about the 'final solution' suspect in the eyes of highly placed Americans and Englishmen, who had found it

---

*See appendix, 'The British Foreign Office and the News from Poland'.

†Typical of the careless way in which Riegner's information was handled in the United States was the fact that everything that had been sent from Geneva including information which was clearly not scheduled for publication was published in the *Congress Weekly* of 4 December 1942.

inconvenient in the first place. One of them was Cavendish-Bentinck, the chairman of the British Intelligence Committee, who wrote as late as July 1943 that the Poles and to a far greater extent the Jews, tended to exaggerate German atrocities 'in order to stoke us up'.[18]

It was said that the news about the systematic mass murder could have 'embarrassing repercussions'. Whom could it embarrass? It was believed in London and Washington that stories like these would at best sidetrack the Allies from the war effort, at worst, as it was argued by the head of the Southern Department of the Foreign Office in September 1944, it would compel various heads of offices 'to waste a disproportionate amount of their time in dealing with wailing Jews'.

As the Riegner report reached London, a senior British official noted that 'we have, of course, received numerous reports of large-scale massacres of Jews, particularly in Poland'.[19] Where did these numerous reports originate? Some came from the usual intelligence sources, others from prisoners of war who had succeeded in escaping from the continent and had accidentally witnessed such scenes. One of the escapees who later became famous was Airey Neave, a prominent Tory parliamentarian who was killed by Irish terrorists on the premises of the House of Commons in 1979. He had witnessed the early stage of the 'final solution' in Poland. A British officer who had been hiding in Warsaw and escaped in early June of 1942 was said to be the source of the OSS report from Lisbon quoted below.

Some reports came through ordinary diplomatic channels. Thus David Kelly, head of the British legation in Switzerland, in a letter dated 19 November 1941 to Frank Roberts of the Central Department of the Foreign Office:

Here are a few miscellaneous items I have just heard from colleagues. The Pole told me ... that 1½ million Jews were living in Eastern (recently Russian) Poland have simply disappeared altogether; nobody knows how and where.[20]

The report is of considerable interest: it is one of the first, if not the very first, indication that the activities of the *Einsatzgruppen* had reached the West and also the fact that hundreds of thousands of Jews had been killed. The source was Alexander Lados, the Polish diplomatic representative in Bern. He was neither a naïve man nor a sensationalist; he had been Minister of the Interior in the exiled Government before moving to Switzerland. He had no radio contact with Poland; the information could have reached him only through a Polish courier on his way to the West. The news was substantially correct: one and a half million Jews had lived in the territories occupied by the Germans since the invasion; those who had not escaped had been killed. There were other such reports from various sources.

But there were, in addition, two other major sources of information, one highly secret, the other quite open. The story of the enigma decrypts ('Ultra', 'Triangle') became gradually known during the 1970s. Throughout much of the war British intelligence was able to intercept internal radio signals inside Nazi Germany and to read them. In the headquarters of this operation in Bletchley, which employed thousands of people, the *Luftwaffe* code was first deciphered and subsequently other codes. The ss code was broken in late 1941 and also the *Abwehr* code. Many studies of the Second World War which did not take this into account will have to be rewritten, for it does make a difference whether army, navy or air force commanders were reliably informed about the strength of the other side and its intentions. True, much vital information was not transmitted by wireless telegraph but by telephone, teleprinter or courier, which was always preferred over shorter distances. Thus communication between Berlin and Madrid was by wireless and could be read, whereas the letters exchanged between Berlin and Paris could not be intercepted. British intelligence could have known about the 'final solution' through the enigma decrypts. But did it? It will not be possible to provide a conclusive answer to this question for a long time. Many Ultra signals have been released in recent years but these almost exclusively concern naval and air operations and these too are incomplete. Material pertaining to army and ss intelligence is not accessible so far, and some of it may never be released. The same refers to us decrypts; Britain was not the only country to intercept German radio communications in Eastern Europe during the war. Thus the evidence available is incomplete and indirect, and it has to be analyzed in terms of probability rather than certainty.

The ss code, it will be recalled, was broken by British intelligence. But most of the signals read in Bletchley apparently dealt with foreign intelligence, not the 'final solution'. I have been assured that those reading the cables to and from the Main State Security Office (RSHA) in fact learned about the mass murder of Jews from MI6 sources.* It is also argued that up to 1943 when a computer was installed only a relatively small part of the material intercepted was, in fact, decoded. It was a matter of hit and miss and signals dealing neither with the military build up nor with high grade political intelligence were given low priority. Information about Jews was hardly considered top priority. It has been said furthermore that, for technical reasons, reception from Eastern Europe was uncertain. But this did not prevent Ultra in spring of 1941 from collecting important evidence about the build up of the German army and air force against the Soviet Union in Poland.

Did the ss *Einsatzgruppen* actually use wireless for their progress reports? Yes. The *Einsatzgruppen* reports state that they used not only teleprinter but also radio stations. Operation Report 131, dated 10 April 1942, announces, for instance, that *Einsatzgruppen* A and B used Radio Smolensk; Group 6, Stalino; 7A Klinzy and Orel; 9 Witebsk; 10 Feodosia; 12 Federowka. Radio stations at Kiev, Charkov, Nikolaev and Simferopol were also used.

There was in any case yet another source of information which had a direct bearing on the 'final solution'. British intelligence was closely analyzing on a daily basis the movements of German trains. There was a special 'Railway Research

---

*But the relevant documentation is not accessible. It is not known and probably will not be known for a long time by whom and in what circumstances the ss code was broken. We do know, however, that the Polish Second Bureau had deciphered the SD code and was regularly reading it well before the outbreak of the Second World War. This has been described in some detail in the memoirs of the head of this task force, Marian Rejewski, a gifted mathematician. (M. Rejewski, *Wspomnienia o mej pracy w Biurze Szyfrow Oddzialu II w latach 1930–45*, unpublished, Warsaw, Military Historical Institute. See Richard S. Woytak, *On the Border of War and Peace; Polish Intelligence and Diplomacy in 1937–1939 and the Origins of the Ultra Secret* (New York, 1979), p. 101.) It is quite likely that the SD code was changed after August 1939, but we do not know whether it was changed radically and for this reason it cannot be said with any certainty whether the British services simply continued where the Poles had stopped in 1939 or whether a major new effort was needed to break it. All that matters in this context is that the ss–sd code could be read in Britain by late 1941.

Service' with the Ministry of Economic Warfare which, with the help of Enigma, broke the German railway code in February 1941. At the same time, quite independently, SIS also discovered the code and this made it possible to follow the movement of German trains all over Europe.[21] Railway intelligence was, of course, especially interested in irregular patterns, and the trains carrying the Jews to Poland and inside Poland to the camps, cannot have escaped their attention. If German railway staff reached the conclusion that Auschwitz had become one of Europe's most important and populous centres in view of the many trains directed there, the same thought must have occurred to Allied intelligence too. Was it perhaps a place of great importance for the German war effort? Thus, quite probably, an attempt was made to find out more about what, if anything, was produced in Auschwitz and the other camps. Such studies were probably undertaken, but they have not been declassified.

Was information concerning the extermination of European Jewry suppressed by the intelligence services? The answer seems to be 'yes', but in view of the fact that many of the files of these services have been destroyed it may not be possible to prove conclusively whether this was indeed the case, and if so, for what reason. This is not to question the integrity of those intelligence officers who in later years have denied all knowledge. As Churchill once observed: memories of war should never be trusted without verification. But verification has been made impossible in this case.

But there were other equally important sources of inform-ation on which one can report with greater certainty. Unlike the Soviet Union, Germany was not a hermetically closed country even in wartime. Tens of thousands of foreign citizens continued to live and to travel in Germany and some of them also went to the occupied territories in the East. North and South American diplomats and journalists (with the exception of Argentina and Chile) left Germany in January 1942. But there were still the neutrals such as Spain and Portugal, Sweden and Switzerland, Ireland and Turkey and, of course, Germany's allies and satellites. They had embassies in Berlin and there were many local consular offices – Sweden had fifty-three such offices, Finland thirty-two, Denmark thirty, even Portugal had twenty.

Many of these consuls were German citizens, but those in key posts (such as Hamburg, Prague or Vienna) were usually foreign nationals; Swiss consuls were always Swiss citizens. It was not the main assignment of consular officers to provide political intelligence, but nor would they be reprimanded for picking up and passing on gossip and news items. Thus, to provide an example, a Swiss citizen who had by accident witnessed a massacre in Ukraine did inform his consul in Hamburg. Consuls would extend help to citizens of the countries they represented. Among these citizens there would invariably be some Jews who foolishly had stayed in Germany. There were others, whose claims were shaky, widows or descendants of Turkish or Spanish citizens. But investigations had to be made in each case and thus diplomatic and consular personnel were bound to learn that Jews were deported, that their property was seized, that they were disappearing without trace. When two of the secretaries at the Turkish embassy in Berlin who happened to be Jewish suddenly vanished or when a similar lot befell the German-language teacher of the ambassador of Siam in Berlin, questions would be asked.

It has been mentioned before that foreign nationals living in the Reich would learn about the fate of the Jews. Thus Goebbels in one of his staff conferences (on 11 March 1941) mentioned with evident indignation that he had just learned that half the foreign students in Berlin were staying in Jewish apartments. The Finnish ambassador, Professor Kiwimaeki, was a personal friend of Felix Kersten, Himmler's masseur, who was one of the best-informed people in the Reich. Kersten warned Kiwimaeki in July 1942 that Himmler wanted the Finns to surrender their Jews. The Swedes received information from a variety of sources. It was a Swedish diplomat, Baron von Otter, who was approached by Kurt Gerstein in the Warsaw–Berlin express. Gerstein, Chief Disinfection Officer of the *Waffen* SS, was in charge of supplying the poison to the camps. He had just returned from an inspection tour attending to technical details such as the relative advantages of Zyklon B (hydrogen cyanide) and carbon monoxide in killing people and he told Baron von Otter who informed Stockholm. This was an accidental meeting, but others were routine. The Swedish Embassy parson was in constant touch with oppositionist elements in the

German Protestant Church and tried, unsuccessfully, to rescue some of the converted Christians, such as, for instance, the adopted daughter of Jochen Klepper, the well-known author. Counsellor Almquist of the embassy also participated in these rescue attempts. Swedish businessmen in Warsaw were in touch with the Polish underground and some were arrested. Swedish diplomats were bound to learn about the mortal danger facing the Jews. It is unlikely, to put it mildly, that they and other neutral representatives in Berlin, which sometimes included even Germany's allies (such as Italy and Hungary), would have gone out of their way trying to prevent the enforced journey of a Jew from Germany, Holland or France to some East European destination, unless they also knew that deportation was a sentence of death. Only very few, such as Baron von Otter, had received a briefing on the technology of mass murder. But these were technical details. Of the net result there was no doubt.

The diplomats constituted only a small part of the foreign community in wartime Germany. Even after the exodus of the American journalists in December 1941 there were still some hundred foreign journalists stationed in Germany. Their number slightly increased in 1942–3 and it was only during the last year of the war when the lines of communication broke down that many of them left. The majority came from satellite countries, which is not to say that they were always enthusiastic about Nazi politics. There were also quite a few correspondents from neutral countries. The main Swedish newspapers were represented: *Svenska Dagbladet*, *Dagens Nyheter*, *Stockholm Tidningen*, *Nya Daglight Allehande* and even *Social Democraten* had permanent Berlin correspondents. Their reports were, of course, strictly censored but this does not mean that they did not know about the fate of the Jews.

Nazi officials did not always keep even top secrets. Thus Professor Karl Boehme, head of the foreign press department of the Ministry of Propaganda, announced at a reception at the Bulgarian embassy in May 1941 that he would soon be *Gauleiter* of the Crimea. Following this incident he was indeed sent to the eastern front, but as a soldier and it was only owing to Goebbels' personal intervention that he was not shot. If military secrets of this importance were accidentally revealed, the 'final solution' was more widely discussed and commented upon. True, foreign correspondents were not permitted to travel freely in Eastern Europe during the war, but there were still guided tours for both resident journalists and those specially invited. Thus a group was taken to Kiev in October 1941 to see the destruction wrought by the Bolsheviks, Captain Koch, who was in charge of them, was asked about the murder of many thousands of Jews in the Ukrainian capital – this was merely a few days after Babi Yar. He denied all knowledge whereupon the journalists (according to an *Abwehr* report) told him that they knew about it anyway – '*dass sie darüber doch genau Bescheid wüssten*'.[22] Journalists could not print such stories, but they could still talk about them. Most of them went on home leave quite frequently and would inform their editorial offices, their families and friends. Albert Müller, foreign editor of the *Neue Zürcher Zeitung* from 1934 to 1965, wrote in retrospect that there was no 'direct news', but that the deportations and the concentration in ghettos were impossible without announcements in the German press in occupied Poland, which were read by the foreign correspondents in Berlin. 'We received no picture of photographic exactitude, only silhouettes.'[23] But the silhouettes were quite revealing, and Müller also remembers the information he received early on in the war from an unimpeachable source, a lawyer and reserve officer stationed now in the Warthegau (the Polish region annexed by Germany in late 1939) about the mass graves for Jewish victims. The officer added in his message that the incident was less uncommon than the fact that it had reached the court at all. On another occasion the Dutch Government-in-exile informed Müller and his colleagues that the central register office in Amsterdam had been destroyed by the resistance because there were certain indications that there were in Poland installations for the mass murder of the Jewish deportees or that these were about to be finished.

The presence and the movements of the neutrals in wartime Germany will still preoccupy us later on. It has been mentioned here simply because this was another important channel through which the Allied governments would learn about conditions in the Nazi-occupied countries and also about the fate of the Jews. Some of the neutrals would report to British and American connections, just as, for instance, some of the Spanish diplomats stationed in London would pass on information to Berlin. But even those who had no direct Allied connections would report to their superiors in Stockholm, Bern and other capitals, and they would talk to their friends, colleagues and business associates. 'Gossip' of this kind would be picked up by Allied diplomats and agents in the neutral capitals.

Letters sent out of Germany and neutral countries were read with attention in various Allied censorship offices; the headquarters were in Bermuda. Read in conjunction with press and news agency reports they were an important source of information. A report on 'Conditions in Germany and occupied countries', dated 18 February 1942 and based entirely on material of this sort, noted 'a ruthless new drive to clear the Reich of the Jews'. A large proportion of the Red Cross postal messages out of Germany during January 1942 'were from unfortunates on the eve of their departure to Poland or unknown destinations'. There were exact data about many cities. As regards the conditions awaiting the deportees it was said that direct information was not easy to come by – an obvious understatement. But it was also stated the 'rumours leaking through into Germany are reported to have caused a number of Jews to prefer suicide to deportation' (letter from Lugano, dated 9 January 1942). From America there came a 'horror story of thousands of the inmates of a ghetto' somewhere near the Russian front put to death 'in an attempt by the authorities to stamp out typhoid'.[24] Such reports were periodically put together; they show that much of interest could be culled from seemingly unpromising sources.

By late summer of 1942 the information about the mass murder was available in London but no great publicity was given to it. Various reasons can be adduced for the decision to play down the news; other Allied governments, it has been noted, reacted in a similar way. The issue is of importance, for if the information about the 'final solution' had been publicized more widely, more people in occupied Europe would have heard about it, and earlier at that. The role of the British Ministry of Information, headed at the time by Brendan Bracken, remains to be explored in this connection. I have been assured by some who worked with him and knew him well that he believed that the news was so horrific that it would be discounted as a propaganda lie of Goebbels-like dimensions. He did chair a press conference in July 1942 arranged by the Polish Government in London and spoke with horror and indignation about the atrocities committed against the Jews. He also declared that retribution would be administered when victory was won. But there was also the consideration that politically it would be unwise to give too much publicity to this specific Nazi crime.

The planning committee of the Ministry of Information (MOI) had reached the conclusion in July 1941 that while a certain amount of horror was needed in British home propaganda, this was only to be used sparingly 'and must always deal with the treatment of indisputably innocent people. Not with violent political opponents. And not with Jews.'[25]

Why not with Jews? Were they perhaps not 'indisputably innocent'? No, the reason was more complicated. According to the experts of MOI the public thought that people singled out as victims were probably a bad lot. Thus paradoxically MOI referred in 1942 to the 'holocaust of Catholics' in Europe, but to the Jews it referred only rarely and not in terms of a holocaust even after the facts about the 'final solution' had become known.

There was a further reason. As a senior official of the MOI wrote at the time: for twenty years between the two World Wars there had been a well-conducted campaign against atrocity stories and some people had become 'contra-suggestible'. He personally did not know whether there was a 'corpse factory' but most people believed there was not.[26] The same argument was quite frequently used in the United States. When John Pehle, director of the War Refugee Board, wanted to publish the Auschwitz report of the two escaped prisoners in 1944, Elmer Davis, head of the Office of War Information, protested: publishing these reports would be counter-productive; the American public would not believe them, considering them First World War style atrocity stories. But the OWI pundits also used the opposite argument: in occupied Europe the truth about the final solution would be believed and this would strike such mortal fear into the heart of the non-Jews that all resistance to the Nazis would collapse.

But there was a third argument and it was probably the decisive one. There is, in the words of the historian of MOI, a complete absence of minutes and memoranda relating to this issue but he is in no doubt that 'the ministry almost certainly hesitated because of the widely reported prejudice in the British Community against the Jews'.[27] Anti-semitism figured throughout 1940 and 1941 in almost every single issue of the 'Home Intelligence Weekly Report'. For unknown reasons there were much fewer such reports during the second half of 1942 but then, towards the end of the year, 'anti-semitism appears actually to have been revived by the authoritative disclosures of the Nazis' systematic massacres of the European Jews'.*[28] The weekly reports of 8 and 15 December 1942 announced extreme horror, indignation, anger and disgust. But in the weekly report of 29 December the conclusion was reached that as the result of the publicity 'people became more conscious of the Jews they do not like here'. This then was undoubtedly the main reason for playing down the murder of the Jews, and if MOI used this argument with regard to the home services of the BBC, the intelligence services and the Foreign Office used similar reasons with regard to its European services. The PWE (Political Warfare Executive) was certainly well informed about the 'final solution'. In its headquarters at Electra House in London it received not only relevant items from all other British intelligence services, it had a group of thirty analysts at the British Embassy in Stockholm to read all newspapers from Axis and neutral countries; once a week a special RAF plane would fly the material to London. But the PWE was as uneasy about the use of the 'Jewish theme' in leaflets dropped over the continent or in broadcasts. Even towards the end of the war Sir Robert Bruce Lockhart, director of the PWE, explained to a fellow British diplomat that it was quite pointless to intensify the appeals to save the doomed Jews: such declarations would only result in increased maltreatment. Furthermore paper, planes and broadcasting hours were limited and the PWE had many other commitments. Whatever the reasons, and there were at least half-a-dozen arguments, the conclusion was always the same. No one in the West suggested suppressing the information about the mass murder altogether, and, in any case, the control

---

*The editorial writers of the leading British newspapers were certainly less self-conscious than the bureaucrats at the time. There were strong, detailed and frequent editorial comments in *The Times*, the *Manchester Guardian*, the *Daily Telegraph* and other daily newspapers throughout December 1942.

of institutions such as the MOI and PWE over the media was far from absolute. But the official consensus was to refer to it only sparingly.

In October 1942 the Jewish Telegraphic Agency learned of the Riegner cable and published its gist without attribution. In November Rabbi Stephen Wise was asked to come to Washington and was told by Undersecretary Sumner Welles that the additional information received by the State Department confirmed the deepest fears, releasing him from silence. He told a press conference in Washington that he had learned through sources confirmed by the State Department that half the estimated four million Jews in Nazi-occupied Europe had been slain in an 'extermination campaign'.[29] On 17 December 1942 the eleven Allied governments and de Gaulle's Free France Committee published a common declaration which announced that the German authorities were now carrying into effect Hitler's oft-repeated intention of exterminating the Jewish people in Europe. This was followed by editorials, broadcasts and public meetings. There seemed to be no more doubt about the authenticity of the terrible news.

But on 10 February 1943, after the US minister to Switzerland had forwarded yet another message from Riegner on the 'final solution', he was asked by Breckinridge Long, Assistant Secretary in charge of the Special War Problems Division, not to accept and transmit any more such reports to private persons in the United States.[30] There were influential circles in Washington who did not want reports of this kind to be circulated. They felt even more strongly than their colleagues in the British Foreign Office that these reports could have embarrassing repercussions.

Or were attitudes perhaps motivated by genuine doubts about the veracity of the 'horror stories'? News about Nazi atrocities had been widely published in the American press from 1939 onwards. Commenting on some of these reports, the *New York Herald Tribune* wrote editorially on 5 December 1941 that 'the sum of it all indicates that the fate reserved for the Jews by the Nazis is worse than a status of serfdom – it is nothing less than systematic extermination.' During the first six months of 1942 there were reports of mass executions and all the important messages coming out from Poland were also published. US embassies in Budapest and Bucharest reported the Kamenets Podolsk massacre and the deportation to Transniestria. The cables on these events of Mr Franklin M. Gunther, US ambassador to Bucharest, apparently created some displeasure in the department but all that matters in this context is that the relevant information was available in Washington. US diplomatic personnel were still stationed in the Axis countries up to the end of 1941, and in Vichy for a year after. Jewish institutions furthermore provided a steady stream of information. The files of the State Department are full of such material: information, queries, appeals for help, suggestions for action, protests. As early as 7 October 1941 Atherton of the European Division of the State Department sent a sixty-page memorandum 'Poland under German Occupation' to Colonel Donovan, at that time still 'Co-ordinator of Information'. A member of the US Embassy in Berlin who had formerly served in Warsaw had received this document from a Pole. It described conditions in Poland before the German invasion of the Soviet Union and said that it was the endeavour of the German authorities in Poland to 'ruthlessly and entirely exterminate the Jewish element from the life of Aryan communities'. Terms such as 'extermination', 'elimination' and 'liquidation' were repeatedly used, and it was stressed that Nazi policy was to make the Jews disappear from Europe.* Although reports such as these did not specifically refer to physical extermination, they left little to the imagination. A long signal datelined Lisbon, 20 July 1942, begins as follows: 'Germany no longer persecutes the Jews, it is systematically exterminating them. . . . These facts moreover have been corroborated by many returning citizens of European origin now here.'[31] But were these reports read in Washington? When three months later Professor Felix Frankfurter voiced his apprehension about the fate of the Jews to President Roosevelt he was told not to worry, the deported Jews were simply being employed on the Soviet frontier to build fortifications.[32]

---

*NND 750140. The document is of considerable interest because it is the first detailed statement on the situation in occupied Poland prepared by the Polish underground. There is reason to believe that it was actually taken to Berlin by one of the Swedish businessmen living in Warsaw on whom more below.

It is certain that Roosevelt knew more than he admitted to Frankfurter. One month before, on 22 August, he had said in a White House press conference that

the communication which I have just received . . . gives rise to the fear that as the defeat of the enemy countries approaches, the barbaric and unrelenting character of the occupational regime will become more marked and may even lead to the extermination of certain populations.

Who were the 'certain populations'? Certainly not the people of the Netherlands and Luxembourg from whose governments-in-exile he had received information. Roosevelt's general attitude was perhaps most succinctly stated in a reply to a letter from General Sikorski early in July 1942 in which the Polish head of state had suggested drastic action as a deterrent against German terrorism. Roosevelt said that he was fully aware of these actions but there was no answer except the crushing of the military might of the Axis powers. America was deeply incensed about the barbaric behaviour of the Nazis but it would not stand for acts of retaliation such as the indiscriminate bombing of the civilian population of enemy countries.[33] Roosevelt was kept fully informed by, among others, long cables from A. Drexel Biddle, ambassador with the exiled governments in London and a personal friend. But given his belief that the only politically and strategically sound course was 'the most effective prosecution of the war' he did not pay attention to the news about the 'final solution' and he may have even considered it inopportune.

To continue with the information which reached Washington in spring and summer of 1942, another report, probably from the same source, begins with a discussion of the chronology of the 'final solution':

The exact date when Hitler decided to wipe the Jews from the surface of Europe in the most literal sense of the word, namely by killing them, is unknown. Evacuations and deportations accompanied by executions date as far back as the Polish campaign, but the organized wholesale slaughter of whole communities and trainloads of Jews appears to have been practised not before the German attack on Russia.[34]

It ends with the description of the working of gassing vans outside Minsk.

The OSS report just quoted was by no means the only one. One of the first on the 'systematic liquidation of the Jews' is dated 14 March 1942, but some leading OSS officials had known, and written about it, even before. One of them was Fred Oechsner, formerly head of the United Press Bureau in Berlin, who went on to cover the war in the East with the German and Romanian army and had been to Odessa and other places. He knew to report in October 1941, from German sources, about the special treatment of the Jews in Kiev, Zhitomir, Kherson and other places ('the Ukrainians took care of matters').[35] Major Arthur Goldberg, who worked for the OSS in London, was given details about the 'final solution' by Shmuel Zygielbojm and passed the information on to Washington.[*] Perhaps the best informed American on things German in 1941–2 was the legendary Sam Woods (1892–1953), commercial attaché, first in Berlin and later in Zürich, from early 1943. A Texan who knew no German and pretended not to have the slightest interest in politics, Woods engaged with great success in freebooting intelligence activities outside any organizational framework. In Berlin, in February 1941, he received a copy of the German battle order for 'Barbarossa'; later, in Zürich, he received information that the Germans were debating whether to work on the atomic bomb – to mention only two of his major scoops. There is much reason to assume that Woods knew from his German contacts about the fate of the Jews. But, more often than not, he conveyed his information to his superiors by word

---

[*]Arthur J. Goldberg, subsequently US representative to the United Nations, was asked in late August of 1942 by General Donovan, whose special assistant he was, to organize a London office of the Labour Division of the OSS which Goldberg directed. Adolph Held, president of the Jewish Labour Committee, suggested Shmuel Zygielbojm as one of several useful contacts. The two became friends in autumn 1942. They met both officially and socially: 'In the course of these meetings Mr Zygielbojm informed me about Hitler's programme for the "final solution". He also provided me with evidence supporting the information he furnished. I forwarded this information to General Donovan through OSS channels. At this point my memory becomes faulty. I believe that he not only advised me about the death camps but also about the uprising in the Warsaw ghetto and requested either a bombing of Auschwitz and/or the Warsaw ghetto. . . . I recall that upon receiving an answer to my urging that his request be honoured and that it was negative, I asked him to have dinner with me at Claridges where I was staying. With understandable pain and anguish I told him that our government was not prepared to do what he requested because in the view of our high command, aircraft were not available for this purpose. The next day he committed suicide – this I recall vividly. . . .' (letter to author, 15 November 1979).

of mouth, and it is doubtful whether this will ever be proven. The Germans apparently never suspected Woods during his Berlin period (1937–41); they became interested in him only after his appointment in Zürich.

In another account, a soldier of the Italian expeditionary force to Russia is quoted: 'God will chastise us terribly for the assistance we render to all these crimes.' A report dated August 1942 was a copy of a message sent to Rabbi Wise and intercepted by the US authorities: 'There is hardly a Jew to be found in the whole of Eastern Poland, including occupied Russia ... the Jews deported from Germany, Belgium, Holland, France and Slovakia are to be slaughtered. .... Since this slaughter would attract greater attention in the West, the Jews must first be deported to the East, where other countries are less likely to learn of it.' Reports, from French officers who escaped or were repatriated from prisoner-of-war camps in Poland as well as M. Charles Mercier (a Red Cross representative?), mention not only 'choses incroyables sur les massacres des Juifs' ('unbelievable things about the massacres of the Jews') but also concrete details such as the extermination of the whole Jewish population of the town of Rawa Russka.[36] Yet another message says that 'Jews in the East not excluding Eastern Galicia and Lwow are being systematically murdered. There are none left in the larger Soviet Ukrainian towns, in Lithuania they will be soon completely exterminated.'[37] A signal datelined 'German frontier – November 15, 1942', probably based on the report of a journalist, deals with the murder of Jews in the Baltic countries and says that the procedure will serve as an example elsewhere.[38] Lastly, the OSS received, through liaison officers, much information from Polish sources in London. Reports dated August and September 1942 included details about camps such as Treblinka as well as Polish and German eyewitness accounts.

In the light of these and other reports, published and secret, one would have assumed that as 1942 drew to its close not only the US intelligence community and officials of the State Department but average newspaper readers were aware that the Jews of Europe were being systematically exterminated. But this was by no means the case and while one can think of various explanations the reasons still remain something of a riddle.

President Roosevelt was too busy to study the newspapers in great detail, and he was certainly a less avid reader of intelligence reports than Winston Churchill. But what about the diplomats and the intelligence agents in the field? Two examples should suffice. On 5 April 1943, Hershel Johnson, US ambassador to Sweden, sent a cable to Washington in which he reported that of the 450,000 Jews in Warsaw only 50,000 remained. There were also some incorrect details in his cable: the stories about the lethal methods used (gas) were said to be a distortion of the facts, the Jews had all been killed by German army firing squads and some of the German soldiers had revolted. This report is remarkable, however, for a very different reason. By April 1943 the great majority of Polish (and European) Jewry was dead. Ambassador Johnson surely must have been aware of the fact. An experienced diplomat, he was serving at the time in one of the most exposed and most interesting listening posts as far as Nazi-occupied Europe was concerned. He had no doubt read in the American press about the fate of the Jews; he had seen translations from the Swedish press. The year before he had sent a cable to Washington about the destruction of Baltic and Ukrainian Jewry. Yet he ended his cable of April 1943 with the following words: 'So fantastic is the story told by this German eyewitness to his friend, my informant, that I hesitate to make it the subject of an official report.'[39]

It is possible, though not very likely, that the news from Poland had somehow bypassed the US ambassador to Sweden. But no one was better informed during these years about events inside Nazi-occupied Europe than Allen Dulles representing the OSS in Bern – which makes the following incident which took place in June 1944 all the more difficult to explain. Two inmates of Auschwitz, Vrba and Wetzler, had succeeded in escaping to Slovakia and wrote a long and detailed report about their experiences which later became famous and was widely circulated by the War Refugee Board. The report contained many new details but all the essential facts had, of course, been known for a long time. The report was taken by a courier to Budapest and from there to Switzerland. Garrett, the representative of the British news agency Exchange Telegraph, received a copy which he took to Allen Dulles on 22 June 1944.

Dulles read it in his presence: 'He was profoundly shocked. He was as disconcerted as I was and said: "One has to do something immediately. . . ."'⁴⁰ Dulles sent a cable to the Secretary of State the following day. Eighteen months earlier the *New York Times* and other American newspapers had repeatedly featured news items such as 'Two-thirds of Jews held in Poland slain – only 1,250,000 said to survive of 3,500,000 once there'.⁴¹ Even if it is assumed that not a single additional Jew had been slain since December 1942 it is impossible to understand Allen Dulles's surprise and shock.

What follows from these and similar incidents is that the process of perception and learning is more complex than commonly assumed: the fact that some information has been mentioned once or even a hundred times in secret reports or in mass circulation newspapers does not necessarily mean that it had been accepted and understood. Big figures become statistics, and statistics have no psychological impact. Some thought that the news about the Jewish tragedy was exaggerated, others did not doubt the information but had different priorities and preoccupations.

A moving interpretation based on personal experience has been given by W. A. Visser't Hooft, a Protestant theologian and the first secretary of the World Council of Churches, who spent the war years in Switzerland. In October 1941 he received alarming reports about the deportation of Jews from Germany and other occupied countries to Poland, but, writing thirty years later, he noted that it took several months before the information received entered his consciousness.

That moment occurred when I heard a young Swiss businessman tell what he had seen with his own eyes during a business trip to Russia. He had been invited by German officers to be present at one of the mass killings of Jews. He told us in the most straightforward and realistic way how group after group of Jewish men, women and children were forced to lie down in the mass graves and were then machinegunned to death. The picture he drew has remained in my mind ever since. From that moment onward I had no longer any excuse for shutting my mind to information which could find no place in my view of the world and humanity.

Why, in the view of this prominent churchman, did the outside world remain indifferent? Was it because the victims were Jews?

Visser't Hooft replies:

I do not underestimate the reality of such anti-semitism but I have found little evidence that it has played the main role in this situation. It was rather that people could find no place in their consciousness for such an unimaginable horror and that they did not have the imagination, together with the courage, to face it. It is possible to live in a twilight between knowing and not knowing.*[42]

But there is more than one explanation for the indifference. Everyone went through a period of doubt with regard to the terrible news from Eastern Europe. Some decided to act, once there was no reasonable doubt that the information was correct. Others preferred to prolong the twilight period, and some who knew kept their knowledge to themselves.†

* In the course of my search for the German industrialist who first conveyed the news about Hitler's decision to destroy European Jewry to Sagalowitz (see p. 78), I was greatly intrigued by the personality of Robert Boehringer, an industrialist and poet of German origin who had settled in Basel before the First World War. During the Second World War Boehringer played a certain role in the International Red Cross. But though this most secretive man probably was active in transmitting information from Germany, he was not the mysterious messenger. Elizabeth Wiskemann, British press attaché in Switzerland during the war, mentions in her autobiography, *The Europe I Saw* (London, 1968), that she had two informants in Basel: one a Jewish lawyer married to a German wife, the other a German, working for Hofmann LaRoche, who had a Jewish wife. Wiskemann refers to the "industrialist" as "Mr. Y." There is reason to assume that it was Georg Ernst Veiel, director of Hofmann LaRoche in Berlin until 1938. Veiel was a friend of Goering; they had been to the same flying school in the First World War and Veiel had kept contact with him and other fellow veterans. Veiel also received important information from Robert Bosch, the leading South German industrialist, apparently via Bosch's private secretary, Willy Schlosstein. These connections are of interest, for Wiskemann writes that the 'final solution' was reported to her by the end of 1941. In the meantime, however, I had established that the name of the "industrialist" began with S, which made me doubt whether it was Veiel after all. But Elizabeth Wiskemann mentions yet another Basel source. Investigations have shown that this was probably Seligmann-Schuerch, the Basel banker. Swiss friends also drew my attention to the role of Dr. Eduard Schulte, general manager of the Georg von Giesche mining company in Breslau. Schulte frequently visited Switzerland during the war and eventually became a defector. He, too, seems to have brought important information out of Germany. Though so far inconclusive, the search has not been in vain, for it shows that the information about the mass murder reached Switzerland simultaneously through various channels.

† Since *The Terrible Secret* was first published in hardcover, important new evidence about the extent of Allied knowledge of the massacres has come to light. I wrote on pages 84–85 that the Allies probably knew about the killings through the Ultra decrypts. Since then, the second volume of the *Official History of British Intelligence in the Second World War* has been published (September 1981), which states in an appendix that the Allies, beginning in spring 1942, decrypted daily reports on prisoners in seven camps, including Auschwitz. In the words of the *Official History*, the daily reports consisted of a series of unheaded, unexplained columns of figures which British Intelligence worked out to mean (a) number of inmates at the start of the previous day, (b) new arrivals, (c) departures by any means, and (d) the number at the end of the previous day.

4

THE NEWS FROM POLAND

THE first authentic and detailed news about the 'final solution' came from inside Poland. Hitler had decided to make that country the slaughterhouse of Europe and the Polish sources of information were, therefore, more important than all others. Poland had been defeated and occupied by the Germans in the autumn of 1939 and then divided between Germany and the Soviet Union. Then, within a few days after the German invasion of Russia in June 1941, eastern Poland was reoccupied and so were the Baltic countries and parts of White Russia and the Ukraine.

Soon after the defeat a Polish Government-in-exile came into being and was recognized by the other Allied governments. This Government had a representative, the *Delegat*, inside Poland who was in constant touch with London where the Government was located after the fall of France. Independently, a country-wide armed organization had come into being, the ZWZ (*Zwiazek Walki Zbrojnej*) which in 1942 became the AK – *Armia Krajowa* – the army in (or of) the country or Home Army. The commander-in-chief of ZWZ/AK, General Stefan Rowecki, was responsible for all military affairs, whereas the *Delegat* was the supreme authority on political issues. But the dividing line between political and military questions was by no means clear cut and the division of labour between the two institutions less than perfect. Furthermore, Polish domestic politics were not only complicated but had lost little of their pre-war acrimony. The Polish Socialist Party (PPS) and the Peasants Party (SL – *Stronnictwo Ludowe*), were the strongest forces inside the resistance, whereas some of the leading figures in and around the Government-in-exile – Sikorski, Sosnkowski, Haller and Kukiel – as well as among the AK command, were the men of the centre or the right. The *Delegat* during the early period was Ratajski, later Professor Jan Piekalkiewicz took his place. Both depended on the ZWZ/AK for practical help, for in the beginning they did not have their own radio contact with London nor did the money arrive regularly. Piekalkiewicz was seized by the Germans in 1943 and killed.

A detailed description of the various forces which made up the Polish resistance cannot be given in this framework. Suffice it to say that the only important group which had refused to join the general camp were the Communists. But they became important only later on. In 1941–2 they barely existed: the party had been subjected to a massive purge by the Comintern in the late 1930s and eventually it was dissolved. Individual Communists established radio contact with Moscow in 1942. A post-war Polish publication quotes a cable sent to the secretary of the Communist International reporting the deportations from the Warsaw ghetto. It could well be that this is the only such communication in existence, which is not to say that Soviet intelligence was ignorant of the facts.

If the Communist underground was not a significant force in 1942, how strong was the AK? As a military organization it was far from impressive, and the schemes for armed insurrection against the Germans prepared by some of its leaders were quite fantastic. But it did have a wide net of sympathizers and informants all over Poland, and this in the context of the present study is of great importance.[1] In Poland, unlike in France and most West European countries, there were no political collaborators. The Germans would find an informant among the criminal classes, but not among the elements of which the underground was constituted. For the Germans had no wish to give the Poles even limited political autonomy. The Poles were an inferior subject race; on this basis there was no room for collaboration. Furthermore, German rule in Poland was far more bloody and repressive than in Western, Northern and even Southern Europe: about a million Poles were killed during the war. Thus there was a great reservoir of good will for the AK, and none at all for the Germans.

The Polish Government-in-exile maintained contact with Poland mainly through the Polish section of the SOE (Special Operations Executive), which, together with the Sixth Bureau of the Polish General Staff, developed communications with Poland, delivered supplies to Poland and carried personnel to and from Poland. SOE contact with Poland was established in various ways. From 15 February 1941 onwards parachutists were dropped in Poland; from summer 1942 such drops became quite routine. It is mistakenly believed that Poland remained outside the reach of Allied aircraft until late in the war, but this is not so. It was admittedly a long flight from London and special planes had to be used such as a modified Whitley, later twin-engined Dakotas and Hudsons with special tanks, and later yet four-engined Liberators. Two-way 'bridge operations' as practised by the SOE in Belgium and France with small Lysander aircraft were impossible in Poland; the first landing operation took place in April 1944 near Lublin.[2] Couriers from Poland to London had to make their way to London in long, cumbersome ways. Some went via Sweden, others through Western Europe. The reports they were carrying would take weeks and sometimes more than a month or even two. But short messages could be radioed daily to London, longer ones had to be taken out of Warsaw where the danger of detection was not as great. In this case there would be inevitable delays in transmission.

During 1941 and up to late July 1942, however, there was yet another link between Warsaw and the outside world, more important than the SOE, which the Poles had established with the help of sympathizers among the Swedish colony in Warsaw. These 'Warsaw Swedes' were instrumental in getting long messages out of Poland on behalf of both the Home Army and the *Delegatura*. They also carried their return money and foreign passports. The Swedish connection was of particular importance with regard to information about the fate of Polish Jews. Carl Wilhelm Herslow and Sven Norrman, the two leading figures among the Swedes – there was a third, Carl Gösta Gustafsson, but very little is known about him – had many Jewish acquaintances with whom they kept in touch and whom they tried to help. On one occasion in 1942 Norrman went into the Warsaw ghetto and shot several films until the ghetto police stopped him. These films as well as much other material was passed on to Mieczyslaw Thugutt who at the time was in charge of the Stockholm base of Polish intelligence (No.3, 'Anna'); later in 1942 Thugutt was moved to London and became chief co-ordinator of communication with the homeland on behalf of the Government-in-exile.

Herslow, who had been a career army officer and military

attaché in both Moscow and Berlin, was director in Warsaw of the Polish safety-match state monopoly, which was part of the old Ivar Kreuger business concern. Norrman was head of ASEA, an electro-technical corporation connected with the Wallenberg interests. Both men had lived in Poland for many years and identified with the Polish cause for which they worked with energy and at great risk.[3] On their frequent visits to Sweden they would report on the situation in Poland to the Foreign Minister, to Eric Boheman, the State Secretary of Foreign Affairs (who seems to have been in on many, though not all, of their activities), and the chief of staff of the army. Herslow would also report from time to time to King Gustav V and the Crown Prince.

The Swedes knew a great deal about the secret reports they were carrying because they had been involved with the resistance since the early days. Some of them had even met General Rowecki ('Kalina'), the commander of the Home Army, which was, of course, strictly against the rules of conspiracy. The reports on the situation inside the country (*Sprawozdanie sytuacyjne z kraju*) published by the Polish Government-in-exile were based mainly on material carried by the Swedes. Together with letters from Jews in Poland (such as the *Bund* letter of May 1942 and the Chelmno account sent by Ringelblum) these were the chief sources on the fate of Polish and East European Jewry during the first half of 1942. The Swedes would collect the material, usually on 35mm film, in Warsaw, and would either carry it on their person or ship it through the Swedish chamber of commerce to Stockholm. Thugutt or some other representative of the 'base' would hand it to British intelligence and it would be sent on to London by the weekly RAF plane.*

Thus the progress of certain reports from Poland can be followed almost on a daily basis. The famous (second) letter of

---

*The same plane would take the daily and weekly reports ('The Digest') of the press-reading bureau at the British Embassy in Stockholm, headed by Cecil Parrott, which were prepared on the basis of the perusal of newspapers from many occupied countries (as well as Germany) for the Political Intelligence Department. These surveys also occasionally contained material concerning the fate of European Jewry. See, for instance, FO371/26515 3410. The department was made up by about thirty people, most of them Jews; it produced a 'wonderful daily record of all indications of anything we were looking for'. (Sir Cecil Parrott to author, 10 December 1979.)

the *Bund* which will again feature in this story was written during the first half of May 1942. It was collected by Sven Norrman in Warsaw on 21 May and reached London a mere ten days later, admittedly a case of exceptionally quick delivery. The Chelmno account reached London apparently with the same messenger but it had been on the way much longer.

This was Norrman's last visit to Poland. He was warned not to return. His colleagues were seized by the Gestapo in a series of arrests beginning late July 1942. Four of the Swedes were sentenced to death, others to lengthy prison terms. But the death sentences were not carried out whereas most of the imprisoned Poles were executed. Himmler in a special report regretted that Norrman, the most important figure in the network, had not been caught.[4] It was also said during the interrogation that the films smuggled out by Herslow had been shown in British and American cinemas stirring up anti-German sentiment, clearly a reference to pictures taken in the ghetto.

Thus the most important direct connection for carrying bulk mail to the West was cut precisely at the time the liquidation of the Warsaw ghetto began. The Polish underground continued to maintain radio contact with London and tried to send out longer reports by way of its bases in Switzerland and Istanbul ('Bey'). But it was only when Jan Karski, on whom more below, arrived in London in November 1942 that detailed information was again available abroad.

Polish Jews had no connections with the Allies, nor could they send couriers as the Polish underground did. They did send letters and postcards to Switzerland, Hungary and Turkey, which did not always arrive, and in which the writers could only intimate in aesopian language what happened. From time to time mysterious couriers would arrive from neutral countries but it was never certain whether these could be trusted. The Polish underground was in an infinitely better position not only to transmit news abroad but also to collect information. Jews were confined to ghettos whereas Poles could, within limits, move freely in their country. Polish SOE operators even went to White Russia and Ukraine, visiting Kiev, Minsk, Zhitomir, Pinsk and other places. The AK got information on a fairly regular basis from its agents among the Polish police and the railway workers.

The records, to repeat, show that the first authentic news about the 'final solution' was transmitted to the West by the couriers and the radio station of the Home Army. The overall issue of Polish-Jewish relations during the Second World War is complicated and painful; it cannot, for instance seriously be disputed that few weapons were passed on to the Jews by the AK. But the question which preoccupies us in this study is a more narrow one: did the Polish underground transmit the news about the massacres as quickly and fully as it could? And was this news suppressed or given full publicity by the Polish authorities in London?

The Polish case is very briefly that they did what they could, usually at great risk and in difficult conditions. If the news about the mass murders was not believed abroad this was not the fault of the Poles. It was, at least in part, the fault of the Polish Jews who, in the beginning, refused to believe it; it was also the responsibility of the Jewish leaders abroad who were initially quite sceptical.[5] Some Polish-Jewish historians on the other hand argue that while the Home Army did transmit some information to London, it could have done more to inform Jews inside Poland. Furthermore, the Polish Government is accused of having delayed publication during the 'evacuation' of the Warsaw ghetto between July and September 1942. According to this version the Poles did not mind publicising the slaughter in the eastern provinces which had been under Soviet control. But they became more reluctant to transmit the news as the process of extermination came under way inside Poland. If they had made it known that 400,000 Jews were deported from Warsaw to a nearby death camp the world would surely have expected the Polish underground to do something about it. For this reason the Warsaw events were a major embarrassment which had to be played down or at least delayed.

How much truth is there in these allegations? That there has been a great deal of anti-semitism in modern Polish history is not a matter of dispute, but it is also true that help was extended to the Jews after 1939 precisely by some who had been their bitterest enemies before. Those who represented Poland after 1940 were by and large people who had been in opposition in the 1930s to the rabidly anti-semitic Government and they tried to eliminate the forces who had caused Poland's ruin. All this is not to say that the Government-in-exile and its representatives at home were liberal internationalists who saw their first duty in helping the persecuted Jews. If the Poles showed less sympathy and solidarity with Jews than many Danes and Dutch, they behaved far more humanely than Romanians or Ukrainians, than Lithuanians and Latvians. A comparison with France would be by no means unfavourable for Poland. In view of the Polish pre-war attitudes towards Jews, it is not surprising that there was so little help, but that there was so much.

But again, as far as this study is concerned, the issue is not help but transmission of information. The Poles did not realize immediately the scale of the Nazi plot to exterminate all Jews. But most Polish Jews were even slower in understanding that they were not facing isolated pogroms but something infinitely worse. In the writings of Ringelblum (about whom more below) and others one finds only too often complaints that the seriousness of the situation was not understood in the ghetto.

It would have been far better if the Jews had not depended entirely on the transmitters of the AK or the *Delegat* for their contact with the outside world. This dependence is one of the many riddles of that period. It was difficult to produce weapons in the ghettos, but the construction of wireless transmitters was a less formidable task. There were dozens, if not hundreds, who had the expertise. Thousands of Jews were employed in workshops or little factories. The necessary materials could have been stolen or bought, a code could have been agreed upon with Jewish organizations abroad. By 1942 no second Edison or Marconi was needed to build a transmitter of twenty or thirty watts which would have been received abroad. The Polish resistance had eventually about a hundred such transmitters. They were relatively small and the Germans, hard as they tried, succeeded in locating only a few of these. In Palestine, the know-how, needless to say, also existed. Paradoxically, in early 1942 British Intelligence (ISLD) asked the Jewish Agency to provide short-wave instructors for parachutists trained in Egypt, and the *Hagana* sent four of its experts to these camps. In the absence of any such initiative, Jewish dependence on the Poles for transmitting their messages was almost total.

In the beginning the Jews in the ghetto had great difficulties even to reach the Polish underground. There were sporadic contacts between *Hashomer Hatzair*, the Zionist - socialist youth movement, and the leadership of the Polish Boy Scouts. One of them, 'Hubert' (Kaminski), was now editor of the AK *Biuletyn Informacyjny* and Ringelblum's report about Chelmno, the first account of mass murder by gassing, was probably conveyed to the West through this channel. But far more important were the ties between the socialist anti-Zionist *Bund*, represented by Leon Feiner, and the Polish Socialists of the PPS. Feiner ('Mikolaj', 'Berezowski') was transmitting news for 'Artur' through the AK radio and through couriers, first intermittently, and later fairly regularly. 'Artur' was Zygielbojm, the *Bund* representative in London, who, having escaped from Poland in 1940, had arrived there from America in April 1942, and who became the most vocal Polish-Jewish spokesman abroad. Leon Feiner was a lawyer by profession who had shown great courage in a number of political trials. He had been arrested for a while under the rule of the colonels. Another illegal, a young Jewish woman who met him during the war, described him as follows:

... my attention was called to a guest who had just entered. He too had an air of self confidence. A tall, elegant, elderly man with silvery hair and an upturned moustache, bright eyes and rosy cheeks. He was the image of a Polish country gentleman. . . .[6]

Jan Karski (Kozielewski), the courier whose mission to the West in late 1942 had a considerable impact, also met Feiner and wrote about him:

[He] lived outside the ghetto but was able by secret means to enter and leave it as he pleased and carry on his work there. Inside the ghetto he looked, talked and acted like the other inhabitants. To carry on his tasks outside he succeeded in changing his appearance so completely as to go absolutely undetected by the keenest scrutiny . . . with his distinguished grey hair and whiskers, ruddy complexion, erect carriage and general air of good health and refinement, he passed easily as a Polish 'nobleman'. He appeared before the German authorities as the owner of a large store, prosperous, dignified and unruffled. How great an effort of will this pose must have necessitated I realized later when he accompanied me to the ghetto. . . .[7]

Feiner lived to see the German retreat from Poland but died shortly afterwards in a hospital in Lublin.

Some time between November 1941 and February 1942 a

'subcommittee for Jewish affairs' was set up at the Bureau of Information and Propaganda of the AK which was headed by two intellectuals – the historian Stanislaw Herbst (Chrobot) and the lawyer Henryk Wolinski (Zakrzewski). But contact between them and the Jews was still sporadic and regular communications between the Jews and London was established only the following winter, after most of the Warsaw Jews had already perished. During 1941 the AK transmitted only a few situation reports concerning Jewish affairs; this began to change towards the end of the year when information was received in the Polish capital about the massacres in the East. According to a Polish source communication was slow and the alarming news from Lwow, Vilna, Bialystok and Volhyn province did not reach Warsaw until the beginning of 1942.[8] But a perusal of the records shows that the Lithuanian and Ukrainian massacres were known already in November 1941. An article in the illegal organ of a small socialist group (*Barykada Wolnosci*) dated November 1941 stated, *inter alia,* that in Vilna only 3,000 Jews stayed alive and that there had been large-scale massacres elsewhere.[9]

Similar information was contained in the AK bulletins. According to one such report only 12–15,000 Jews had survived in Vilna out of 70,000; the Kovno ghetto no longer existed; in Minsk and Motel (Chaim Weizmann's birthplace) all Jews had been killed, and the same was true broadly speaking for the Jewish population of Polesia, Volhynia and Pinsk.[10] An even earlier Home Army report dated October 1941 reports 'horrible and repulsive news' from Lithuania and Vilna district, where the Lithuanian police with the active help of students from universities and high schools had murdered 170,000 Jews. In short, the news about the actions of the *Einsatzgruppen* had been received in Warsaw well before the end of 1941. Early in the New Year these items became quite specific. A report covering the period from 16–28 February 1942 mentions not only individual killings in Warsaw, Miedzyrzec, Jaslo, Poznam and Ostryna, but massacres on an unprecedented scale in eastern Poland, Lithuania and Ukraine.

A few examples from this survey: Molodeczno: in November the Lithuanian police shot all Jews with the exception of one physician. Nova-Wilejka: all Jews killed in November. Vilna:

according to recent arrivals of 70,000 Jews only 11,000 remained in late December. Stanislawow: on 16 November 1941 killing of the Jews by Germans with the help of Ukrainians. Kosow: several thousand Jews killed by Gestapo and a Ukrainian battalion. Mass executions of Jews in Staro-Konstantinow, and Zhitomir (17,000 victims) and Kiev (70,000). This obviously referred to the Babi Yar massacre. There were more names, more figures, more gruesome details.

So far the worst news had all come from the territories in the East which had been occupied by the Germans after June 1941. But in January 1942 the first information about the gassing vans in Chelmno was received in Warsaw; this is the six-page account which has already been mentioned. A small group of grave-diggers succeeded in escaping; their evidence was taken down by Ringelblum's friends in Warsaw. The report was trans-mitted, apparently by courier, to London and the United States where it was widely publicized.[11]

Then in late March and April news was received about the 'deportations' from Lublin, the killing of 2,000 Jews on the spot and the dispatch in closed railway carriages of 26,000 to Belzec to be killed there by means of poison gas. But the Home Army had apparently no accurate news about how exactly the inmates of Belzec were killed: on subsequent occasions mass electro-cution and various other techniques of murder were mentioned.[12]

Even before (on 16 March) a long letter from the *Bund* had described the Warsaw ghetto as 'one big concentration camp' in which the Jews were cut off from the world and the rest of the country. They were dying in many horrible ways, thousands were systematically sent away and their traces were lost. Some were killed by gas. The letter ended with the incongruous request for information about the balance of power in the 'Jewish street' in the United States – shades of the ideological debates of previous decades.[13]

There had apparently been a request from London for confirmation of the rumours about mass murder in the eastern territories. On 8 April 1942 there was the answer of the *Delegat* – the previous news seems to have come mostly from the Home Army. He confirmed that the information about the murder of thousands of Jews in Eastern Galicia, in the Vilna region, in

White Russia and in Lublin was correct. In Vilna alone, 60,000 Jews had been killed.[14]

The reports were transmitted either in the form of short radiograms which reached London within a few hours, or a few days at most, or more often in the form of longer reports – *Pro memoria o sytuacji w kraju* – 'Notes about the situation in the country'. Some detailed accounts appeared in the *Biuletyn Informacyjny* edited by the Bureau of Information and Propaganda of the Warsaw district of the Home Army. It was already mentioned that the longer reports sent by courier would take considerably longer to reach London since the breakdown of the Swedish network; thus, the review of events during August 1942 was published in London only in late December.

The Polish underground did not consider Jewish affairs its main concern and in its exchanges with London news regarding the fate of the Jews was not given high priority. But neither was such information suppressed: of the eighty-five pages of the *Sprawozdanie* 6, 1942, more than one-third deals with Jewish affairs. The general feeling seems to have been that there was nothing the Poles could possibly do to save the millions of Jews. They could, after all, not extend help to their own. There was furthermore the tendency to stress the part of Ukrainians, Lithuanians and Latvians in the killings and the implication that Polish police would not be involved in actions of this kind.[15] But this, on the whole, was in accordance with facts.

On occasions the Polish underground did not get its information right, but this was probably inevitable in wartime. Thus, the AK got the truth about Auschwitz with some delay. During 1942 three illegal brochures were published by the Home Army, all were written by women – but the authors were not yet aware that this had become the largest of all the extermination camps.[16] They were apparently confused by the fact that Auschwitz consisted of several camps and that some prisoners were actually released from Auschwitz. According to their experience no one was ever freed from a death camp. The first more or less accurate report on the true character of Auschwitz seems to have been published only in September 1942. It reported the presence of 70,000 Jews from all over Europe and the installation of gas chambers and three crematoria working around the clock.[17]

The Polish underground regularly used several lines of communications: *Delegat* would address his communications to 'Stem', Stanislaw Mikolajczyk, the Minister of Interior, and his reports would usually cover 'civilian' affairs. Military affairs on the other hand would be radioed or dispatched to the Prime Minister (Sikorski) by the commander of the Home Army, General Rowecki, or his deputy, Bor Komorowski. They would be read by Sikorski, his chef de cabinet, Sosnkowski, the commander-in-chief, and a few others. It stands to reason that 'military' news, i.e. Home Army affairs, was not widely circulated, but the information concerning Jews did not belong to this category. On Zygielbojm's part there were no complaints that information had ever been withheld from him, and he was not by nature the most trusting of men. Even if the Government had tried to keep such news from him he would have heard from friends: the Polish socialists were after all represented in the Government, and secrets could not be kept for long in these conditions. When it appeared in June 1942 that Polish Jewry faced not mere pogroms but extinction, the London Polish National Council commented in its resolutions of 10 June and 8 July about the 'planned slaughter of practically the whole Jewish population'. General Sikorski's broadcast on 9 June 1942 has already been mentioned. Few Jewish organizations were willing at the time to use such extreme terms. Western disbelief puzzled the London Poles and their 'Bulletin for Home Affairs' wrote: 'If the Polish reports from the homeland do not find credence with the Anglo-Saxon nation and are considered to be unreliable, they surely must believe the reports from Jewish sources.' (*Sprawozdanie*, 5 August 1942.) But they still did not believe the reports, or in any case thought them grossly exaggerated, and this seems to have influenced the Polish coverage from the homeland. Perhaps they should understate the enormity of the events in order to gain greater credence?

On 22 July 1942 the deportations from Warsaw began which was, of course, an event of the first magnitude. But neither the Poles in London nor the British Government paid much attention. General Bor Komorowski later wrote in his auto-biography that 'as early as 29 July we had learned from reports of railroad workers that the transports were being sent to the concentration camp at Treblinka and that there the Jews disappeared without trace. There could be no further doubt that this time the deportations were but a prelude to extermination.'[18] According to General Bor Komorowski, the Home Army was transmitting daily reports to London on the situation, but the BBC maintained complete silence: 'There seemed to be only one possible explanation for this silence on the part of London. The news was so incredible that it had failed to convince. We ourselves had, after all, been loath to believe the first reports we received of the exterminations. I was to learn later that this was, in fact, what happened.'[19]

Stefan Korbonski was chief of *Kierownictwo Walki Cywilne* – the Civilian Struggle Directorate – and later became the last *Delegat* in Poland. He tells essentially the same story. Official Polish bodies in London and the BBC took no notice of the reports about the deportations from Warsaw to the death camps which he had sent independently:

This game lasted for a couple of days and evidently due to the daily alarm of the London station, the government finally replied. The telegram did not explain much. It said literally: 'Not all your telegrams are fit for publication.' I racked my brains trying to understand the meaning. Here they were deporting and murdering 7,000 people a day and London believed that this was not fit for publication. Had they lost their heads – or what? It was only a month later that the BBC gave the news based on our information and only many months later the matter was explained to me by a government courier parachuted into Poland: They didn't believe your telegrams, the Polish government did not believe them nor did the British. They said you were exaggerating a bit in your anti-German propaganda. Only when the British received confirmation from their own sources the panic set in and the BBC broadcast your news.[20]

The signals sent from Warsaw during the first four weeks after the deportations started have not been published. A radiogram transmitted by the Wanda radio station on 25 August announced that on some days 5–6,000 Jews were taken out of Warsaw, on others 15,000 – altogether some 150,000 had been deported.[21] But this was an AK radiogram from Rowecki to Sosnkowski, the Polish C-in-C in London. Since it has been the policy of the Polish archives in London (like, unfortunately, most other archives) to grant only selective access, it cannot be checked whether frequent cables were sent by the non-military

Polish underground from Warsaw during late July, August and early September 1942. The *Biuletyn Informacyjny* in its issue of 30 July commented at length on the complete destruction of the Warsaw ghetto, about the manner in which the deportations were organized, about the suicide of Adam Czerniakow, the head of the *Judenrat* (Jewish Council), and it correctly predicted that the deportations would last several weeks.* But the *Biuletyn* was unlikely to reach London for many weeks. The copies of the many signals mentioned by Bor Komorowski and Korbonski have not been located, but this does not mean that they did not exist.† There is no reason to assume that there was a decision in Warsaw suddenly to stop the flow of information after wide coverage had been given to the killing of the Jews during the previous months, not only in eastern Poland but also in the General Government proper. It seems far more likely that the arrest of the Swedes accounts in part for the interruption in the flow of information and that, on the other hand, the explanations given by Bor Komorowski and Korbonski were basically correct: to the extent that the information from Warsaw was played down, the reason was in London. Who were the culprits?

Dr I. Schwarzbart, who was the other Jewish representative on the Polish National Council, wrote in his diary on 24 October 1944: 'I shall never forgive Mikolajczyk for having remained silent about the reports concerning the extermination of the

---

*On 30 July 1942 there was no accurate information as yet with regard to the destination of the Jews. It was announced that they were brought 'to the East, in the direction of Malkinia and Brest on Bug'. There was no precise news 'but there is room for the most pessimistic assumptions'. Even in the next issue of the *Biuletyn* the information given was not correct: the Jews, it was said, were brought to 'two death camps, Belzec and Sobibor' (6 August 1942). In *Biuletyn* of 13 August it was said that the number of those deported was 120–150,000. *Biuletyn* of 20 August gave a figure of 200,000 and the editorial commented on the 'bestial murder of millions of Jews living among us before the eyes of our people'.

The Ministry of the Interior of the Polish Government-in-exile distributed the *Sprawozdanie* reports in English translation to public figures, Members of Parliament, journalists etc. Thus report 6, 1942, covers the period from 1 July–1 December 1942 with special attention to the period 16 July–16 August. 'The Polish authorities in London receive reports on the situation in Poland. . . . We feel that this information should be given to the British public.'

†Polish materials covering the Second World War are dispersed over many archives. I have looked in vain for copies of the signals from Korbonski's station in the two London Polish archives and I have been assured by General Tadeusz Pelczynski that they are not there. They could be in American archives or in private hands.

Jews between July 1942 and September 1942 . . .'[22] Perhaps the Minister of the Interior did not reveal the whole truth; the reasons which may have induced him not to have already been mentioned. But it is also possible that Schwarzbart felt uneasy. Had he himself not warned against 'exaggerations' at the time? The figures about survivors which Schwarzbart conveyed to Jewish institutions were more optimistic than those of the Polish Government-in-exile. Thus in November 1942 he mentioned a figure of 140,000 survivors in the Warsaw ghetto.*

The Warsaw deportations began on 22 July 1942. Five days later, on 27 July, the Jewish Telegraphic Agency reported on the authority of Zygielbojm and the Polish Government-in-exile that the Germans had started mass expulsions from Warsaw aiming at mass extermination. On the following day there was another JTA report to the same effect and the news item was also carried by the *Manchester Guardian*. The information could have reached the Polish Government only through one of the underground wireless stations.

In speeches on 22 August and 1 September, Zygielbojm made it clear that he was aware of what was happening in Warsaw: a whole people was being exterminated in poison gas chambers. The Germans had chosen Poland for the place of execution of the Jews of all occupied countries as well as Germany herself. It was not a pogrom according to Zygielbojm; the executioners harboured no hatred towards their victims, they were simply doing their job. It was a case of studied and cold-blooded extermination.[23] Thus the beginning of the deportations from Warsaw was certainly reported and after four weeks information came through that 150,000 Jews had disappeared. It was after the initial announcement that the Polish Government-in-exile, for whatever reasons, seems to have decided to play down the news of the deportations.

There were some sceptics in its ranks and it is certainly true

---

*Schwarzbart to World Jewish Congress, 16 November 1942, Institute of Jewish Affairs Archives London, Schwarzbart did, in fact, know about the beginning of the deportations from Warsaw. On 27 July he sent a cable to the executive of the World Jewish Congress which begins with the words: 'The Germans have begun mass murder in the ghetto of Warsaw . . .' There is a handwritten note: 'This information I received today from Minister of Interior, Mr. Mikolajczyk.' WJC, Institute of Jewish Affairs Archives, London.

that the British Foreign Office, by and large, thought the information either unreliable or exaggerated. There might well have been an inter-departmental wrangle whether to believe the reports or not. Baroness Hornsby-Smith was in 1942 the principal private secretary of Lord Selborne, Minister of Economic Warfare, who was responsible for the SOE and its activities in Poland. In 1979 she said that the news from Poland was initially not credited in London: 'The SOE, never very popular with the regular Services, as we had our own sources of intelligence and communication, gathered evidence in, not through diplomatic channels, but through men daily risking their lives in the Underground. Again, initially, it was dismissed as unreliable or exaggerated propaganda from a suffering people.'[24]

Thus, those mainly responsible seem to have been some officials in the Foreign Office Intelligence Department. But we know from Polish sources that Lord Selborne did not at this date quite believe the news either. If the Polish radio station in London (*Swit*) which pretended to broadcast from inside Poland did not carry the news about the deportations from Warsaw, the ultimate decision was British, because though the station employed Poles it was a British station. Such disbelief was by no means limited to the British Foreign Office. One example chosen at random should suffice. Hillel Storch, who represented the World Jewish Congress and the Jewish Agency in Stockholm during the war, went to the US Embassy one day in 1942 and told the first secretary that a Jew named Sebba had arrived by way of Finland and had provided information about the extermination in Latvia. 'Dear Mr Storch,' he was told, 'On propaganda we know more than you do.'[25] Yet the US Embassy had received the same information from a Polish source (Wieslaw Patek, head of the consular section of the local Polish legation) including figures about victims in Vilna, Riga, other parts of Latvia and Estonia. The source was an Estonian officer who had watched mass executions; he had passed it on to Helsinki whence it had reached Stockholm.[26] The information existed all along only it was not believed.

As a result the Polish Government-in-exile, whose estimates of the number of victims had been on the whole accurate up to July 1942, began to provide figures that were too low after that date.* Until all files from British and Polish archives are released, which may not happen for a long time, there will be no certainty with regard to the responsibility for this change in 'information policy'. It was not a systematic cover-up. The news was simply played down, and it was made the easier because it was always possible to claim that there was no confirmation from independent sources.

Meanwhile the news about Warsaw had also reached the Jewish institutions in London and New York. Richard Lichtheim in Geneva reported on 15 August that:

On August 14 another person (an Aryan) straight from Poland, a very trustworthy and well known person, reported the following: The ghetto in Warsaw is being liquidated. Jews, irrespective of age and sex, are being taken in groups from the ghetto and shot. ...

We owe the survival of this report to the watchfulness of a certain Mr Yates in the State Department: 'The German text had been inserted between the leaves of the letter to Rabbi Wise. ... I was accordingly suspicious and had copies made for our records.'[27] His superiors took the report seriously. When on 23 September Sumner Welles, the Undersecretary, asked Myron Taylor, US ambassador at the Vatican, to find out what was known in the Vatican about the 'final solution' he quoted the text of this cable in full.[28]

On 21 August 1942 the London *Jewish Chronicle* and other newspapers reported the suicide of Adam Czerniakow, the head

*In November 1942 the Polish Government still talked in its communiqués about 'more than a million Jewish victims'. On one occasion it was said that Himmler had ordered the execution of half of the Jewish population by the end of the year (*New York Herald Tribune*, 25 November 1942). No one, to be sure, not even Himmler himself, knew exactly at the time how many Jews had been killed. But it should have been known in London that the figure was closer to three than to one million. In late 1943 a Polish refugee, a clerk from Warsaw, arrived in Britain. He had left Gdynia on 1 November and arrived in London via Stockholm on 10 December. He was interrogated by MI19 in great detail and reported, among other things, that 3.3 million Polish Jews had been killed, that some 200,000 were in hiding and another 130,000 were passing as non-Jews. These figures were remarkably accurate. Cavendish-Bentinck, chairman of the joint intelligence committee, passed this report on to Cadogan of the Foreign Office because he thought it of exceptional interest. But he added that the Poles 'find some difficulty in believing the figures given for the extermination of the Jews' (FO 371 39449 xk 6699). This seems to have been the general consensus among Allied intelligence services at the time. According to an Allied official announcement published in August 1943, 1,702,500 Jews had been killed up to that date (*New York Times*, 27 August 1943). The actual number of victims was more than twice this figure.

of the *Judenrat* (Jewish Council). This was said to have been his response to the Nazi demand for the deportation of 100,000 Jews from Warsaw 'which was tantamount to death'. On 10 September the Jewish Telegraphic Agency reported the deportation of 300,000 Jews from Warsaw. On 20 September from the same source: 'Pogroms on unprecedented scale in Poland. The Nazis have begun the extermination of Polish Jewry. Save us.' On 2 October 1942, again in the *Jewish Chronicle*, 'Nazi's Master Plan for Jews' (the Riegner report without attribution). The news item was published in the middle of the paper. As so often information of this kind was not considered front-page news and there was no editorial comment. One could not, after all, be certain and so one preferred to wait.

During the remaining months of 1942, Zygielbojm continued to receive signals and letters from the remnants of the *Bund* in Warsaw. One dated 2 October said that 300,000 Jews from Warsaw had been killed and that half a million remaining in the whole of Poland faced the same lot.[29] On 15 December: 'About 40,000 Jews remain in the ghetto.'[30] A long report datelined Warsaw, August 1942, dealt with the Jewish death camps, mainly Treblinka I and II, the process of selection and many other details. There was also a ten-page, single-space letter from Feiner which had been written on the last day of August and which reviewed once again the whole process of extermination from the beginning. Feiner described how the Germans had succeeded in deluding the doomed, paralyzing their will to resist: those temporarily staying behind firmly believed that they had been saved. The ghetto police had participated in the organizational preparations of the deportations. After reviewing the process of extermination in other parts of Poland such as Lwow, Feiner concluded with a number of suggestions. Those dead could not be resurrected, but there still was a chance to save the remnant of Polish Jewry. He proposed an appeal to the whole world by the United Nations, and a stern warning that Nazi criminals would be punished. Furthermore, the Polish Government-in-exile should appeal to the nation so that every Pole would give all possible help to the Jews. A special appeal should be made to the working class and the intelligentsia. But above all, it should be clear that in this unequal war the

Hitlerites understood only one language: Germans living on Allied territory should be taken as hostages for the Jews about to be killed.[31]

The same suggestion had been made in a previous message by the *Bund*. Feiner was a lawyer, but he also knew the limits of law – *de maximis non curat lex*. The appeal was, of course, quite fruitless. The Allies published a statement in December 1942 but its terms did not inspire Hitler with great fear – he took no notice. The proposal to take hostages was not practical either and as for threatening the war criminals with punishing them for their crimes, there were differences of opinion among Western statesmen. While Churchill thought that a declaration would 'strike a chill to the evil heart', Anthony Eden, on the contrary, feared that such pronouncements would simply cause Hitler and his companions to 'harden their hearts'.

In November 1942 another Polish courier, Jan Kozielewski ('Witold', 'Jan Karski'), arrived in London. A young man who had joined the Polish Foreign Ministry before the war, this was his third and last mission. Once before he had fallen into the hands of the Germans. In contrast to previous couriers he had actually talked to Jewish leaders, to Leon Feiner and a young Zionist whose identity is not altogether clear to this day. As he sat with them 'in a huge, empty, and half ruined house in the suburbs', Karski realized that the prospects facing them were horrible beyond description. The Zionist leader said: 'You other Poles are fortunate, you are suffering too, many of you will die, but at least your nation goes on living.' After the war Poland will be resurrected.[32]

They told him that the Jews were helpless, that the entire Jewish people would be destroyed. The Polish underground could save a few but three millions were doomed: 'Place this responsibility on the shoulders of the Allies. Let not a single leader of the United Nations be able to say that they did not know that we were being murdered in Poland and could not be helped except from the outside.' They then suggested all kinds of schemes including a massive bombing campaign of German cities, and public executions of Germans in Allied countries. But that was utterly fantastic, Karski said, such demands would only confuse and horrify all those in sympathy with the Jews. 'Of course,' the Zionist answered, 'do you think I don't know it? We ask it because it is the only rebuttal to what is being done to us. We do not dream of its being fulfilled.' The Jewish leaders then said that if American and British citizens could be saved, why could not Jewish women and children be exchanged? Why couldn't the lives of a few thousand Polish Jews be bought by the Allies? But this was opposed to all war strategy, Karski said. 'That's just it. That's what we're up against,' the *Bund* leader said. 'Tell the Jewish leaders that this is no case for politics or tactics. Tell them that the earth must be shaken to its foundations, the world must be aroused. Perhaps then it will wake up. . . .'[33]

He then suggested that the Jewish leaders should go to all important English and American government offices, that they should not leave, not eat and drink, until a way had been decided to save the Jews. 'Let them die a slow death while the world is looking on, let them die. This may shake the conscience of the world.'

Having visited the ghetto twice and smuggled himself into Belzec death camp, Karski made his way to London.[34] He met Zygielbojm and conveyed the message from Warsaw, including their call for a hunger strike. 'It is impossible,' Zygielbojm said, 'utterly impossible. You know what would happen. They would simply bring in two policemen and have me dragged away to an institution. Do you think they will let me die a slow lingering death? Never . . . they would never let me die.'[35] But he promised he would do everything they demanded, if he was only given a chance. Karski writes that at bottom he thought that Zygielbojm was boasting or at least thoughtlessly promising more than he could perform.

Karski went on to see public figures; he even met Eden and later, in America, Roosevelt. He made a profound impression on all those he met as Count Edward Raczynski, Polish Foreign Minister, noted in his diary. In May 1943 the news reached Karski that Zygielbojm had committed suicide. In a last letter to the Polish President and Prime Minister in exile he wrote that while the crime of murdering the whole Jewish population of Poland rested in the first place upon the murderers themselves, indirectly it rested on all humanity, the governments and peoples of the Allied states which had not undertaken concrete action to stop the crime: 'By passively watching the extermination of millions of defenceless, tortured to death children, women and men, those countries became accomplices of the murderers.' Though the Polish Government had contributed to a large extent towards influencing world opinion, it had done nothing commensurate with the scale of the drama taking place in Poland:

I cannot remain silent, I cannot go on living when the remnants of the Jewish people of Poland of whom I am a representative are eliminated. . . . By my death I want to express my strongest protest against the extermination of the Jewish people.

The world was not shaken to its foundations and Zygielbojm's death was forgotten, except by his comrades.

As the war ended and the full enormity of the catastrophe began to register there was bitter recrimination. On one side the help extended to the Jews during the war was magnified, in an apologetic literature, sometimes out of all proportion; instances of help rendered were singled out, cases of indifference or hostility were disregarded. On the other side there has been the urge to throw out indiscriminately accusations of neglect and sabotage, within the Jewish camp, and *a fortiori* outside, with the Poles as an obvious target. Such charges and generally speaking the search for scapegoats are psychologically intelligible, but they do not contribute to a better understanding of what happened. The record of the Polish underground and the Polish Government-in-exile was not perfect, as far as the publication of news about the 'final solution' is concerned. But the long report submitted by Edward Raczynski, the Polish representative to the Allied governments, of 9 December 1942 contained the fullest survey of the 'final solution'. No other Allied government was remotely as outspoken at the time and for a long time after.* If one finds fault with them what is one to say about the Russians who deliberately played it down from the beginning to this day? What about the British Foreign Office which decided in late 1943 to delete any reference to the use of gas chambers because the evidence was untrustworthy?† What about the American officials who tried to suppress the 'unauthorized news' from Eastern Europe? What about the Jewish leaders who continued

---

*The note was forwarded by Biddle to Cordell Hull on 18 December 1942.
†This refers to the Stalin-Roosevelt-Churchill declaration of 1 November 1943.

to doubt the authenticity of the news well after it should have been obvious that there was no more room for doubt? In a search for scapegoats few are likely to emerge unscathed.

5

THE JEWS IN NAZI-OCCUPIED EUROPE: DENIAL AND ACCEPTANCE

IN a speech on the sixth anniversary of his rise to power, Hitler said:

Today I want to be a prophet once more: if international-finance Jewry inside and outside of Europe should succeed once more in plunging nations into another world war, the consequence will not be the Bolshevization of the earth and thereby the victory of Jewry, but the annihilation of the Jewish race in Europe.

Among Jewish leaders in continental Europe, England and America, not too much attention was paid to this and similar declarations. Politicians were known always to use exaggerated language and Hitler was thought to be no exception. Jewish leaders were not blind and it was, of course, no secret that Nazi Germany persecuted the Jews more relentlessly and harshly than any state in modern times. But the Jews in their long history had frequently been the victims of persecution; they had outlasted all haters of the house of Israel, they would survive Hitler as well. There was in any case a long way from persecution to annihilation. No one in his right mind thought that Hitler actually intended to kill all Jews. About half of German and Austrian Jews left before the outbreak of the war; more would have done so if emigration had not been almost impossible. No country wanted them. Even Palestine was virtually closed to all but a few after 1936. Jewish leaders expressed fear, they protested against the Nazi policy, some of them were greatly concerned that emigration from Germany and Austria was not proceeding quickly enough, especially as persecutions became more violent in 1938. The Jewish communities in the countries near Germany had, of course, heard and read about the plight of their co-religionists in Germany and many were apprehensive that this kind of anti-semitism would spread. But by and large they did not see the mortal danger.

After Poland had been defeated in 1939 and divided between Germany and the Soviet Union, many thousand Polish Jews who had fled to the Soviet Union returned to German-occupied territory. The older generation remembered the German army from the First World War when it had occupied much of Poland and the Ukraine. Even if their rule was harsh, even if they did not like the Jews, the Germans were after all a *Kulturvolk*, a civilized nation, there was no arbitrary killing. The same pattern recurred in the regions occupied by the Germans after their invasion of the Soviet Union in June 1941. East European Jewry was not aware of the fact that in 1940 it was confronting a different kind of German authority. The Jews like the Slavs were *Untermenschen*, 'subhuman', only much more so; there was quite literally no future for them in the German New Order in ·Europe. They were expelled from the parts of Poland which were incorporated in the Reich, they were concentrated in ghettos, they lost all rights, they were mistreated and starved. Mortality in ghettos was very high. There were some voices even in 1940 claiming that East European Jewry was doomed, but this referred to a long-term perspective. No one was prepared as yet for the mass killings which began with the invasion of Russia.

The Jews in the western regions of the Soviet Union were even less prepared than those in Poland. Relations between Russia and Nazi Germany had been fairly close since the agreement of August 1939. The Soviet press had certainly not reported that anything untoward had happened to the Jews under Hitler. As the leaders of the *Einsatzgruppen* realized with evident surprise when they were gathering the victims for the slaughter, the Jews seemed to have no idea at all of their fate. It was only months later, after hundreds of thousands had been killed, that they noted that the news about SS practices had spread and that they no longer met the whole Jewish population whenever they arrived in a new place. But the Jews in the Soviet Union were not organized, there were no links between communities, and by the time the nature of the danger had been understood it was usually too late.

This was true even with regard to the areas which had been annexed by the Soviet Union as recently as 1940 such as the

Baltic republics, Bessarabia and Bukovina, in which there were substantial Jewish concentrations. The 'special units', helped by local cut-throats, went to their work systematically from the day they entered a new town or village. But the stories of the survivors of the massacres – and there were almost always a few of those – were not believed. Dr M. Dvorzhetski, a physician in Vilna, related many years later his own first reactions as follows:

One day I saw in the streets a woman barefoot, her hair dishevelled. She gave the impression of being out of her mind. I took her into my room and she said: 'I come from Ponary.' 'From the labour camp at Ponary?' I asked. 'There is no labour camp at Ponary, they kill Jews there,' she said.

The woman told Dr Dvorzhetski about the executions and described her escape from the pit into which the corpses had been thrown. She had been hit only in her arm. The doctor still did not believe her but when he dressed her wounds he found creeping ants from the woods.

Dvorzhetski then went out and told others what he had heard about Ponary. 'Doctor,' they said, 'are you too a panic monger? Instead of giving us a word of consolation you tell us nightmares.' 'After all, this is Europe, not the jungle,' people argued, 'they can't kill us all.' News about mass murder was met with incredulity or at most ascribed to the savagery of a local commander.[1]

But the killings in Ponary did not stop and news was filtering in from Kovno and from the smaller communities in the neighbourhood of Vilna. Leaders of the Jewish youth organizations met and on 1 January 1942 published a manifesto which said that 'all ways of the Gestapo lead to Ponary', that Ponary meant death, that it was not a concentration or labour camp and that everyone there was killed by shooting. Above all, the manifesto stated that Hitler intended to kill all Jews of Europe and Lithuanian Jewry was to be the first.[2]

This was the first time that such a warning was issued. The leaders of the Vilna underground decided to alarm the Jewish communities in Poland with whom they had traditionally close links. But even before their emissaries went out, a first messenger had arrived from Warsaw in late October or early November 1941. Sinister rumours had reached Warsaw and it had been decided to check whether they were true. The courier was a young Pole named Henik, a member of the Boy Scouts who was on friendly terms with the members of *Hashomer Hatzair*, the Zionist-socialist youth organization. He contacted the leaders of the Vilna underground and apparently even witnessed a massacre (at Troki). According to another source his mission took place even earlier, in September 1941, but there is general agreement that his report was not believed in Warsaw: it seemed altogether incredible.[3] But in the following weeks and months several emissaries from Vilna began to arrive in Grodno, Bialystok and Warsaw, mainly 'Aryan-looking' Jewish women. In early 1942 a whole delegation representing the Vilna underground came to Warsaw and met representatives of the main Jewish groups. Their reports appeared without attribution in the illegal newspapers. *Jutrznia* (of *Hashomer Hatzair*) reported on 21 March 1942 that the period of slow killing was ending and the Jews now faced total physical liquidation. *Slowo Mlodych* (of *Gordonia*) in its issue of February/March 1942 reported that of 400,000 Lithuanian Jews only 100,000 remained and that they had been led like sheep to the slaughterhouse: Hitler's threat to destroy European Jewry was carried out. Meanwhile Frumka Plotnicka, a youth movement emissary, had been to Volhynia, the region in eastern Poland–north-west Ukraine and reported that all Jews had been killed except a few thousand in Kowel.

The illegal press which carried these reports played an important role in keeping the ghettos informed. There were many such newspapers, in Polish, Hebrew and Yiddish, including a *Daily Bulletin* of three pages which mainly featured news from foreign broadcasts. Another daily sheet (*Morgen Frai*) was published by the Communists. The most important of the periodicals in addition to those already mentioned was *Biuletyn* and *Der Vecker* (of the *Bund*), *Plomienie* and *El Al* (of *Hashomer Hatzair*), *Yedies* and *Unser Weg* (*Dror*), *Yugentshtimme* and *Proletarisher Stimme*. The *Daily Bulletin* appeared in 200 copies; the average circulation of the others was about 300–500. They were also distributed outside Warsaw. Each copy was read by many people who passed the news on by word of mouth. Thus the illegal press reached tens, perhaps hundreds of thousands.

But how great was its political and psychological impact? When the emissaries from Vilna met with the leading representatives of the Jewish parties in Warsaw in early 1942, the majority no longer doubted the authenticity of the news from Lithuania. They even feared that it was possible that similar events might occur elsewhere. But on the whole they were inclined to see in these outrages manifestations of German revenge against 'Jewish Communists' in the formerly Soviet territories. As one of those present put it: this is Warsaw, in the centre of Europe; there are 400,000 Jews in the ghetto, a liquidation on this scale is surely impossible.[4] The news from Eastern Galicia received in Warsaw at about the same time was no better, but the same reasoning applied to these territories which had also been part of the Soviet Union after September 1939: it couldn't happen here.

Then in late March there was alarming news of the removal of the Jews from Lublin district. No one seemed to know their destination. Lublin was Poland proper; furthermore, this was precisely the area which at one time had been set aside by the Nazis as the place where most (or all) East European Jews were to be 'resettled'. Even before, in February, there had been reports about Chelmno, the first extermination camp.*

Chelmno on the Ner (Kulmhof) is in western Poland some forty miles west of Lodz and had been incorporated in Germany after the campaign in 1939. In October 1941 a special unit took quarters in the village – this was the *Sonderkommando Lange*, called after its commander, Herbert Lange, a police officer. This unit had received its training in mass murder in eastern Prussia, liquidating some 500 patients suffering from various mental disorders. In early December 1941 – well before the Wannsee Conference – it began operating in Chelmno.

The reports which reached Warsaw and subsequently also the West† said that Jews from the neighbourhood, places such as Kolo and Sompolno but also from Lodz ghetto, had been taken to Chelmno where they had simply disappeared. First the Jews had been told that a new community would be created somewhere in the vicinity. Then they were taken to a castle, a one-storey ruin from the First World War. At first they were treated kindly and reassured about the continuation of their

---

*It was published in *Der Vecker, Slowo Mlodych* and other underground papers.
†The report was given publicity by Zygielbojm in London, appeared in New York (*The Ghetto*, 5 August 1942) and the Yiddish press, and was widely reprinted.

voyage. Then they were taken in groups to a large, well-heated closet which led to an underground corridor at the end of which was a ramp-like structure. There an elderly German addressed them: the entire transport would be sent to a new ghetto, the men would be employed in factories, the women in housekeeping, the children would be sent to school. Prior to continuing their trip they would have to subject themselves and their clothes to disinfection. They were told to disrobe and to hand over personal documents and valuable articles. Then they were led into large grey trucks, which were hermetically sealed. The trucks would then be driven into the Lubrodz woods, a distance of some seven kilometres. There, having satisfied themselves that the victims were dead, the drivers would empty their load into a pit five metres deep and almost two metres wide, which had been prepared by a group of Jewish gravediggers who, in turn, were watched by some thirty gendarmes. The emptying of the truck was described in considerable detail. It was mentioned, for instance, that each layer of corpses was covered with chloride powder so as to remove the nauseating odour. The gravediggers tried to inform the outside world about what was happening at Chelmno; they threw letters out of the vans taking them to their work. Eventually three of them succeeded in fleeing and made their way to Warsaw where they arrived in February.

Rumkowski, the head of the Lodz ghetto, the second largest in Poland, seems to have learned about the purpose of Chelmno independently. This appears from a letter he had written to the rabbi of a nearby community (Grabow) who had turned to him with the request for information.[5] But on the whole Rumkowski kept silent and if the story of Chelmno reached the Jewish public in Poland and abroad this was to the credit of a small group in the Warsaw ghetto which was running a clandestine documentary centre and intelligence service under the name of *Oneg Shabbat*. The gravediggers were interviewed by members of this circle who passed it on to the Jewish illegal press and also to the Polish underground.* The driving force behind this group was

*It has been established that the three gravediggers arrived in the Warsaw ghetto about four weeks after their escape. They had been apparently advised to direct their steps to the capital by the rabbi of Grabow (not far from Chelmno) whom they had seen earlier on. *Oneg Shabbat* passed the news on to the Polish underground press, to the left-wing paper *Barykada Wolnosci* (see 'Satanskie Zbrodnie Hitlera', March 1942) and,

Emanuel Ringelblum, a leader of the left-wing Marxist-Zionist party *Poale Zion*. Born in 1900 in Eastern Galicia, he had studied at Warsaw University and taught history in Warsaw high schools until in 1938 he became involved in the organization of help to refugees from Nazi Germany. From this time on he was one of the leaders in the movement for self-help and mutual assistance. Together with A. Gutkovski and Hersh Wasser, as well as a group of younger people, he established an archive on the condition of the Jews in Warsaw and the process of liquidation. Information was also collected from refugees from smaller communities all over Poland. The weekly news sheets which contained this information were distributed 'to public men and editors of underground papers, both Jewish and Polish'. It alerted public opinion to the extent of the killings and their likely continuation and 'also served as a source of news for outside the country on the appalling things that were being done to the Jewish population'.[6] Ringelblum was caught by the Gestapo in March 1944, tortured and shot. Wasser, one of his close collaborators, survived the war. The materials collected by the group were hidden in three containers after the destruction of the ghetto. Two were found after the end of the war, the third has been lost. They constitute the most important single source for our knowledge about Warsaw during these tragic years.

But the news about Chelmno had reached not only Ringelblum through the gravediggers; it had been transmitted to Warsaw in January in a less dramatic way – through the mail. In the archives of the Jewish Historical Institute in Warsaw there are five letters and postcards in which Jews living in the vicinity of Chelmno neighbourhood informed their friends and relations in Warsaw about what had happened and asked them to inform Jewish leaders at once about the impending danger.[7] They are dated 9, 21, 22 and 27 January. If five such letters have been found after the total destruction of Warsaw it is not unreasonable to assume that there were many more such

lastly, through the lawyer Henryk Wolinski, head of the Jewish department at the *Delegatura*, it was transmitted to London and the United States. Wolinski also helped Ringelblum to get the reports about the extermination of the Jews in Lublin and other regions to the West (March–April 1942). They were sent by courier, not telegraph, since these were longish reports; they reached London only with a delay ranging from four to eight weeks. See Ruta Sakowska, 'Archiwum Ringelbluma', *Biuletyn Żydowskiego Instytutu Historycznego w Polsce*, July–December 1978 and chapter 4 above ('News From Poland').

messages. The letters about Chelmno quite apart, there were many others about massacres, deportations and gassings all over Poland. Post offices in Poland continued to function, warnings continued to arrive from all over the country; perhaps the Nazis thought that since the Jews were doomed anyway it did not greatly matter whether calls for help were transmitted from one place to another. The existence of these letters shows, in any case, that many Polish Jews did know at an early date about the 'final solution'. If so, why were they so reluctant to believe it? Perhaps they thought like the woman from Krushniewiza who wrote to her husband on 24 January 1942, one week before her deportation to Chelmno: 'We face a great disaster, we know beforehand what will happen to us. It is better if one does not know, if it happens suddenly. . . .'[8] Or to provide another example on a higher level of sophistication: the underground newspaper *Der Vecker* had been one of the first to carry the news about Chelmno. But in its next issue (15 February 1942) it attacked the 'alarmists and panicmongers' who were spreading the news that deportations would soon start from the Warsaw ghetto. Such rumours, the paper said, were 'criminally irresponsible'.

The first document that has survived about the existence of the first death camp dates back even further. This is a postcard written by an unknown Jew to a resident of Posbebice and was later forwarded to Lodz. It reads as follows:

Dear Cousin Mote Altszul,   31 December 1941
    As you know from Kolo, Dabie and other places Jews have been sent to Chelmno to a castle. Two weeks have already passed and it is not known how several thousands have perished. They are gone and you should know, there will be no addresses for them. They were sent to the forest and they were buried. So, address all Jews that they should pray for the Jewish people, and may God declare: so far and not further. With regard to the Jews of Zagzewo, their address is the same. Do not look upon this as a small matter, they have decided to wipe out, to kill, to destroy. Pass this letter on to learned people to read. . . .[9]

It is not known whether this postcard was read by anyone but the recipients. But there was another letter which in all probability reached a wider circle. Having been seen by the gravediggers from Chelmno, the rabbi of Grabow wrote to his brother-in-law in Lodz:

My dearest,   19 January 1942

Until now I have not replied to your letters because I did not know exactly about all the things people have been talking about. Unfortunately, for our great tragedy, now we know it all. I have been visited by an eyewitness who survived only by accident, he managed to escape from hell. . . . I found out about everything from him. The place where all perish is called Chelmno, not far from Dabie, and all are hidden in the neighbouring forest of Lochow. People are killed in two different ways: by firing squad or by poison gas. This is what happened to the cities Dabie, Isbica, Kujawska, Klodawa and others. Lately there have been brought to that place thousands of gypsies from the so-called gypsy camp of Lodz, and for the past several days Jews have been brought there from Lodz and the same is done to them. Do not think that I am mad. Alas, this is the tragic, cruel truth. Tear off your garments, put ashes on your heads, run through the streets and dance in madness. . . .

I am so tired by the suffering of Israel and I can no longer write. I feel that my heart is bursting. And maybe the Most High will after all have mercy and will save the remnants of our nation. O creator of the world, help us! [Jakob Schulman][10]

It appears from this letter that there were rumours in Lodz about Chelmno even before and that the rabbi was writing in reply to a request for more information.

One of those who had few illusions was Ringelblum, whose diary became one of the most important documents on the last days of Polish Jewry. He wrote in his diary about Chelmno; in April he knew about Belzec and in May about Sobibor, the two other camps which had just started operating.[11] But his diary also reflects his terrible frustration. As April passed and May and there was no sign that the information he had passed on to the Polish Government-in-exile and through it to the Western world about the first death factory and also about the Lublin killings in March–April had indeed reached its destination.

Then on Friday 26 June he was at last sure that his messages had reached London. He noted in his diary that there had been a transmission of the BBC in the morning in which there was said 'all that we knew so well – Slonim and Vilna, Lemberg and Chelmno'. For how many months had he waited, thinking that the world was deaf and dumb? For a long time he had suspected the Polish resistance: perhaps they wanted to keep silent about the Jewish tragedy so as not to detract from their own tragedy.

Ringelblum noted with satisfaction that the broadcast had not merely mentioned individual acts of cruelty, as on previous occasions. For the first time the number of victims had been mentioned – 700,000. Thus the *Oneg Shabbat* group had fulfilled a great historical mission and perhaps saved hundreds of thousands of Jews. Even their death would not be in vain as the death of so many other Jews for they had made known the devilish plan which the Germans wanted to keep secret to destroy Polish Jewry. If only England would take suitable counter-measures the Polish Jews could perhaps still be saved.

Ringelblum's words about the 'great historical mission' and his implied optimism were, of course, tragically wrong in retrospect. But it is now generally accepted that he and his group were indeed the first to alert the West to the fact that East European Jewry was no longer facing just pogroms but that a new stage had been reached – extinction.[12] It was not the fault of *Oneg Shabbat* that suitable counter-measures were not taken – perhaps could not be taken by the British or anyone else.

A few days later, on 30 June, Ringelblum returned to the same topic in his diary:

These last days the Jewish population has been living in the sign of London. For long months we tormented ourselves with the question: does the world know about our suffering? And if so, why does it keep silent? Only now have we understood the real reason: London did not know. Now, following these revelations there is great excitement, joy mixed with fear.

According to Ringelblum even most Germans in Poland had not known until recently about the mass killings. Some of the Germans who had heard about Chelmno were greatly perturbed and were reported to have said that they and their families would pay dearly for these crimes. Hence Ringelblum's conclusion: quite possibly the Nazis were afraid of German public opinion. But a sober appraisal showed that the Jews could not expect any mercy from the Germans. It all depended how much time Hitler had to pursue his designs. If he had sufficient time, then the Jews were lost.

Even before the news from London had reached him Ringelblum had pondered in his diary the meaning of another death camp, Sobibor. On 17 June he wrote that a friend from another town who had assisted with the 'population transfer' to

Sobibor where Jews were choked with gas had asked him, 'How much longer will we go as sheep to slaughter?' Ringelblum commented that the deportations were carried out in such a way that it was not always clear to everyone that a massacre was taking place. As a result the urge to defend the whole community and the feeling of solidarity were lost, there was a spiritual breakdown, a disintegration caused by three years of terror. He continued:

Nonetheless it will remain completely incomprehensible why Jews from villages around Hrubieszow were evacuated under a guard of Jewish policemen. Not one of them escaped, although all of them knew where and towards what they were going. No expert will be able to explain why 40 pioneers (*halutzim*) from an agricultural kibbutz consented to be led to the slaughter though they knew what had happened in Vilna, Slonim, Chelmno and other places. One gendarme is sufficient to slaughter a whole town. . . . In Lublin four Gestapo men set up and performed the entire operation. . . . They went passively to death and they did it so that the remnants of the people would be left to live, because every Jew knew that lifting a hand against a German would endanger his brothers from a different town or maybe from a different country. That is the reason why 300 prisoners of war let themselves be killed by the Germans on the way from Lublin to Biala, brave soldiers who had distinguished themselves in the fight for Poland's freedom. . . .

But was this explanation entirely convincing? Ringelblum had said himself that the phenomenon was inexplicable in the final analysis. On some occasions he noted that it was not always clear to the victims what fate was in store for them, and on other occasions he wrote that they knew perfectly well. There was an inconsistency in his comments but this inconsistency was inherent in the situation. It was an essential part of it.

Yizhak Zukerman, one of the leaders of the Zionist-socialist underground, wrote in 1944 that the Jewish underground press had carried extensive reports about the mass murders,

but Warsaw did not believe. . . . Simple commonsense refused to accept the possibility of the mass destruction of tens and hundreds of thousands of Jews. . . . The press was decried for panicmongering even though the descriptions of deportation action were strictly true. The news about the German crimes was received with incredulity and mistrust – not only abroad. Even here in the immediate neighbourhood of Ponary and Chelmno, Belzec and Treblinka these reports found no credence. Unfounded optimism went hand in hand with ignorance.[13]

If some did not believe the reports, others did. Haim Aron Kaplan, unlike Ringelblum, was not in the centre of the Warsaw stage, nor did he have a private information service at his disposal. He was an elderly educator, the head of an elementary Hebrew day school. His diary was discovered after the war – Kaplan and his family died in December 1942 or January 1943 in Treblinka – and it clearly shows that there were no secrets in the ghetto. Thus on 16 May 1942:

Alfred Rosenberg has stated explicitly: 'The Jews are awaiting the end of the war; but the Jews will not live to see it. They will pass from the earth before it comes.' Vilna, Kovno, Lublin, Slonim and Novogrudok have proved that the Nazi may be relied upon to keep his word.[14]

On 3 June Kaplan wrote in his diary that 40,000 Jews of Lublin had disappeared, but no one knew their burial place. Aryan messengers had searched for them but found no trace: 'But there is no doubt that they are no longer alive.' On 7 June: 'The English radio, whose listeners endanger their lives, strengthens our hope. We listen to Reuters with great respect.'

On 10 July 1942 Haim Kaplan, the teacher in the isolated ghetto, knew about the 'final solution'. One refugee had escaped from Lublin and he had brought dreadful news:

It has been decreed and decided in Nazi ruling circles to bring systematic physical destruction upon the Jews of the General Government. There is even a special military unit for this purpose which makes the rounds of all the Polish cities according to the needs and the requirements of the moment. But a total slaughter such as this can't be put into practice in one day. . . . Therefore the Nazis have established a gigantic exile centre for three hundred thousand people, a concentration camp located between Chelm and Wlodawa. . . . Jewish exiles from all the conquered countries are brought to this exile camp. . . .

One day later:

As long as there is no knowledge hope still flows in the heart, but from now on everything is clear, and all doubt for our future is removed. . . . In every generation they have risen up against us to destroy us. The experiences from our history are not, however, like the current experience. There is no similarity between physical destruction which comes about as a result of a momentary outburst of fanatical mobs incited to murder, and this calculated governmental program for the realization of which an organized murder apparatus has been set up.

On 22 July the deportations from Warsaw began. One month earlier, on 22 June, Ringelblum had asked himself: why should the Warsaw Jews be so privileged as to avoid the curse of deportation? Brutal deportations were carried out in Cracow, the capital of the General Government under the eyes of the highest (German) authorities. Why should the waves of eviction, which had come so close, spare the Warsaw Jews? The chairman of the *Judenrat* had said that he had been given firm promises that there would be no deportations from Warsaw.[15] But then the deportations did come under way, and before the second consignment left Czerniakow committed suicide; if he did not know what the deportations meant, he certainly guessed. The destination was Treblinka, north-east of Warsaw. The Jews in the ghetto had heard of Chelmno, about Belzec and Sobibor. But all they knew of Treblinka was that it was a prison camp. Nor did the Home Army know any more at the time. It was decided to send a scout, Zalman Friedrich, another 'Aryan-looking' Jew, to collect information about this new camp. He went to Sokolov, the main railway station nearest Treblinka, where he met an acquaintance, bloody and in rags, who had just escaped from the camp. This man told him that Treblinka was another death factory which had become operative the very day the first transports from Warsaw had arrived. Friedrich returned to Warsaw the sixth day after the deportations had started (28 July) and reported to the *Bund*, of which he was a member. The illegal press immediately published his report. But as usual there was more than one source: another Warsaw Jew, Eli Linder, had escaped in a heap of disused clothing from the camp. Later yet more details were revealed by Abraham Krzepicki who had fled after eighteen days in Treblinka and returned to Warsaw. Railway workers who had accompanied the trains confirmed these stories. And lastly the smell of the burned corpses hung over the whole neighbourhood like a 'cloud of pestilence' as the German commander at Ostrow put it in his report. All the residents of the nearby villages knew it.

Those left behind in Warsaw knew that they were under a sentence of death. But they still hoped that help would come from outside and they realized that it was of paramount importance to inform the world. The Zionists, while very active in the ghettos, were not in a good position to do so. Many of their leaders and their most active members had left Poland before the war or just after its outbreak by way of Vilna. They were in contact with Slovakia, Hungary and Switzerland but their letters and postcards included only hints which were not always understood and believed. A few of them succeeded in escaping to Slovakia and from there to Hungary where, for the time being, they were in relative safety.

The Jewish Communists were not in a much better position. They had comrades outside the ghettos but for them like for the Home Army assistance to the Jews was not a top priority. The Polish Communists, in any case, had been 'purged' over and over again in the 1930s. The party had in fact been dissolved by the Comintern; it was re-established in Warsaw only in 1942 and a Communist fighting organization came into being only in 1943. By the time a rudimentary Communist network had come into existence and news could be transmitted to Moscow, most Polish Jews were no longer alive. There still was the *Bund*, the big, well-organized working-class party; it had always opposed emigration; some of its leaders had escaped to the Soviet Union where they found a tragic end (the execution of Alter and Ehrlich). Those who remained had fairly close relations with the Socialists (PPS) and since the PPS was part of the Polish underground they were in a position to transmit full accounts to their comrades in London and New York. In the beginning these reports took a fairly long time to reach the West, but from late 1942 the *Bund* also had access to the underground radio stations through which messages could be relayed to London very quickly.

About the main actors in these exchanges, and the messages sent, more will be said elsewhere in this study. But among all these reports there is one which should be singled out because it provides a unique insight into the many fears and few hopes of Polish Jewry in mid-1942. This is the report of the *Bund* written in early May 1942 which reached London later the same month, and was broadcast (in part) over the BBC on 2 June. It was published in America in August and begins with the following words:

From the day the Russo-German war broke out, the Germans embarked on the physical extermination of the Jewish population on Polish soil, using the Ukrainian and the Lithuanian Fascists for this job.

It mentions a great many facts and figures about the number of Jews killed in various places (including Chelmno) and the beginning of the extermination in the General Government. It gives a figure of 700,000 victims and says that this indicates that the German Government has begun to carry out Hitler's prophecy that in the last five minutes of the war, whatever its outcome, all the Jews in Europe would be killed. The *Bund* therefore suggested that the Polish Government should ask the United Nations immediately to apply the policy of retaliation against the fifth column living in their midst: 'We are aware that we are requesting the Polish Government to apply unusual measures. But this is the only possibility of saving millions of Jews from inevitable destruction.'[16]

Dr Feiner, the representative of the *Bund*, made the same suggestions even more forcefully in a subsequent dispatch to the West which will be discussed later on.[17] The Polish Government-in-exile also made similar suggestions on various occasions. The idea of Allied retaliation had, in fact, crossed the minds of some German officials, and one of them, the Undersecretary in the Foreign Ministry, had written earlier in the war that Germany was in this respect in an unfavourable position (*wir sitzen am kürzeren Hebel*). But he was referring to a specific problem – the arrest of US citizens of Jewish origin in France in 1941. The situation of Polish and other European Jews was, of course, quite different. The threats that could have been made by the Allies to save Polish, German or Austrian Jewry would not have been credible. And even if there had been such ways and means to threaten the Germans with retaliation by 'unusual measures', most Allied leaders would have argued that such measures, or even the threat of such measures, were indefensible even if it was a matter of saving human lives. Others would have said, openly or in private, that there were always a great many victims in time of war and that it was hardly worth while to take such risks on behalf of the Jews. But all this does not excuse the unwillingness to believe and to publicize the reports from Poland in 1942. And it seems certain in retrospect that at least some Jews could have been saved if greater pressure had been exerted at the time on Germany's satellites. In June 1942 the underground newspaper of one of the Jewish youth movements in Warsaw published a last desperate cry: 'The number of the victims of total murder is daily growing. European Jewry goes up to the gallows – German, Czech, Slovak Jews. SOS. SOS. SOS.'[18] Like so many calls for help this one went unanswered.

This then was the situation in Poland. But well before the death camps began to operate two events had taken place elsewhere in Eastern Europe which became known almost immediately in the West. Normally they would have caused a major outcry but in the event there were hardly any repercussions at all: I refer to the Kamenets Podolsk massacre and the killing of more than 100,000 Romanian Jews in Transniestria.

The Hungarian Government had entered the war against the Soviet Union on 27 June 1941. In July some leading civilian and army officials in Budapest decided to get rid of as many alien Jews as possible. This referred above all to people of dubious citizenship in Carpatho-Ruthenia who were to be handed over to the Germans. The Hungarian Government, which had to give its blessing to this initiative, was told that the aliens would be resettled in Galicia. Some 18,000 Jews were rounded up in Budapest and Carpatho-Ruthenia and transferred to Kamenets Podolsk across the Dniestr, an area from which the Russians had just retreated. The local German military commanders were anything but enthusiastic about this unexpected influx and wanted at first to return the Jews to Hungary. But then the SS was called in, and with the help of some Ukrainian units and a Hungarian platoon killed 15,000 Hungarian and 8,000 local Jews on 27–8 August 1941. It was, to quote Randolph Braham, 'The first five figure massacre in the Nazis' final solution program'.[19]

Of those who had been deported, 2,000 survived, mainly perhaps because the Germans were not yet quite ready to deal with them. One of the survivors returned to Budapest and went with a Jewish delegation to see the Hungarian

Minister of the Interior, who claimed that he was surprised and shocked. He put an end to the expulsions.

The news about Kamenets Podolsk was widely known in Budapest at the time. The US Embassy was informed by Bertrand Jacobson, the representative of the Joint Distribution Committee, and perhaps other sources as well. In a message dated 26 September 1941, Paul Culbertson, Assistant Chief, Division of European Affairs in the State Department, informed the Joint head office in New York that according to 'eye witness accounts of returning Hungarian officers between 7,500 and 15,000 Jews had been killed, and, that their corpses were floating down the Dniestr river'. Four weeks later this news found its way into the press; it was published by the Jewish Telegraphic Agency on 13 October, the *New York Post* on 23 October, and the *New York Times* on 26 October 1941.

Budapest was to remain an important source of information in the months to follow: Hungarian officers returning from the eastern front reported at home about the mass killings perpetrated by the *Einsatzgruppen*. They witnessed mass executions near Dnepropetrovsk and elsewhere in early October. Similar reports, incidentally, also came from officers and soldiers serving with the Italian expeditionary corps on the southern sector of the eastern front.[20] There is no certainty, on the other hand, that the Finnish army and the foreign components of the *Waffen* SS witnessed the *Einsatzgruppen* at work; these were front-line units and they saw action mainly on the Karelian sector of the Russian front where there were few, if any, Jewish communities. But the news about Kamenets Podolsk passed almost unnoticed. It was apparently assumed that this was an isolated incident and since the deportations from Hungary ceased thereafter it was perhaps thought that such events would not recur. True, Hungarian units were also responsible for the killing in 1941 of some 700 Jews in the Hungarian-occupied zone of Yugoslavia. But the commanders responsible for the murder were actually brought to trial in Budapest in December 1943. The Hungarian Government of the day was not exactly philosemitic in outlook but it clearly thought actions of this kind incompatible with the nation's values and traditions.

If Kamenets Podolsk was ignored it is more difficult to

understand that little attention was paid a: first to the decision of the Romanian Government to deport almost 200,000 Jews to Transniestria, meaning the Romanian-occupied sections of the Ukraine adjacent to Bessarabia. At first the Germans refused to accept the Jews. But within the next six months some 120,000 of them were killed; the rest survived and eventually returned to Romania where in the meantime second thoughts had prevailed about the wisdom and the political effects of the Transniestrian slaughter.

The deportations from Romania were not kept secret; they were reported in German as well as Allied newspapers almost immediately after the event. True, conditions in Transniestria were not fully known until a courageous Jewish lawyer fled from Kishinev to Bucharest in a Romanian officer's uniform and informed the leaders of the local community. The deportation of the Kishinev Jews to Transniestria began on 8 October 1941. Three days later W. Filderman, president of the Jewish communities in Romania, was already fully informed and wrote to Marshal Antonescu, the Romanian supreme leader: 'This is death, death, death . . .'[21] Antonescu sent a totally negative answer to Filderman: the Jews had misbehaved and they only got what they deserved. But the very fact that he thought it necessary to reply is of some interest and, largely no doubt as the result of the wide publicity abroad, Antonescu halted the deportations in mid-November 1941.*

Publicity had much less effect in the case of Slovakia, the first foreign country to dispatch its own citizens to the Polish death camps. The first train for Auschwitz left on 26 March 1942. By the end of the year some 57,000 Jews had been deported, about three-quarters of Slovak Jewry. Again it did not take long for the news to filter through. By late April some of those deported had succeeded in returning to Slovakia. According to the evidence of the late Aron Gruenhut, a leader of the orthodox community, Petschuk, assistant director of the Jewish Department in the Slovak Ministry of the Interior, informed him and Ludwig Kastner (not to be confused with the Budapest Kastner, about

---

*There were two further waves of deportations in 1942 but these affected much smaller numbers of Jews. A full report on the massacres was published by the World Jewish Congress in New York on 27 January 1942.

whom more below) in late January 1942 that all Slovak Jews would soon be deported and killed, and that the official version – that they would be used as labour battalions – was just a lie. Is it possible that a Slovak ófficial should have known about the final solution just a few days after the Wansee Conference? It is more likely that Gruenhut's memory was at fault. But there were some other curious coincidences which make it appear that there might have been a leak, or several leaks, in Slovakia. A group of leading rabbis wrote a letter to Monsignor Tiso, the President of the Republic, in March 1942 in which they said that the meaning of the deportations was the physical destruction of the Jews of Slovakia. Perhaps it was just hyperbole, but how to explain that Nuncio Burzio, the papal envoy in Slovakia, in a cable to the Vatican dated 9 March 1942 used exactly the same language: '*Deportazione 80,000 persone in Polonia alle merce dei tedeschi equivale condammare gran parte morte sicura*' ('Deportation 80,000 persons to Poland at the mercy of the Germans means to condemn a large part to certain death').[22]

Rabbi Michael Ber Weismandl, one of the best informed and most reliable witnesses from Slovakia, wrote in his recollections published after the war that in early 1942 he did not yet know about the 'final solution'. But he also mentions that one of his friends had been told even a year or two before by Wisliceny, one of Eichmann's closest assistants, that if the Jews would not leave on *Viehwagen* they would be taken out on *Schlachtwagen* (meaning that if they would not escape leaving behind all their belongings, they would be carried to the slaughterhouse).[23] In the months and years to come the indefatigable Weismandl was to play a central role in trying to stave off further deportations: bribing Gestapo and Slovak officials, sending emissaries to Poland and couriers to Switzerland and Hungary, trying to alarm the world. He was one of the few to survive the war.

During May and June 1942 more and more evidence came to light about the fate of those who had been deported. This information was sent on by the UZ (*Ustredna Zidov*, the Slovak Central Jewish Office) to Jewish leaders in Switzerland, Britain, Palestine and, of course, also to Hungary. An underground railway to Hungary began to function. R. Kastner, the Hungarian Jewish leader, later wrote that he and his colleagues were informed by late summer 1941 about the mass executions

in the Ukraine, the Baltic states, Bessarabia and Bukovina, and
that they had also heard from Hungarian contacts about the use
of gas vans. Kastner reports that at a conference on the second
day of Christmas 1941 in the building of the Budapest Jewish
community he informed those present about the mass killings
and about the gas vans. He said in his speech that perhaps more
than a million Jews had already been killed. But he also wrote
that 'the participants voiced scepticism having listened to my
report'.[24] The fact that most Hungarian Jews rejected the
information about the mass murder in Poland has been attested
by many witnesses. The refugees from Poland and Slovakia who
reached Budapest in 1942 were accused of lying and spreading
panic. Warners such as Otto Komoly, the head of the Budapest
rescue committee, and a few others were the exception.

Joel Brand, who was to play the leading role in the tragic
mission to Istanbul of 1944, on which much has been written,
was even more specific:

The *Waada* (The Hungarian Rescue Committee) set up a regular
intelligence centre in Budapest. Immediately on their arrival the
refugees were closely questioned so that we could ascertain and record
the situation in the ghettos from which they had come. We were as
much interested in the personalities of the officials who ran the German
extermination apparatus as we were in the behaviour of the various
Jewish councils. . . . We sent hundreds of these records by way of
Istanbul and Switzerland to our head offices abroad. It has often been
said in the press and in books on the subjects that the Allies were
informed too late of what was going on in the Polish cities in 1942 and
1943. We cannot agree with this. The official representatives of the
Jewish people were, by means of hundreds of individual memoranda,
fully and immediately informed of the situation. We also know that our
warnings were passed on at once by the Jewish Agency to the Allies.[25]

Joel Brand perhaps exaggerated somewhat. However, the flow
of information certainly became fuller in 1943 when dozens of
young Jews arrived from Poland carrying the news about the
destruction of the ghettos. But some had arrived already in 1942,
and a few even earlier. The first to make the dangerous journey
was Shlomo Zygielnik in 1941, who immediately sent messages
to his comrades who had remained behind: escape was a
practical possibility. He was followed by Zvi Goldfarb (who
went from the Warsaw ghetto to Budapest), Josef Kornianski

and others.[26] Sometimes these journeys would take weeks and even months. But the borders were not really well guarded; many hundreds went from Poland to Slovakia and some six to ten thousand Slovak Jews passed into Hungary in 1942 and early 1943. Those who had escaped from Poland went on to Palestine by way of Romania and Turkey. This too was to become an important channel of information. But professionals were needed to convey information quickly and reliably to places abroad and a leading role was played in this connection by Samuel Springman, a diamond merchant whose links and experience were far superior to those of Joel Brand and his friends from the *Waada*.

The report of a young Slovak Jew about his experiences in Majdanek in early summer of 1942 serves as an illustration.[27] The anonymous writer described in great detail over dozens of pages the abysmal conditions in which the Slovak Jews were kept in Poland: the constant hunger, the work in inhuman conditions. The writer reported that some 400–500 people were daily dying in the camp, 'half of natural causes', and that families had been divided in disregard of the promises which had been made prior to the deportation. He wrote that he could not sleep at night as uncertainty was tormenting him: what had become of his fiancée and his parents? And he said in conclusion that his main task was now to reach Slovakia and to warn those remaining behind. He fled from the camp and within a few days in late June or early July 1942 he was back in Slovakia.

From accounts like these the leaders of Slovak Jewry drew the conclusion that while the situation was desperately bad, most of their relations and friends were still alive. They set out to establish contact. With the help of Jews and non-Jews living in border towns such as Presov, Kezmarok, Cedca and Stara-Lubovna, couriers were sent to the deportees with money, valuables and food. Distances were not great – Auschwitz was only some forty miles from the Slovak border. Border controls were not too rigorous and within a few days messages would sometimes arrive from the deportees in their own handwriting that they had received the vital help.[28] At the same time, the Slovak Jewish leaders bribed some key figures in the Slovak administration and even the Gestapo. They established contact with the Jewish rescue organizations in Switzerland, and repeatedly visited Hungary. In 1943 they even succeeded in smuggling whole groups of young people and children from Poland into Slovakia. Outstanding among these leaders were Rabbi Weismandl and Gisi Fleischmann, a remarkable woman of Bratislava who had sent her children to Palestine at the outbreak of the war but stayed behind to direct the rescue operations. But despite their excellent private intelligence they were apparently not aware for a long time of the totality of the extermination.

One day in November 1942 Rabbi Weismandl arrived in Gisi Fleischmann's office and in a state of great agitation told her that news had just come in from returning couriers: hundreds of those deported had again been deported 'further to the east'. But most of them would probably not survive the journey, they were in mortal danger. But even then the full extent of the tragedy did not register, nor do the Slovak Jewish leaders seem to have known for another year about the gas chambers in Auschwitz, the main camp. Yet a first transport from Slovakia numbering some 1,500 people had been killed in these gas chambers already on 12 May 1942.

The leaders of Slovak Jewry and, to a lesser extent, the leaders of the Polish Jewish youth movements were in constant touch during the war with two of the Zionist emissaries in Geneva, Dr Silbershein and Nathan Schwalb, the representative of the *Hehalutz* (the Zionist pioneer group). Some of these communications are in the Yad Veshem archives (for instance Gisi Fleischmann's letters – M–20/93), others are in the possession of Mr Schwalb. But they have not been made accessible so far to historians. I have found copies of some of these reports in the archives of the International Red Cross in Geneva. From these it emerges that it was already known – but not accepted – in Slovakia in late summer of 1942 that those who had been deported would not return. According to a long account, written probably by Gisi Fleischmann in Bratislava (27 July 1942), the Slovak Jewish leaders had tried to trace those of their compatriots who had been deported to Poland but had addresses for only two thousand out of sixty thousand who had disappeared. They also reported that there was a high rate of mortality, that the situation was tragic and that there was cause for the gravest concern. But they had obviously not yet heard of the extermination camps: Auschwitz is mentioned, but apparently in the belief that this was a labour camp. Subsequent letters dated 27 August and 1 September 1942 convey a similar picture. But at the same time it is quite clear that the writers of these letters knew that no one would ever return from Poland. Thus the letter of 27 August says:

The news which we just got from our emissaries [to Poland] is unique in history. . . . We have lost 60,000 and I only request that the remnant should be saved. . . . The thought that the mass dying continues without interruption drives us mad. . . . I think there is not much chance that we shall ever see again any of our comrades.

How can these obvious contradictions be explained? The Slovak Jewish leaders had warned even before the deportations had started that deportation meant certain death. By July 1942 rumours were rife all over Eastern Europe that Jews were killed in great numbers and 'boiled into soap'.[29] But even Weismandl and Gisi Fleischmann refused to accept this. In a letter to the Palestinian rescue committee in Istanbul, Gisi Fleischmann wrote in April 1943 that they had heard in July 1942 that in the course of another major 'purge' those deported to Poland had been sent further to the East. But despite 'passionate efforts', despite the fact that emissaries were on the way all the time, they had not found any traces. Only in February 1943 had it become known that hundreds of thousands had disappeared in the Rawa Ruska-Przemysl region. A few survivors had been found hiding in the forests. In her earlier letters Gisi Fleischmann had actually used the term physical destruction (*Vernichtungsaktion*). Yet even this wise and courageous woman refused to accept the finality of death.

There were always some rays of hope. Some transports had been dispatched to work camps; many inmates were indeed still alive by late 1942 and even in 1943. If some had survived, others were perhaps also alive somewhere and thus the search for the traces of the deportees went on. There were, so far, no eyewitnesses; no one had returned from a death camp to Slovakia. Thus it was only in 1944, when Rudolf Vrba and Alfred Wetzler arrived with most detailed news about the greatest of all death camps, that the 'rumours' became a certainty.* By that time most of the death camps had already ceased to function. It was not that the information did not exist but, as Oscar Neumann, another Slovak Jewish leader, later wrote: 'There was total resistance in our hearts to believe the news. . . . Of course, there had been certain rumours about the horrible events in Auschwitz. But they were flying about like bats at night, they were not tangible. . . .' But there could be no more tangible information in the circumstances. The letters acknowledging receipt of money and food had stopped arriving long ago; there were no other signs of life. But this was purely negative evidence and therefore unconvincing: perhaps somewhere, cut off, unable to write, most of the relations and friends were still alive.

Slovakia had been the first satellite to participate in the 'final solution'. Deportations from France, Holland and Belgium, Germany, Austria and the Czech Protectorate came under way between June and August 1942. What was known among Jews in these countries about the ultimate destination of the transports? They were living far from Treblinka, Belzec and Auschwitz; these names did not mean anything. But there was still deep concern from the very beginning. In Germany there were 'rumours' based on letters and postcards from the East that those who had been sent to Riga and other ghettos had disappeared and that they had apparently been killed. According to the official explanations deportation meant simply resettlement in Eastern Europe. Instructions were given not to use the term deportation but 'mobilization of labour' – *Arbeitseinsatz*. It was implied that those transported to the East would work in agriculture and industry and perhaps eventually get some autonomy. For a while this version seems to have been widely believed. German eyewitnesses who were present when the trains with Jews from the Reich arrived in November 1941 in Minsk, Riga and Lodz 'prepared for their new life' were amazed that they 'laboured under complete misapprehension as to their future, looking upon themselves as pioneers to be utilized in the colonization of the East'.[30] Russian and Polish Jews had reacted in the same way at first: according to a situation report of

*But in March 1943 Gisi Fleischmann had already informed Geneva about Auschwitz-Birkenau and Lublin and that no Jews remained in the entire General Government. *Yad Vashem Archives* M-20/93.

the *Einsatzgruppen* (dated 3 November 1941), '30,000 Jews gathered (following an appeal) who owing to an exceedingly clever organization believed in their impending resettlement right up to their execution'.

Norbert Wollheim, who had been a prominent youth leader and who was in close touch with various Jewish public figures in Berlin, relates that he had not heard of Auschwitz (and the death camps) until the day, in March 1943, when he arrived there with his family. He had been in contact with Jews living in mixed marriages who had been permitted to keep their radio sets and who were listening to foreign stations, which was, of course, strictly forbidden. But the BBC, the main source of the information at the time, mentioned the camps only on fairly rare occasions. If the news had been heard at all, it had not been believed.[31]

Some Jews received information directly from German friends or acquaintances; the separation between Germans and Jews was by no means complete even in wartime. The case of Dr Herman Pineas, a Berlin Jewish physician, was not unique. He received a letter, written by a former Social Democratic official serving on the eastern front, according to which all Jews in the occupied Russian territories were shot after having been compelled to dig their own graves. The letter had been sent to Paul Loebe, the former head of the Social Democratic faction in the Reichstag (and for several years speaker of the Reichstag), who had passed it on to Dr Julius Moses who had also been a member of the German Parliament. Moses and Pineas were friends and lived in the same building. Pineas translated the letter and passed it on to the American Embassy in Berlin, where it arrived two days before Pearl Harbor. During the last week of 1941 Pineas was visited by Dr Erwin Rehwald, a young doctor who had been his assistant and who was serving then as a German air force physician in Russia. He confirmed the information contained in the letter which had been sent to Loebe.*

There was deep fear and not only because no one likes to be uprooted and to lose his (or her) belongings. Letters mailed in this period (summer and autumn 1942) repeat the same refrain:

*Dr H. O. Pineas, New York, to author 11 February 1980. Pineas decided to go underground following the news which he had received and survived the war in Berlin.

we have not heard from those who were deported, no one has heard, the same is true with regard to other cities in the Reich.[32] Hundreds in Berlin committed suicide, thousands went underground. In part these fears concerned general conditions in Eastern Europe: lack of housing, diseases, starvation. It was suspected that the majority of those who had to leave would not survive for long.

Nor did the selection carried out by the Gestapo make sense. For if the purpose was to employ the Jews in agriculture and industry out in the East, how to explain that precisely those Jews who were working in factories and farms were left behind in Germany at least in the beginning? These doubts grew stronger after August and September 1942, partly as the result of foreign radio broadcasts, partly because of the stories told by soldiers on home leave from the eastern front.

Did the leaders of the *Reichsvereinigung*, the supreme Jewish body, know any more? According to one account Leo Baeck, the central figure of German Jewry, was told by a Mr Gruenberg, a fellow inmate at Theresienstadt (which was not a death camp) in August 1943, seven months after his deportation from Berlin, that in Auschwitz the Jews were gassed to death except those who were used as slave labourers. 'So it was not just a rumour,' Baeck is said to have responded.[33] Baeck, again following the same source, went through a hard struggle whether it was his duty to inform the Council of Elders, but finally decided that no one should know about it. For if the Council of Elders was informed, the whole camp would know about it within a few hours. 'Living in the expectation of gassing would only be the harder and this death was not certain at all; there was selection for slave labour; perhaps not all transports went to Auschwitz. So I came to the grave decision to tell no one. . . .'

This account has been disputed by some who knew Baeck well. If the news about Auschwitz had reached Theresienstadt in 1943 and even if Baeck had decided to keep silent (which his friends maintain would not have been in line with his character) nothing would have prevented Gruenberg talking to others. As the result everyone would indeed have known about it within a short time; but it seems certain that most inmates did not know. It is unlikely that the full truth about this will ever be known. Most of those in leading positions must have heard rumours, but there were, as cannot be repeated too often, a great many rumours, good and bad during the war.

Georges Wellers wrote that among French Jews in Drancy, the chief transit camp to Auschwitz, strange as it may appear, one did not know up to the very end about the fate of the deported. True, one knew that London radio had broadcast horror stories about gas chambers, but one could not believe it. One thought that these were exaggerations of British propaganda and did not pay much attention.* Even Jacob Kaplan, the chief rabbi, wrote after the war that only in early 1944 were there no more doubts that Hitler intended to exterminate all Jews. Such ignorance seems to justify the case made by those who claim that there was total secrecy and that no one could have possibly known and that those who now profess to have been informed speak with the benefit of hindsight.

But the historical record does not bear this out. In late August 1942 the *Consistoire*, the supreme Jewish body in France, sent an appeal to Laval in which it was said that according to precise reports hundreds of thousands of Jews had been massacred in Eastern Europe and that the aim of the deportation was not to make the Jews work but to exterminate them *impitoyablement et méthodiquement.*[34] It can perhaps be argued that the writers of this memorandum did not believe their own words; if so, why should they have bothered to compose it in the first place? To repeat once again, the information existed, but the psychological mechanism of suppression was also at work.

In Holland there was apprehension, but again there were no certainties. As Professor Cohen, head of the Amsterdam Jewish council, put it after the war:

The fact that the Germans had perpetrated atrocities against Polish Jews was no reason for thinking that they would behave in the same way towards Dutch Jews, firstly because the Germans had always held

---

*G. Wellers, *De Drancy à Auschwitz* (Paris, 1946). There are countless such reports from all over Europe. Michel Mazor tells the story of a conversation which he had with a history professor in the middle of the great deportation wave from Warsaw in August 1942. They were waiting to be taken away in a small carpentry shop in Gesia Street. They knew with absolute certainty what 'deportation' meant, they had been told about Treblinka by Polish railway workers, by peasants and even a Jew who had escaped. But the professor refused to accept undeniable facts and talked instead about the numerous examples in world history of collective anxiety psychoses afflicting groups of people facing non-existent dangers. Michel Mazor, *La cité engloutie* (Paris, 1955), p. 127.

Polish Jews in disrepute, and secondly because in the Netherlands, unlike Poland, they had to sit up and take notice of public opinion.[35]

By September 1942 some 15,000 Dutch Jews had been deported to Eastern Europe. True, a few dozen letters had been received but this was hardly enough to still the fears. Radio Oranje, the Dutch station in London to which many Dutchmen listened, had announced on 27 June that 700,000 Jews had been killed. Even before the Communist underground newspaper *De Waarheid* (June 1942) had written that in some territories such as the Ukraine not a single Jew had survived, men, women, children and old people had been exterminated one and all.

In his massive study, a model of writing contemporary history, de Jong has analysed the evidence available at the time in Holland. The speeches by Nazi leaders, German and Dutch, left little room for doubt. According to internal Gestapo reports, Dutch volunteers returning from Russia were freely talking about the bestial murder of Jews.[36] Some Dutchmen and women who had been prisoners in Auschwitz returned in 1942; ss men and prisoners (!) from the same camp were brought over to help with the establishment of camps in Holland; a Dutchman who had been to the Ukraine complained in a letter to Mussert, the leader of the Dutch Nazi Party, about the atrocities which he had witnessed. In retrospect, a great many people, non-Jews and Jews, had heard about the massacres in Eastern Europe. For every instance that can be documented, there were probably many more for which there is no record. Some people may have dismissed the 'rumours' out of hand, but many were at the very least deeply troubled. The deportations continued and while there was a growing number of Jews who did not turn up at the meeting places but went into hiding, the majority still appeared at the railway station after the receipt of a mailed instruction.

This leads to the inescapable conclusion that with all the misgivings about the deportations, most Dutch Jews either had not heard, or did not want to hear, about the death camps. A year later it was the turn of Danish and Greek Jews and two years later of Hungarian Jewry. Yet the reaction was the same. The Danish Jews had the good fortune to get an emphatic warning about the impending 'action'. But they dismissed this at first as an act of provocation despite the fact that the warning came from leaders of the resistance whose competence and integrity was beyond all doubt. David Sompolinsky, a leading member of the Danish community, later tried to provide an answer:

We did not understand the situation. Despite all the indications of an imminent action against the Jews we continued to be sceptical. This was the country I had grown up in, where I had no quarrel with anyone; I had no form of contact with German soldiers, and it was unreasonable to suppose that they would without reason, without a trace of moral justification, seize, arrest and deport citizens of the country. But theoretically we knew that it was possible and that it happened in other countries, but we could not get used to the idea that it could happen to us. Inhumanity, brutality, the absence of any consideration for human feelings and of any sense of justice – it was incredible that people could be capable of all this.[37]

Sompolinsky describes how towards the end of the Jewish New Year's service 1943, which took place in private homes, a young Dane appeared and began to explain quietly that the Jews should disappear at once, since the Germans might arrest them within the next few hours. But all those present had heard such stories before and they were not greatly impressed. Then a sudden change took place in the young man's behaviour: 'With choking voice he asked us to leave the house. . . . He begged us to believe him and left the house with tears in his eyes.' It was only then that most Jews were willing to consider that there might be something to the rumours after all. They still were not fully convinced but they went to hide in the country and later on they escaped to Sweden.

These were the lucky ones. The great majority of Greek Jews was not saved, and hundreds of thousands of Hungarian Jews also perished in 1944. Most European Jews had been dead for a long time; the fact had been mentioned in broadcasts and in the underground press all over Europe. But the hope still prevailed that what had happened elsewhere would not necessarily occur in one's own country. Polish Jews believed for many months that the massacres would be confined to the Nazi-occupied areas in the Soviet Union. When the 'actions' began inside Poland, it was widely thought that these were individual, unauthorized operations undertaken by local commanders on their own initiative. After whole ghettos had already been liquidated it was still assumed in Warsaw that the Nazis would not dare to kill hundreds of thousands in the capital. When deportations started in Warsaw it was thought that only those not employed in workshops and factories connected with the war effort would be affected. Among German and Austrian Jews it was believed that while Nazis were quite capable of committing any conceivable cruelty vis-à-vis Russian and Polish Jews whom they regarded as inferior species, they would treat Jews from their own *Kulturkreis* ('region of cultural influence') differently. French, Italian and Dutch Jews, on the other hand, were convinced that the Nazis had always hated and despised their own (German) Jews but that they would not necessarily transfer these feelings to Western European Jews whom they hardly knew. And so forth.

The strategy of deception did, of course, also play a certain role. Hitler, Goebbels and other Nazi leaders had threatened the Jews with extinction but this could have meant a great many things other than mass murder: forced emigration to Madagascar or Patagonia or some other place. To this day no written order by Hitler has been found to kill European Jewry; in all probability there was no written order. Later in the war Himmler explained that the whole matter had to be kept in strict secrecy and that for this reason the SS and not the state bureaucracy had to be given this assignment. Terms such as killing were not used even at the Wannsee Conference in which the organizational preparation of the mass murder was discussed. It was always the 'final solution', 'resettlement', 'special treatment', 'mobilization of the labour force'. Nazi officials outside Germany stressed in their contacts with non-Jews and Jews that life in the East would be hard at first but healthy, productive and ultimately rewarding. When the news about the mass murder first circulated outside Germany in 1942 Fritz Fiala, the editor of *Grenzbote*, the organ of the *Volksdeutsche* in Slovakia, was sent by Eichmann to visit some of the Jews who had been 'resettled' in the East. His article, featured all over Europe, showed pictures of a Jewish coffee house with a Jewish policeman in front, a group of smiling Jewish nurses and of well-nourished young men.[38] According to Fiala all the Jews with whom he had talked were satisfied with their lot: 'All their fears had been dispersed, not a single one of the arguments [against deportation] had been justified.' One of them went as far as saying to him: 'I wish the whole world knew with how much humanity Germany has treated us here.' Though Fiala did not mention the name of the camp, it was in fact Auschwitz, as appeared from post-war evidence.[39]

There were other means of disinformation. When later in the war the Slovak leaders, slightly perturbed, mentioned to the Germans the 'fantastic rumours' about the fate of the evacuated Jews, pretending they had no idea about what was happening to them in Poland, Eichmann referred to more than one thousand letters and postcards which had been received in Slovakia from evacuated Jews within the previous two months. This technique had been used from the very beginning. Arriving in the death camps the deported Jews were advised (and sometimes compelled) to write letters, usually undated, to their families and friends: they had ample food, the housing was satisfactory, their state of health excellent. The dispatch of these postcards and letters was staggered over several months by the camp authorities; several dozen would arrive every month in Holland or other foreign countries long after the senders had been killed. But some of the deportees did survive three or even six more months in Auschwitz; they had been selected for work in a factory or the services or perhaps in the orchestra. They, too, continued to write, and as a result there was a steady trickle of correspondence. Each such message had a great echo: if some friends and relations were still alive, perhaps others were too. Perhaps they were just too busy to write.

As Jacob Presser, the leading Dutch-Jewish historian, wrote: 'For those who wanted to believe the best, and believe it at all costs, the letters, more than anything else, it was said, weighed far heavier in the balance than any amount of rumours about German threats of "extermination".'

Between July 1942, when the deportations started, and October 1943 a total of 1,700 letters and postcards had been received in Holland from the camps in the East. This means that only one family in ten had written – just once. At this stage the forebodings should have become certainties. But they did not; the psychological defence mechanisms were too powerful. De Jong mentions the case of Leo Laptos, a Polish prisoner who had worked as a pharmacist in Auschwitz-Birkenau, was transferred to Holland and told Dr Van der Hal, an inmate of the Jewish

camp in Vught, that when the Jewish transports reached
Auschwitz, most were immediately gassed and cremated. He
provided details of the procedure followed. When Van der Hal
was transferred to another camp he informed several Jewish
doctors, but the impression he gained was 'that they simply
refused to believe me, although they were visibly shaken by the
news'.[40] When this case came up in a post-war trial, two of the
three doctors had no recollections of ever having discussed the
matter with Van der Hal. Physicians more than other people
come in frequent contact with death and have to be aware of the
transience of human existence. But if even physicians fell victim
to self-deception it is easy to understand the reaction of others.

The inclination not to accept unpleasant realities can be
found to a greater or lesser extent among most of mankind. The
denial syndrome occurs frequently at the time of dying. To
quote a leading medical expert: 'An adequate realization of the
true state of affairs is no bar to the use of denial.'

Few wish to hold constantly in mind the thought that death is coming
very close. After all, it is not absolutely certain that they are dying,
there is no reason why grim foreboding should not be softened by some
comforting inconsistency.[41]

Denial of reality manifested itself in the willingness to believe in
rumours, however fantastic, as well as the unwillingness to talk
about death, assuming that such talk would somehow bring the
evil nearer. There were constant rumours that somehow the war
would soon end, that Hitler had died, that the Allies had used
some miracle weapon, that all Jews would be permitted to
emigrate to Palestine.* The belief in these rumours can be
compared with the faith in miracle cures of dying men and
women.

But the comparison between the attitude of the Jews and the

---

*This is what Juri Becker's novel *Jacob the Liar* (New York, 1969) is about. Jacob has
intimated that he has a radio set in the ghetto and ever since he has to invent news, for the
curiosity of his neighbours is insatiable: 'We want to know if it's true that they intend to
sell us for a ransom. If so, where is the money? We want to know if it's true that a Jewish
state is to be established. If so, when? If not, who is hindering it? Above all, we want to
know where the Russians are. . . . Tell us how they are breaking through the battle lines,
what tactics they're using, whether they're treating prisoners as prisoners or as criminals,
if they're having a great deal of trouble with the Japanese in the East, whether or not the
Americans can at least relieve them of that, if they are not invading Europe? And
we also want to know about Kiepura's fate and how he is getting along in America' (pp.
90–1). Jan Kiepura was one of the leading European lyric tenors of the inter-war period.

denial syndrome in dying people is also misleading: the refusal to surrender, the vain hope among dying people may be preferable to utter hopelessness. The situation of the Jews who remained behind after the first waves of deportation had taken place was different. Some of them survived; more would have stayed alive if they had rejected the false hope and accepted reality, however terrible.

Could it be that Danish or Dutch or French Jewry lived in genuine ignorance and that it was not, therefore, a case of rejecting reality? This seems to be true with regard to most of them. But the nearer people lived to the location of the death camps, the more and the sooner they were bound to know. Russian Jews, cut off from the outside world and isolated, were unaware of the purpose of the *Einsatzgruppen*. But after a few months the news had spread and enough was known in Poland by spring of 1942 to make genocide at the least a likely proposition. True, these were only rumours, but they were persistent and they came from many sources. True again, the rumours had not reached everyone, but among the leaders of the community and among educated people there cannot have been many who had not heard them. In the case of the dying individual greater determination does not prevent death. In the case of East European Jewry the acceptance of reality might have induced more people to flee or to resist. Most would still have died but less than actually perished.

Much blame has been put on the leaders of the communities who knew more than others about the 'final solution'. But for all one knows some of them were also victims of the denial of reality syndrome, while others had accepted reality but pursued what seemed to them the only possible strategy, that of winning time, which proved ultimately futile. In a passage which contains all that can be said on the subject, Louis de Jong admits that all this is very difficult to explain to a younger generation which learns history in a shortened form that cannot but distort the reality of a thousand dreadful days and nights:

Hitler had said it plainly: let war come and the whole of European Jewry will be exterminated. And the war had come. Why then did no one draw the correct inference? It is easy for us to wonder, looking back as we do at the German extermination camps and gas chambers through the years, and free as we are of the tremendous psychological tensions of the war, above all of fear, of mortal fear in its most naked form. *Le soleil ni la mort ne peuvent se regarder fixement* – man cannot stare at the sun or at death, wrote La Rochefoucauld, but then he was only thinking of men as lone individuals. The gas chambers, however, spelt death – and what a death! – not only to individuals but to all those they held dear: their parents and grandparents, their children and grandchildren, their relatives and friends. Small, indeed, must have been the number of those among the millions driven to death, who could face that awesome truth. And we should commit an immense historical error were we to dismiss the main defence mechanisms employed by the victims – not constantly mind you, but by way of intermittent distress signals – as mere symptoms of blindness or foolishness; rather did these defence mechanisms spring from deep and inherent qualities shared by all mankind – a love of life, a fear of death, and an understandable inability to grasp the reality of the greatest crime in the history of mankind.[42]

If the Jews of Nazi-occupied Europe needed a defence in the court of history, the case could not be put more succinctly and fairly. But who is there to judge them? Not surely those who survived because they were safely out of Hitler's reach, or those born after the Second World War: they will not even begin to understand. But even those whose life experience has not been so distant in place or time can provide satisfactory explanations only for some of the questions arising out of the catastrophe. Others may forever remain inexplicable.

6

WORLD JEWRY: FROM GENEVA
TO ATHLIT

'WORLD JEWRY' is a term that has frequently been used by Jews, and their friends and enemies. As a political reality it has, of course, never existed. When the Second World War broke out the Jewish communities were no more united than they had been in the past. They co-ordinated their international activities during the war but there was never a central leadership or organizational unity. The Zionists had their emissaries in non-occupied Europe, so had the various unpolitical aid and rescue organizations such as the Joint Distribution Committee; the orthodox religious groups had their own small network, keeping their distance from the rest. There was no central body collecting and sifting the news from Nazi-occupied Europe. Most Zionist leaders were in Palestine and almost wholly preoccupied with the dangers facing the Jewish community in that country. Some were in America, far away physically and psychologically from events in Europe; even Chaim Weizmann, who normally resided in London, was in the United States for most of 1942.

The Zionist leaders were also preoccupied with the future. They realized, quite correctly, that just as the First World War had given Zionism its chance, there would be another opportunity after the end of the Second World War, and they wanted to be prepared. 1942 was the year of Biltmore, the programme in which David Ben Gurion outlined his plans for a Jewish state. This blueprint involved the immediate transfer of two million Jews to Palestine. Weizmann was not enthusiastic about invoking such astronomical figures. He feared that one-quarter of the Jewish people in Europe might not survive the war. But whatever their differences, both 'maximalists' and 'minimalists' in the Zionist camp were planning for the post-war world. 'A home for whom?' Chaim Greenberg, the noted Jewish writer, asked in February 1943, 'for the millions of dead in their temporary cemeteries in Europe?' But this was an isolated voice at the time.

The only body in existence uniting several organizations was the World Jewish Congress, a voluntary association of representative Jewish communities and organizations founded (to quote its constitution) 'to assure the survival and to foster the unity of the Jewish people'. It had come into being in 1936 at a meeting in Geneva attended by delegates from thirty-two countries. Its president was Rabbi Stephen Wise, the elder statesman of American Jewry; Nahum Goldmann was the chairman of its executive board. Wise was an influential figure in American domestic politics: he had been on close terms with President Wilson and was the one Jewish leader who could reach Roosevelt. He had attended the Versailles peace conference and spoken there on behalf of the rights of the Jews (and the Armenians). But while he was a man of great charm and moral force, a staunch fighter for many a good cause, his experience was basically in American domestic affairs and there was in him a streak of naïveté. Goldmann was different; he had met all the famous leaders of his time (and never made a secret of the fact). He was a man of the world *par excellence*, equally at home in Berlin and London, in Paris and New York. But with all his travels and talents as a diplomat of the old school, there was something suspect with regard to his political judgment. In 1931 he had been instrumental in overthrowing Weizmann as leader of the world Zionist movement because Weizmann was too soft vis-à-vis the Arabs; in early 1933 he had assured the German Jewish leaders that it was quite unthinkable that Britain and France would permit a takeover on Hitler's part. There had been more such misjudgments both before and after.

It was not at all clear why the two leading figures of the WJC should be in New York far away from the scene of the tragedy. Since Wise obviously had to stay there in view of his many commitments and also because of his connections, Goldmann's place should have been in London. It could be argued that politically Washington was infinitely more important than London: Anglo Jewry had never been an important political factor, nor had it produced in recent times community leaders comparable in stature to a Brandeis or a Wise. But with all this London was an important listening post and also the obvious place to launch political initiatives. But Goldmann did not apparently believe in the possibility of political action. In a speech in November 1941 he said that the problem of European Jewry was more a relief problem than a political one. Political intervention was of no value since most of the governments were practically puppet dependencies of Germany.* This was a strange pronouncement on the part of the man to whom others looked for taking political action. It was also inconsistent with declarations he had made earlier in the war when he had solemnly announced that unless immediate political intervention was attempted to save European Jewry, 'our generation will be burdened with the terrible responsibility before Jewish history'.[1] It was not, of course, that Goldmann did not care about European Jewry. The problem was that despite all the meetings with the mighty and famous his political understanding and foresight were not really very deep, less so in any case than that of Richard Lichtheim who realized early on (and was repeating in almost every letter from Geneva, on which more below) that the one conceivable way to rescue at least part of European Jewry was precisely to exert maximum pressure on the satellites.

Thus, when the first news about the mass killings reached London in late 1941 and 1942, all the leading figures of 'world Jewry' were far away, and none was well informed. The British section of the World Jewish Congress, where some of the early news was received, was headed by Eva Marchioness Reading, the daughter of Alfred Mond. A great lady of much public spirit and some political connections, a specialist in child care, she acted needless to say as a figurehead. The secretaries of the London branch were Noah Barou and Alex Easterman, the former a specialist on co-operative finance. The head of the International Affairs Department of the WJC in New York was Maurice Perlzweig, whose training had been in the rabbinate; he was, furthermore, quite new to the job, having been

*Congress Weekly, 28 November 1941; speech at the Inter-American Jewish Conference: 'It is no use trying to improve the unbelievably tragic position of the Jews in the Nazi dominated countries by political intervention. Of what use is it to intervene with the Romanian, Bulgarian and Hungarian governments, practically puppet dependencies of Germany?' The Romanian, Bulgarian and Hungarian Governments were not puppet dependencies as their attitudes towards the German demands for the surrender of the Jews were to show.

transferred from London to New York in 1942. All these were competent and hard-working men but they themselves would have been the first to admit that they were not equipped to cope with events of such enormity which, of course, no one could have foreseen. Sidney Silverman was chairman of the British section of the WJC, a left-wing Labour Member of Parliament, like Stephen Wise a naïve man but a born fighter who intuitively seems to have understood that European Jewry was facing a disaster unparalleled in their history and that one had to react quickly.

Much has been written about the suppression of the Riegner cable by the State Department. But out of ineptitude the news was suppressed by Jewish leaders in New York and London and even in Jerusalem for a considerably longer time. As Stephen Wise wrote to President Roosevelt in December 1942: 'I succeeded, together with the heads of other Jewish organizations, in keeping them [the cables about the systematic mass murder] out of the press.'[2] There had been reliable accounts well before the Riegner cable but they had all been ignored. The Jewish Agency and the World Jewish Congress leaders were flooded with information by their own representatives. But they did not understand what they were reading and did not believe their own informants.

The fate of Richard Lichtheim's reports from Geneva will be discussed later on. They were read in Jerusalem, London and New York but they did not result in either publicity or political action. Riegner's message fared no better at first. Sidney Silverman in a cable from London informed Wise and Goldmann of the contents of Riegner's cable on 24 August 1942. On 1 September, in another telegram signed Barou-Easterman, the London branch of the WJC suggested immediate action:

Suggest following urgent action: first public declaration leading political religious other authorities in all free countries; second press conference; third you approach Vatican; four, we approach United Nations make formal categorical pronouncement etc. etc.*

In New York there was the inclination at first to go public but then second and less prudent counsels prevailed. It was decided that Rabbi Wise should turn to the State Department for advice:

*This cable was read by US censorship and forwarded to the State Department. A note to A. A. Berle is affixed: 'We will suppress if you approve.' NA 862.4016/2238.

had Washington heard anything about the subject and what kind of action did it suggest? Wise and Goldmann had, in fact, no real doubts about the authenticity of the reports. As Perlzweig wrote to Easterman on 3 September:

The [Riegner] telegram ... had what I can only describe as a shattering effect. Nobody here is disposed to doubt that the information is at least substantially correct. It is desperately difficult to know what to do. We thought at first of publication, but then it occurred to us that when this news seeps through to Europe it will have a demoralizing effect on those who are marked as hopeless victims. We decided to seek the best possible advice.*[3]

But would they get the best possible advice from the State Department which had tried to keep the information from them in the first place? Clearly they did not know how to react and wanted to gain a little time. Perhaps they also thought that there was a faint hope that the news was after all wrong, or at least exaggerated. It is not easy to think of an answer to these questions.

In later years this became the subject of much heart-searching and recrimination. In a letter to a non-Jewish friend Stephen Wise wrote in September 1942: 'I am almost demented over my people's grief.' But he did not shake heaven and earth as the Polish had demanded and for apparent want of another course of action, put his trust in Roosevelt whom he so much admired. If criticism has been heaped on Wise, this was mainly, no doubt, because he was the Jewish leader best known at home and abroad. Other leaders did not act differently, dismissing the information emanating from Poland as the macabre fantasy of a lunatic sadist, for, as one of them put it, such things did after all not happen in the twentieth century.[4] Chaim Greenberg charged the American Jewish Congress with criminal slowness. But he also said that this was the only organization which had at least not removed the extermination from its agenda. The fault was not of a few men or groups but of American Jewry which had put a horny shell over its soul 'to protect it against pain and

*In a speech in November 1944 Goldmann argued that he and Wise had to comply with the State Department's request not to publish the 'atrocity stories' for the time being, for otherwise this would have been the last cable they had received from Geneva. But they had not received the information via the State Department in any case, Washington did try to stop the transmission of news later on (February 1943), and there were other channels to convey information from Switzerland to the US.

pity. We have become so dulled that we have even lost the capacity for madness. . . .'[5]

The State Department, to do it justice, did in fact make some enquiries, and it received some information quite independently in early August. This refers above all to a cable from the US ambassador in Stockholm who had been told by the Poles that 60,000 Jews had been killed in Vilna, and many more in Eastern Galicia and the Ukraine.[6] The Department now asked the Vatican for information; in ancient times kings and rulers used to consult the Delphic oracle with similar results. Meanwhile, Jews were killed in Auschwitz and Treblinka, Sobibor, Belzec and Chelmno at the rate of 5–10,000 a day. 'Desperately awaiting your answer,' Barou and Easterman cabled on 9 September. Wise and Goldmann had some reassurance for their colleagues in London: they had been told that the deportations from Warsaw were meant to supply labour building fortifications at the Polish–Soviet border (this was apparently what Roosevelt had told Felix Frankfurter); one had to wait for the return of Myron Taylor, the US envoy to the Vatican; and the timing for publication had to be suitable. 'We urge postponement publicity until right effect producable [in] entire American press,' was the content of another message by Goldmann, Wise and Perlzweig to London, and in another cable on 9 October they announced 'problem receiving consideration highest authorities whose guidance imperative stop Department deeply sympathetic and cooperative stop.'[7] This information about the 'highest authorities' was quite simply false: neither the President nor the Secretary of State was giving consideration to the problem. Nor was it clear what waiting 'until the right effect was producable' meant. True, it would have been most desirable if the US Government had officially confirmed the news from Geneva and if it had joined the Jewish leaders in their protest and suggested effective counter-measures. But how could they have expected even for a single moment that this was likely to happen? Did they really believe that the State Department was deeply sympathetic?

Meanwhile the London members of the WJC, impatiently waiting, had decided to engage in an investigation of their own: and this resulted in another tragi-comedy, the consultation of Edward Benes. Benes, the exiled President of Czechoslovakia, had acquired the reputation of knowing more than anyone else about events in Nazi-occupied Europe. There was a grain of truth: the Czechoslovak secret service received fairly regular reports from a middle-echelon *Abwehr* officer, Paul Thümmel (A–54), who on several occasions had provided information of some importance.[8] When consulted by Easterman in September, Benes said that the Riegner report was not just false but probably a German provocation scheduled to justify German vengeance in case it was published in the West. He strongly advised against any publicity; he would try to find out with the help of the finest intelligence service in Europe. But this took a fairly long time and on 6 November 1942 Easterman again wrote to Benes with the request for information. Yes, Benes, said in his answer, he did have news and from two independent sources at that: the Germans were not preparing a plan for the wholesale extermination of the Jews. Some Jews had been left in their places of residence and were moving about almost unhindered. It was quite likely that Nazi behaviour would become more repressive as they were nearing defeat. But this would be directed against all the subjugated people. The Jews would not be singled out for special treatment.[9]

This letter was written, to repeat once again, in November 1942, one year after the deportations from the Protectorate had started. By November hardly any Jews were left in Czechoslovakia. Most, indeed, were no longer alive. The question arises whether this was just another intelligence failure or whether the intelligence on which Benes based his judgment was deliberately misleading. No conclusive answer can be given on the basis of the evidence available. During 1941 the Czech resistance was in radio contact with London through several stations but they were all discovered by the Gestapo, the last of them in October 1941. Parachutists from London delivered another station which operated from January to June 1942. During the second half of 1942 the only contact between Prague and London seems to have been by courier. A new station ('Barbora') was in action from mid-November 1942 to early January 1943, that is only after Benes had sent off his letter to Easterman.[10] Furthermore, the Gestapo had received proof in early 1942 that Thümmel was a 'traitor' and he had been released from arrest only in order to lead the German security forces to key members of the Czech underground.[11] But reports on the situation in the Protectorate still reached Benes through refugees and couriers. Thus a detailed account had been received in June 1942 from a teacher who had escaped the month before. This report did mention Auschwitz and poison gas, but there was not a single word about the fate of the Jews. The same month Bruce Lockhart, head of the Political Warfare Executive (PWE), received from Czech intelligence sources a detailed review of conditions inside Czechoslovakia which did indeed mention Jews. But there were only complaints against them: they were the agents of Germanization and it was the general opinion that 'after the war the Jews will not dare to go in for politics or take part in public life, or be doctors or lawyers. If this fact is overlooked it may have very unpleasant political consequences.' On the other hand the Czech Government was perfectly aware of the deportation of the Jews from Slovakia.[12]

What emerges from all this is that Czech intelligence was less well informed during this particular period about events in the homeland than either before or after. It is also true that, generally speaking, Benes' judgment was more often wrong than right. But there was no need to maintain an intelligence network in order to know that Czech Jewry had been deported: the Prague newspapers reported it and even the German news agency *Dienst aus Deutschland*.[13] But Benes' utterly misleading account was overtaken by events. A few days after it was received Undersecretary Sumner Welles summoned Stephen Wise and told him that the news from Europe was essentially true. The question of whether the US Government would do anything about it was left open. Thus, on 24 November, Stephen Wise called a press conference in which he announced that he had learned 'through sources confirmed by the State Department' that half of the four million Jews in Nazi-occupied Europe had been slain in an extermination campaign.[14] The publication in any case could not have been delayed any longer. Two days earlier the Jewish Agency in Jerusalem had officially announced that the horrible news from Eastern Europe was indeed correct.

How had the information reached the Jewish organizations in the first place? There had been many dozens of news items, some seemingly reliable, others of doubtful provenance, and they had come through many channels. The emissaries of the Jewish organizations in Geneva, Stockholm and Istanbul read about the disappearance of European Jewry in newspapers from the occupied countries, both German and vernacular. True, the newspapers in the Reich hardly ever dealt with the subject and the papers from Belgrade and Bratislava, from Cracow and Riga not very often. But from a careful reading of the press a certain pattern emerged which, at the very least, inspired grave fears: for if it was true that, as these papers announced, town after town had become empty of Jews (*judenrein*) including some with a pre-war Jewish population of 100,000 or more (such as Kishinev), if whole countries were 'purged', what had become of the Jews?[15] Taken singly these items did not amount to much, taken together they pointed to a frightening pattern.

There was another even more obvious source of information about which more will be said later on. Postcards and letters sent from Nazi-occupied countries to neutral places did reach their destination. Such messages could even be sent from most ghettos. They took between one and two weeks to reach Switzerland or Sweden, and not much longer to Spain and Turkey. Thus the first, or one of the first reports of the deportation from the Warsaw ghetto came through a letter sent from Warsaw to the Sternbuchs, the representatives of orthodox Jewry in Switzerland. It reported that Mea Alafim (hundred thousand) had been invited by Mr Hunter to his country house 'Kever', meaning grave. There was fairly regular correspondence between most occupied countries and Geneva where the representatives of the Jewish organizations such as Lichtheim, Riegner, Schwalb, Silbershein and Ullmann had their offices. After 1943 Istanbul became more important.

Much important information emanated from those who had escaped from the ghettos and death camps. There is an enormous literature on every level of sophistication about Allied soldiers, sailors and airmen who fled from the POW camps. These books belong to genre that always attracts many readers; there is much to admire about the courage and ingenuity of those who fled from very closely guarded camps. But Jews also escaped. There were, however, fundamental differences between daring Allied officers who tried to reach Switzerland and

a Jew who attempted the same. The worst that could happen to
the officer, if apprehended, was a few weeks' solitary confine-
ment;* the Jew, on the other hand, faced certain death. Once
the Allied officer reached Switzerland he was safe, whereas the
Jew, more likely than not, would be turned back, at least during
the most critical part of the war, up to September 1943. But it is
also true that Jews had nothing to lose and they continued to flee
in considerable numbers, in every direction in which there was
even the faintest semblance of safety. Thousands went underground, hiding in cities or villages or forests or leading a 'normal
life' having assumed another, non-Jewish identity. There were
escapes from Holland and France into Spain and Switzerland;
this refers to the underground railway established by Joop
Westerweel and Joachim Simon (Shushu) in Holland and by
'Croustillon' and 'Pierre Lacaze' in southern France. There
were more or less fixed points at which the crossing of the border
took place – at Pau and Perpignan, near Oloron and through
Andorra. Many hundreds escaped this way from Nazi-occupied
countries. Jews from the Polish ghettos fled both to the East
(into the Soviet Union) and to the South, through Slovakia to
Hungary. There were Jewish smugglers and taxi and truck
owners at the Slovak-Polish border and their help was
invaluable; the border guards on the Hungarian frontier could
frequently be bought. From Hungary some continued via
Romania to Turkey and onwards to Palestine. As from 1942 the
Romanian Government no longer opposed emigration in
principle; the main difficulty facing the Jews was that no country
wanted to have them. The tragedy of the *Struma*, the refugee ship
which was torpedoed, is the best known but not the only one of
its kind. Jews from Croatia and southern France went into Italy
where they felt much safer for the time being. A group of Jewish
agricultural pioneers rowed from the Danish island of Bornholm
to Sweden; some tried to do the same from Holland to the
United Kingdom. Jews even joined the 'Organization Todt',
the Nazi labour service, with false papers. They were sent to
various parts of Europe and eventually escaped. A Polish Jew
who had joined one of these labour battalions walked into
Sweden from Norway. A few reached Sweden as stowaways

*Towards the end of the war there were some executions of escaped POWs but these
were rare exceptions.

from Baltic ports. German Jews walked over the Swiss border in the middle of the war, west of Lake Constance. 'It is a miracle how these people escape,' Riegner wrote to Goldmann in June 1942, 'more than fifty Jews from Germany have arrived here during the last 2–3 months.' A few dozen Greek Jews were taken out from Greece in old caiques by the Cairo branch of MI9, headed by Lieutenant-Colonel Tony Simmonds who had been with Wingate in Palestine in the 1930s. Some Jews were permitted to leave Nazi-occupied Europe legally even after America had entered the war; the information they provided was of considerable importance.

Many thousands escaped and everyone brought some information. True, sometimes they had seen very little such as the two elderly German Jewish ladies who had the good fortune somehow to have acquired US citizenship and who arrived with the *Drotningsholm* in New York in late June 1942. They had hardly left their house in Nuremberg and were not aware of events in far-away Poland. But even they had seen or heard something (that those deported to Riga were not heard of again); the stories of a few dozen, let alone a few hundred witnesses, added up to a great deal of information about what had happened to the Jews in Nazi-occupied Europe. Even in 1942, in the middle of the war, 3,733 new immigrants arrived in Palestine (1,407 'legal' and 1,539 'illegal' immigrants). Most of them came from Europe, mainly from the Balkans but also from Hungary, Slovakia and other countries. 8,500 came in 1943 and 14,460 in 1944. Almost everyone had a story to tell.*

The idea to collect and analyze this evidence occurred both to the Jewish Agency and to British military intelligence and in late 1942 an institution with the innocent and rather vague name 'Inter Service Liaison Department' (ISLD) was established under Colonel Teague in Haifa. The Jewish liaison officers

*How much was known to a single, isolated individual emerges from the story of Leonidas Sebba, a refugee from Riga who arrived in Sweden in January 1943. His written report (in German) extends over ten foolscap pages, it was typed in single space for Hillel Storch, the representative of the World Jewish Congress in Stockholm. Sebba described not only the death of members of his family and acquaintances but reported details about all major Jewish communities in the Baltic countries and reached the conclusion that almost all Jews had been killed. Sebba, who was twenty-one at the time, escaped from the Gestapo for which he had worked as an electrician, found employment on a German ship hiding his identity, 'defected' in Helsinki on 8 January 1943 and continued to Stockholm.

were R. Zaslani (Shiloah) and Gideon Ruffer (Rafael). Interrogating recent arrivals from Europe, ISLD gathered much information of value but the enterprise would have been of even greater value had it started earlier. Nor should it have been limited to those who reached Palestine: debriefing by the Allies in Spain and Switzerland was no more than sporadic.[16] A similar organization, FNIB (Foreign Nationalities Intelligence Branch), was established in the United States later in the war, but it did not apparently produce items of major interest in the context of the present study as it was limited to the analysis of personal letters from Nazi-occupied Europe.

Given the isolation of the remnants of European Jewry, how much could those have known who got away? A great deal, as the example of the exchange transport of November 1942 shows; it played, as will be demonstrated, a crucial role in persuading the Zionist leadership in Palestine that the extent of the 'final solution' had not been exaggerated. Furthermore, someone would always get away at the time of a massacre. The *Einsatzgruppen* and their local assistants were in a hurry, there was so much more work to be done. Some Jews pretended to be dead, and then, during the night, crawled away; others jumped from the cars or trains leading to the place of execution; some succeeded in hiding in the most unlikely circumstances. Those who had miraculously been saved would try to reach the nearest remaining Jewish community and they would, of course, report what they had witnessed.

Nor were the death camps escape-proof. The first escapes from Chelmno and Treblinka took place within a few days of these camps beginning to operate. The most difficult place for escapers was Belzec, but there was one escape even from there, and in any case, the place had been visited by Kurt Gerstein who talked about it to several German friends and foreign diplomats.*

Auschwitz was the largest of the camps, and there were 667 escapes. 270 of the escapers were subsequently caught, but almost 400 got away. In 1942 there were 120 escapes, the year after 310. Among those who fled there were at least 76 Jews;

---

*There were about ten escapes from Sobibor before the revolt and sixty during the fighting; a few dozen inmates fled from Treblinka before the revolt and perhaps twenty during it. I am grateful to Dr Y. Arad, director of Yad Vashem, for these estimates.

altogether there were probably more. In many cases the camp authorities did not fully identify in their records those who fled. In his autobiographical notes Rudolf Hoess, commander of Auschwitz, wrote that it was virtually impossible to stop news from the outside world reaching Auschwitz and *vice versa*. When Himmler visited Auschwitz he complained about the 'high, unprecedented numbers of successful escapes from Auschwitz' and asked the commander to use every possible means to put an end to them. But the escapes continued.

Some Auschwitz inmates were actually released by the German authorities. There were 952 releases during the first half of 1942 and 26 during the subsequent six months. There were releases from Auschwitz even in 1943. In early 1944 a considerable number of Jewish women were freed from the camp owing to the intervention of Oskar Schindler. A German who ran a factory in Cracow, Schindler saved the lives of many Jews; he is remembered in Israel as one of the 'Righteous among the Nations'.

Those who had escaped from the camps had no reason to keep silent, and those legally released were also not unduly worried by the undertaking they had signed – never to reveal anything. But if they were believed as in the case of those who came to Warsaw from Chelmno or Treblinka, there was much more scepticism in Western Europe and also in Hungary. The story of the two young Roman Catholics from Holland who were released from Auschwitz on 12 May 1942 is not untypical. One of them told Louis de Jong: 'The worst thing was that you simply could not get through to those closest to you. That gave you a terrible sense of isolation, as if a steam-roller was about to run you over. You felt like screaming it from the housetops but knew it was just a waste of your breath – no one would believe a word you told them.'[17] The year after, 1943, four Dutch women, Jehovah's Witnesses, returned from Auschwitz to Holland and faced the same reaction: 'Most people refused to believe us.' In many circles it was only in late 1943 and perhaps even in 1944, with the evidence piling up from many sources, that news about the camps was finally accepted. One cannot stress too often that the evidence had been available for a long time but it was not believed.

Nathan Eck, one of the future historians of the holocaust,

escaped from the Warsaw ghetto to Czestochova in 1942. In letters which he sent to Abraham Silbershein in Switzerland, one of the Jewish Agency's emissaries whom he knew from the pre-war period, he reported more than once about the deportations and the mass murder. One day, in September 1942, he received a postcard in which Silbershein asked whether the news was really true; surely there had been at least some exaggeration? Eck replied that if, after all the information that had been forwarded, Silbershein still did not accept it, there was hardly much point in any further correspondence.[18] It is a revealing story because Silbershein was a 'professional' in almost daily correspondence with Jews in the occupied countries. If even he had his doubts, it can well be understood that others did not believe.

Warsaw–London, the Polish underground network, was the most important channel of communications for news about the early stages of the 'final solution'. But there was another of equal, or almost equal, importance which led from groups of Zionists or individuals in occupied Europe to Geneva and from there to Jerusalem, to the head offices of the Jewish Agency for Palestine. Switzerland was a vital listening post on the continent, more so than in the First World War when Copenhagen and Amsterdam had served a similar purpose. The importance of Switzerland had not been foreseen by the Jewish institutions and no special preparations had been made; the presence of Jewish emissaries in Geneva and Zürich was more or less accidental. Once the war had broken out, and especially after the fall of France and Italy's entry in the war, Switzerland was almost entirely cut off. After the occupation of Vichy France by the Germans the isolation became total. Communications with Switzerland were also affected. Airmail from Switzerland to Palestine hardly ever took less than four weeks and frequently longer. Sometimes important news would be transmitted by telegraph by way of Istanbul but these relatively short messages would always raise further questions. There would be many queries and requests for details from Jerusalem and so the emissaries in Geneva got accustomed to writing long letters. They could have phoned Istanbul but this was expensive and their budget permitted this only rarely.* Hence the delays and the misunderstandings which frequently arose. Among the representatives in Switzerland, Gerhard Riegner of the World Jewish Congress has already been mentioned. There were a few others – Nathan Schwalb, representing the *Hehalutz*, the pioneer organization, Ullmann, editor of a local Jewish newspaper, Pazner (Posner) an employee of the Jewish Agency, the Sternbuchs representing orthodox Jewry, and Dr Abraham Silbershein. Each of them had his connections in the occupied countries: the letters they wrote and received throughout the war were one of the most important channels of communications with Jewish leaders and communities all over Europe.

The most senior of them was Richard Lichtheim, one of the early leaders and spokesmen of Zionism in Germany. Born into a wealthy family in Berlin in 1885, at the early age of twenty-eight he became editor of *Die Welt*, the central organ of the world Zionist movement. During the First World War he represented the Zionists in Turkey, engaging in various diplomatic missions. He interceded on behalf of Palestinian Jewry suffering at that time from the mistreatment of malevolent Turkish governors. After the war he was for a number of years a member of the World Zionist Executive in London (head of the Organization Department). He opposed Weizmann's hesitant and 'weak' line and in 1925 he joined the revisionist movement which promised a more forceful and dynamic political line. But the extremism of Vladimir Jabotinski (and *a fortiori* of some of his younger followers) eventually repelled him, and ten years later he rejoined the main Zionist camp. No one doubted his talents and the Zionist leadership was willing to employ him again, but not in a leading position. Lichtheim had always been a little too independent in his judgment for the

*Even in October 1942 when information about the 'final solution' was received in Jerusalem from many different sources there was reluctance to spend money on too frequent and too long telegrams. When Gruenbaum, in a meeting of the Jewish Agency executive, asked for a special allocation of 100 Palestinian pounds for cables, both to get more news and to mobilize Jewish organizations abroad, Elieser Kaplan, the Jewish Agency treasurer, argued that fifty pounds would be sufficient. Some of those present claimed that protests by Jewish organizations would be ineffective; Shertok said that the same information was received in London and New York and it was pointless to urge the Allied governments to turn against the Nazis, since they were in a state of war with Germany in any case. Protocol of Jewish Agency Executive, 25 October 1942, quoted in Y. Gelber, *Toldot Hahitnadvut* (Jerusalem, 1979), 1, p. 682.

bureaucratic apparatus. He had never lived in Palestine for any length of time and his command of Hebrew was uncertain, to say the least. He was a German Jew, which is to say that he never quite fitted into the closely knit group of the East European Jews who dominated Zionist politics and who belonged to a different cultural and social milieu. When he was sent to Geneva in 1939 no one realized how vitally important Geneva would be in the years to come, as a source of information.

In some ways Lichtheim was eminently suited for this assignment: of all the Zionist leaders of his generation he had the surest grasp of world politics. He was widely read in recent European affairs and he had, of course, followed international politics for three decades from a close angle. His analytical skill was impressive. He never had any illusions about Hitler's immoderate aims and mad ambitions, nor did he have any false hopes with regard to the firmness the Western Allies would show vis-à-vis the Fascist dictators. His predictions with regard to the course of the war and developments in the post-war period were remarkably accurate. True, his reports did not have a great impact back home in Jerusalem, but it is more than doubtful whether someone more in tune with the Zionist leadership would have been more successful in explaining the grim realities of Nazi Europe.

Lichtheim was less ideally suited in some other respects. He had not much experience in conspirational work. His training had been in a different world. But such activities were impossible in any case in Geneva; the Swiss authorities were closely watching the Jewish emissaries and would have taken a very dim view if these had engaged in any suspect activities.

Thus, as the war broke out, Lichtheim set up shop in 52 rue des Paquis, Palais Wilson – and began his correspondence with Jerusalem which concerned the fate of individuals and that of whole communities. He became more and more pessimistic as Hitler occupied country after country. But it was not a pessimism that led to passivity. He did have suggestions how to save at least some of the Jews of Europe and he was repeating his proposals relentlessly and without much success.* In a letter

*The following is based on the Lichtheim correspondence kept in the Central Zionist Archives in Jerusalem (CZA). I knew Richard Lichtheim through his son, George, and I discussed with him his work in Geneva on various occasions accompanying him on walks through Rehavia, the Jerusalem suburb where he made his home in the late 1940s.

written after the fall of France he mentioned the existence of a 'specific office dealing with the solution of the Jewish Question' – Eichmann's department in the Main State Security Office. Others were to discover this more than two years later. But at that time the 'final solution' had not yet been put on the agenda; the Nazis were planning 'radical emigration' and settlement in Madagascar. As Berlin saw it, there was sufficient room in Madagascar. Palestine on the other hand, to quote Lichtheim, would belong in the Nazi New Order to a power which would 'either liquidate the Jews there entirely or, in any event, not permit further immigration.'[19]

But to repeat once again, at that time the issue was emigration and economic assistance, not yet physical survival. 'What will become of the Jews of Europe?' Lichtheim asked as 1940 drew to its close:

I feel that a word of warning to the happier Jews of England and America is necessary. It is impossible to believe that any power on earth will be able (and willing?) to restore to the Jews of Continental Europe what they have lost or are losing today. It is one of the superficial beliefs of a certain type of American and British Jew that after Great Britain's victory – for which, of course, the Jews all over the world are praying – everything will be all right again with the Jews of Europe. But even if their civil rights can be restored – what about the property confiscated, the shops looted, the practices of doctors and lawyers gone, the schools destroyed, the commercial undertakings of every description closed or sold or stolen? Who will restore all that and how? ... And what will be left of the Jews of Europe? I am not speaking of the hundreds of thousands who during these years of persecution have managed to escape and are now trying to build up a new life in Palestine, in USA, in South America, Australia, San Domingo or elsewhere. Then there are the refugees in Europe who tried to escape but did not go fast and far enough. ... What will become of them after the war?[20]

It was clearly a problem that could not be solved by simple formulae such as the slogan 'Restore their rights'. As Lichtheim saw it there would be a mass of several hundreds of thousands after the war in a 'permanent no-man's land drifting from one frontier to another, from concentration camps to labour camps, from there to some unknown country and destiny'. It was a remarkably accurate forecast. True, when Lichtheim wrote even in 1940 about 'an ocean of blood and misery' he did not assume that millions would be killed. His predictions may now appear unduly optimistic; among his contemporaries these were considered examples of unwarranted despondency.

The situation was rapidly changing for the worse. After the Nazi invasion of Yugoslavia and the establishment of the Fascist Ustasha state in Croatia the turn came of Croatian Jewry. 'The situation of the Jews in Croatia is desperate,' Lichtheim wrote. The Italians were behaving much more humanely in their occupied zones than Germany's other allies, but 'the Croats are certainly among the worst'. There was no reaction from Jerusalem.[21] Later that year, Lichtheim reviewed the deportations from Germany, Austria and the Protectorate: Jews from German cities were concentrated in Berlin, others were deported to Poland or other East European countries. Similar expulsion orders had been given in Vienna and Prague.

So far no information had been received that anything untoward had happened to those deported to Eastern Europe. Those remaining behind were employed in German war industries. On the whole, everything considered, the picture seemed to be not too bad: some Jews had been arrested but few people had been actually killed in Germany. Yet Lichtheim had dark forebodings for he concluded his report as follows:

With all these degradations added to actual starvation and brutal treatment, the remnants of the Jewish communities of Germany, Austria and Czechoslovakia will probably be destroyed before the war ends and not too many will survive.[22]

In November 1941 the mass deportations had not yet started and the death camps did not yet exist. But Lichtheim again ended a dispatch on a solemn note:

With regard to Germany, Austria and the Protectorate it must be said that the fate of the Jews is now sealed. . . . Generally speaking, this whole chapter bears the title: 'Too late'. There was a time when the us and the other American states could have helped by granting visas. But this was obstructed by the usual inertia of the bureaucratic machine and by red tape.[23]

There was, of course, more to it than the 'usual inertia of the bureaucratic machine'. Was there anything that could still be done to help? Lichtheim noted that America still had some influence with Vichy and could make use of this. At least some of the persecuted Jews in France could be rescued in this way. He returned to this point in another letter sent to Weizmann through J. Linton in London. Again he stressed that the fate of the majority of European Jewry was sealed: of those deported to the East only a minority of the younger and stronger would survive. The whole policy of deportation to the devastated towns of western Russia in the middle of the winter was 'murder combined with torture'.[24] The Red Cross had been informed but what could it do against the will of the Gestapo? He transmitted the most recent information received in Geneva and then noted that:

It is a curious thing that President Roosevelt never mentioned the Jews whenever he spoke of the oppressed nations. The Governments of the democracies may have been led to believe that there would be still more terrible persecutions if they mentioned the Jews in their speeches. I think this to be a mistake. Events have shown that the Jews could not have suffered more than they have suffered if the statesmen of the democracies would have said the word.[25]

But perhaps there was yet another motive, perhaps they wanted to avoid the impression that the war had anything to do with the Jews. Such hush-hush tactics would hardly silence the anti-semites: 'Great Britain and America should say: we are neither Jews nor do we wage war for the Jews we are battling for mankind against the enemy of mankind.'[26]

Where were the voices condemning the atrocities and warning the perpetrators of such deeds *that they will be held responsible* (underlined in the original)? Lichtheim thought that in some cases such as Romania, Hungary, Slovakia, Croatia and Vichy a warning might have had and *may still have* (underlined in the original) 'a deterrent effect'. It was, of course, much more difficult in the case of Germany but even there some persons or circles might be influenced by such warnings.

Why were such warnings not uttered, why were there no words of sympathy and consolation? Was it not true that the world witnessed the most terrible persecution of the Jews which ever happened in Europe, overshadowing by its cruelty and extent even the massacres of the Armenians which at that time provoked a storm of protest in England and America? There was no answer to the questions asked by Lichtheim.

In the winter of 1941 the Nazi war machine suffered its first major setback in the Soviet Union. Lichtheim noted the enormous losses suffered, perhaps the wounded beast would soon feel that the end was near. But he had only scorn for the rumours according to which the generals would take over, forcing Hitler into the background:

> To those who really know Nazi Germany such talk sounds fantastic: Hitler and his party, the Gestapo, one million officials and ss guards, will always be stronger than a handful of generals with nothing but their Prussian lineage behind them.[27]

No improvement in the situation of the Jews could be expected, the picture was getting gloomier and gloomier. From a letter in February 1942 to Arthur Lourie, the head of the emergency committee in New York:

> The number of our dead after this war will have to be counted not in thousands or hundreds of thousands but in several millions and it is difficult to imagine how the surviving will ever be able to return to a normal way of life.[28]

If anything, Lichtheim understated the magnitude of the catastrophe.[29] But such gloomy predictions were rare exceptions at the time: no one wanted to hear of millions of victims in Febuary 1942. These seemed fantastic exaggerations which were not believed among the Jewish leadership nor among the Jewish public. Even some of those who had recently escaped from Eastern Europe rejected such views as unduly pessimistic, indeed as dangerous, because they could well lead to despondency.

Lichtheim frequently returned to his suggestions as to the measures that should be taken to slow down, at the very least, the tide of persecutions. He repeatedly emphasized the necessity of giving public expression over the radio to formal protests and warnings by Allied leaders and urged approaches to the Catholic Church in view of its great influence in some of the countries concerned. Together with Riegner and Sally Mayer, the president of the Swiss Jewish community, in March 1942 he met Monsignor Bernardini, the papal nuncio in Switzerland, and handed him a detailed report about the situation of the Jews. The nuncio stated that he was aware of the unfortunate situation of the Jews and that he had already reported on previous occasions to Rome but would do so again, and recommend certain steps in favour of the persecuted Jews. But soon afterwards Lichtheim sadly noted that the efforts of the Vatican in Slovakia had been of no avail.[30] While Lichtheim watched the slow destruction of European Jewry he was told of plans made by notables in Jerusalem to re-establish their organizations in Europe after the war. For this kind of 'post-war planning' he had nothing but sarcasm. A renewal of the idyllic pre-war Zionism seemed to him totally unrealistic.

My personal prognosis is quite sombre. Those Jews still alive after the war will be engulfed by Russia and the neighbouring countries. I do not share the optimism of those who expect the toleration – let alone the support – of Zionism by Bolshevism. The remnants of European Jewry will have to look somehow for an existence overseas.[31]

The mass killings in Poland were first made public in the world press in late June 1942. At this time Lichtheim reported that Central Europe was to be made *judenrein* (to be emptied of Jews) by means of deportation and direct or indirect killing 'through starvation or even shorter methods':

The Jews in almost all countries of this tormented continent live only in the fear of deportation which aims at their physical destruction quickly or over a longer period, or fear of slave labour in intolerable conditions. Their only thought is towards rescue and escape but this will be possible only in a very few cases.[32]

In August 1942 an English friend sent him a copy of *Hansard* reporting a debate in the House of Commons earlier that month about post-war problems of resettlement. One speaker had mentioned seven, another even nine and a half million Jews who would need homes after the war. Lichtheim wrote bitterly in his reply: 'People in England do not know what is now going on in Europe.' How could even the Jewish leaders believe that there would be five or six million Jews after the war who would have to be resettled? After analyzing the figures Lichtheim stated categorically: 'We now know that deportation means death – sooner or later.'

Of the former Polish, German, Austrian, Czechoslovak, Jugoslavian Jews – altogether 3½m. – and of the others who have been or will be deported, very few will survive. .... This process of annihilation is going on relentlessly and there is no hope left to save any considerable number. .... Therefore it is no exaggeration to say that Hitler has killed or is killing 4m. Jews in Continental Europe and that no more than 2m. have a chance of surviving. With every month that passes this chance becomes smaller and one year hence even these figures might appear too optimistic.[33]

Meanwhile (on 15 August) Lichtheim had dictated a report based on the account of two eyewitnesses who had come directly from Poland, one of them was a non-Jew, 'a very reliable and well known personality'. Both related stories that were, as Lichtheim wrote in an accompanying letter, 'so terrible that I had some doubts if I should forward it or not'. (He kept the report for two weeks before mailing it and sent it out only on 30 August.) It was the report which was also sent to Stephen Wise and was intercepted by the State Department which has already been mentioned in another context (see p. 117). It dealt with the mass killings of the Jews in Warsaw, Lithuania and elsewhere, mentioned Belzec as well as the fact that Theresien-stadt, the showplace (*Musterghetto*) in the Protectorate, was merely an interim station for most of the deportees. The report dwelt upon the death trains and the role of the Lithuanian helpers of the ss; it also said that no Jews were left in the regions east of Warsaw. Among the practical suggestions contained in the report was the request by the author(s) to bring these facts to the knowledge of American Jewry without reference to its source. He complained that cables giving the very same information had been sent from Warsaw to London before but had been publicized in the (British) radio only with delay. American Jewry should not be kept in ignorance for so long. The report contained some incorrect statements such as the allegation that the corpses of victims were used for fat and fertilizers or that the whole non-Jewish population of Sebastopol had been killed. But by and large it gave an unvarnished picture of the situation as Lichtheim pointed out in his comments. Certain facts, he said, had been confirmed quite independently by other sources:

All this gives a most sinister meaning to the other information contained in this report – incredible as it may seem to readers in

England and America. In fact, I believe the report to be true and quite in line with Hitler's announcement that at the end of this war there will be no Jews in Continental Europe.*

The report met with disbelief not only in England and America but also in Jerusalem. Yizhak Gruenbaum, one of the leading figures of Polish Jewry and member of the Jewish Agency Executive, sent Lichtheim a cable in reply which read:

Shocked your latest reports regarding Poland which despite all difficult [to] believe stop haven't yet published do everything possible verify cable.

Gruenbaum did try to ascertain whether the report was true: he sent a cable to Rabbi Marcus Ehrenpreis in Stockholm, as he had done once before in July after Zygielbojm's revelations in London. Had the venerable rabbi heard anything about it? Marcus Ehrenpreis was in his middle seventies at the time. He had been born in Lemberg and had served as a rabbi in Croatia and Bulgaria. He was a prolific author and one of the pioneers of modern Hebrew literature. He was also one of the most unlikely authorities about current events in Eastern Europe, nor was he willing to make a great effort to find out. Lauterbach, head of the Organization Department, was somewhat more cautious in his reply to Lichtheim:

Frankly, I am not inclined to accept all the statements at their face value and, without having, of course, any evidence to the contrary have great doubts as to the accuracy of all the facts contained therein. . . . One must also learn from experience to distinguish between reality, grim as it is, and figments of an imagination strained by justified fear

---

*30 August 1942 (letter 802) CZA. The source of the report was the Polish legation in Bern which served as a base for couriers from Poland. The legation was headed by Alexander Lados among whose assistants was Julius Kuehl who had come to Bern from Poland as a student in 1929 (his dissertation was on Polish-Swiss trade relations). From 1938 on Kuehl was employed in the Polish consular service. He was on friendly terms with the Sternbuchs, an orthodox Jewish family resident in St Gallen. He passed information on to them and to Silbershein in Geneva. In a letter to Dr Schwarzbart in London (8 October 1942 – Schwarzbart Archives) Silbershein says that the above-mentioned report reached him through the Polish legation. But the Sternbuchs also received letters directly from Poland. The most famous, and the most harrowing, were two letters from I. Domb in Warsaw, dated 4 and 12 September in which, in hardly veiled language, the writer announced that virtually everyone around him had been killed. He was now all alone: 'Please pray for me.'

and grows to believe what is whispered without being able, in the circumstances to check its veracity.

But then he added that 'without going into gruesome details' one could not help but accept the main facts and interpretation as contained in Lichtheim's letter.[34] What emerged from Lauterbach's confused letter was that while Jerusalem was by now persuaded that the situation was very bad it was not quite as bad as Lichtheim had described.

During the following days and weeks more evidence came to light in quick succession. On 26 September Lichtheim cabled London that the ghettos of Warsaw and Lodz were nearly empty. Some artisans were left, the majority had been deported to some unknown destination. On 29 September, in a letter to Arthur Lourie in New York: 'The total destruction of the Jewish communities in Belgium and Holland is nearly complete.' On 15 September in a letter to London, again reiterating his old complaint: 'Far too little has been said and done by the Allies to warn the Nazis and their satellites of the consequences of their crime.' But now with the turn of the tide of the war the prospects were better than they had ever been before. He warned that unless this was done the last still existing Jewish communities in Europe, the 800,000 in Hungary and the 300,000 in Romania, would also perish.

On 5 October Lichtheim sent to Jerusalem (and to London and New York) 'a most harrowing report about the situation in Lettland'. For a long time there had been sporadic news about the slaughter in the Baltic countries, which had, in fact, taken place a year earlier. But it had been very difficult to obtain reliable reports; there was no correspondence with Vilna and Riga and very little traffic. The harrowing report was based on the evidence of Gabriel Zivian, a young Jew from Riga, who had witnessed the massacres on the spot, made his way to northern Germany and had worked as a hospital aide in Stettin. Miraculously he had received an entry visa to Switzerland through some relations in Geneva. Riegner interviewed him like an examining magistrate (Riegner's words) for eight hours.[35] This was in August 1942. A little later another young Jew of Polish origin had also reached Switzerland illegally. Since he was quite ill, he could not be sent back to Germany but was hospitalized under police supervision. A physician called

Riegner: they had a patient who was telling them horrible stories. Could Riegner possibly come and find out whether there was anything to this?

Lichtheim forwarded this account and said in an accompanying note: 'We have heard from other sources of similar mass murders in Poland.' Then, on 8 October, he prepared a detailed reply to Gruenbaum who had doubted the veracity of his earlier reports. 'I can easily understand that you are unwilling to believe the report in question.' But the sources were trustworthy. How could one possibly investigate the matter on the spot? No observers were permitted to approach the regions of death, only the SS and some workers. The only available testimony was that of German officers returning from the East. But there had also been letters and postcards from Jews in Poland. There could no longer be any doubt as to the intentions of Hitler and the Gestapo. He ended the letter as follows:

> I have foreseen this development long ago. In my letters to London and New York I have constantly warned our friends of what was coming and I have submitted certain proposals. But I always knew that in the case of Hitler nothing we or others would do or say could stop him. Therefore I have asked our friends in London and New York to try to save at least the Jewish communities in the semi-independent states of Romania, Hungary, Italy and Bulgaria. . . .
>
> But we have to face the fact that the large majority of the Jewish communities in Hitler-dominated Europe are doomed. There is no force which could stop Hitler or his SS who are today the absolute rulers of Germany and the occupied countries. It is my painful duty to tell you what I know. There is nothing I could add. The tragedy is too great for words.[36]

The correspondence with Jerusalem continued. There were more facts but they hardly affected the general picture. On 16 October, in a private letter to Lauterbach:

> I have the impression that my previous reports have not always found the necessary understanding. Some of our friends did not want to believe that something like this can happen, others may have been misled through different (i.e. less alarming) reports. It is pointless to deal now with the motives which have caused this. Events speak an inexorable language and we face these events impotently, or almost so. . . .

On 26 October he transmitted one of the notes, which he had

handed together with Riegner, to the American minister in Bern four days earlier, containing a general survey of the situation. On 20 October he wrote another long summary of recent events: the deportations to Poland and inside Poland had nothing to do with the Nazi war effort and the need for more labour, 'there is a plan behind these measures to exterminate immediately the largest possible number of Jews'. Previously there had been pogroms and mass executions but they had been of a local character, and it had been thought that despite everything, despite slave labour, starvation and all other deprivations at least the younger and stronger might survive and that some of the communities would not be completely destroyed:

But it has become more and more evident in the course of the last three or four months (and you will have seen that from my reports) that even this outlook was too optimistic and the latest deportation measures have made it quite clear what is contemplated.

Lichtheim then mentioned reports according to which there had been discussions in Hitler's headquarters about the annihilation of the Jews within the next few months. At the end of July Hitler had signed a formal order approving the plan of total annihilation of all Jews of Europe on which the Nazis could lay their hands. Reliable witnesses had seen the order signed by Hitler in his headquarters. And he concluded, for once in a spirit of resignation:

For the large majority of the Jews of Europe there seems to be no hope left. They are in the hands of a raving madman who has become the absolute ruler of Continental Europe by the will of his own guilty people and by the tragic blindness of statesmen who from 1933 to 1939 have tried to make a deal with the devil instead of driving him out while there was still time to do so.[37]

Five weeks later, on 25 November, at a meeting in Tel Aviv, Elijahu Dobkin of the Jewish Agency Executive said: 'Perhaps we have sinned as the first terrible news came to us two months ago via Geneva and Istanbul and as we did not believe it.'[38] This sentiment was echoed by many others in the following weeks. But the information had, of course, arrived much earlier and it now remains to be asked what had prevented its acceptance in the first place and what caused the reappraisal in November.

As the war broke out more than half a million Jews lived in

Palestine; most of them had been born in the countries occupied by Nazi Germany. Most had friends and family in Europe and they tried to keep in touch with them in every possible way – through postcards and letters sent by way of neutral countries or short 'Red Cross letters'. These were special forms in which messages up to twenty-five words could be transmitted. In the beginning many such letters and postcards came, then they became fewer and fewer. Thus the public in Palestine came to depend for its information mainly on newspaper reports. Correspondents were systematically picking up news of Jewish interests from newspapers in Nazi-occupied Europe, from the Swedish and Swiss press, and of course, also from the infrequent reports in the British, American and Soviet media.

But just as the Jewish Agency executive thought that Lichtheim was exaggerating, and just as the reports by Riegner and others were thought to be unduly pessimistic, the Palestinian Jewish press quite frequently dissociated itself editorially from the 'alarmist information' published in its own columns. A few examples should suffice. Moshe Prager, a Polish Jewish journalist was the author (in 1941) of the first, and for the time being only, book on the life of Polish Jewry under Nazi occupation. In his preface Y. Gruenbaum praised the supreme ability of Polish Jewry to adjust itself to the horrors and he predicted that its spirit would triumph over degradation, tortures and destruction. Prager himself saw the main Nazi aim as turning the Jews into despicable beggars; the Jews, on the other hand were fighting with their last efforts to keep their honour and not be defeated.[39] Terms such as adjustment, triumph, honour and defeat are, of course, singularly inept expressions in connection with the 'final solution'. But these comments were made in 1941 and at the time they seemed not altogether unreasonable. What happened in Eastern Europe in 1940 had, after all, occurred before in Jewish history: Jews were deprived of their elementary rights, there were sporadic pogroms and economic ruin. But there seemed to be no reason to doubt that the great majority of European Jewry would survive the war. Thus the correspondents and commentators discussed whether the Nazi plan to concentrate the Jews in the Lublin area was not all that terrible (because self-government had its advantages as some argued) or whether this scheme was no more than a fraud which would result in one giant concentration camp, as the New York *Forward* reasoned.

But there was to be no concentration in the Lublin region, no Madagascar resettlement scheme. After the invasion of the Soviet Union the information received was no longer about the closing of businesses and violation of human rights, not even of hunger and disease. It was about mass murder. The perceptions which had been formed in an earlier period did not, however, change. As the press saw it, Jewish life continued in Eastern Europe albeit under very difficult conditions.

There was a frantic search for rays of hope. Thus the left-wing press would report with satisfaction that the agricultural training centres in Poland and other countries in which the *halutzim* (pioneers) were preparing themselves for life in the Palestinian collective settlements continued to operate. The orthodox newspapers noted with equal satisfaction that twenty-four Jewish bookshops were still open in the Warsaw ghetto, and three in Cracow.[40] *Ha'olam*, the organ of the world Zionist movement, published virtually no news about the massacres during the first half of 1942; it did feature, however, an article by Apollinari Hartglass, a Polish Jewish leader who had escaped from Warsaw after the Nazi invasion and who, by tortuous logic, tried to prove that while the world had initially ignored the Jewish catastrophe, it had now discovered that it had its propagandistic uses and was 'actually exaggerating it twofold and more'.[41]

Other Hebrew newspapers reported that Amsterdam was to be the embarkation port for European Jewry to some unknown destination overseas. Another paper quoted a Polish professor who had fled to America, to the effect that while the Jews would merely be deported, the Poles would all be killed by the Nazis.[42] The massacres were reported in the papers but also every possible rumour, however incredible, and unlimited scope was given to wishful thinking, and unwittingly of course, to Nazi disinformation. The news about the massacres was printed but widely doubted; it was assumed that some misfortunes had indeed happened but that the number of victims had been grossly exaggerated. *Hatzofe* called correspondents to order in March 1942: they should show greater responsibility and not 'inflate out of proportion every bad rumour'. *Davar* wrote that one should receive with great caution all the atrocity stories allegedly coming from 'soldiers returning from the front'.[43] According to *Davar* it had been reported on the authority of the Soviet army newspaper *Red Star* that most of those killed in Kiev (Babi Yar) had been Jews. But in fact, (*Davar* claimed) *Red Star* had said that most of the victims had *not* been Jews. *Red Star* had said neither the one nor the other, but the *Davar* editorial was quite symptomatic of the prevailing confusion.[44]

Both *Davar* and *Hatzofe* put the blame on the unbridled sensationalism of irresponsible journalists on one hand and the competition between various news agencies on the other. Each wanted to kill more Jews than the other.

The irresponsible informants ... absorb every rumour, they desperately look for every piece of bad news, every enormous figure and present it to the reader in a way which makes the blood curdle in one's veins. ... Do the informants not feel that the news about tens of thousands of killed, of a quarter million victims does not stir up many emotions because it is not believed in view of the inherent exaggeration. ... We still remember the dispatches from the days of the riots [in Palestine 1936–9] which were sent out all over the globe and which were so much exaggerated.

Hatzofe rejected the Zygielbojm report: all these accounts were repetitive. There had been perhaps a pogrom somewhere, but then the same news would be reported one day from London, another day from Stockholm and on the following day from yet another place. When the Chelmno story reached *Davar* in October 1942 it was introduced by the following editorial note: 'We publish this horrible account on the responsibility of the source ...'[45] Other newspapers ridiculed the astronomical figures of victims which could not possibly be true. When Czerniakow, the head of the Warsaw *Judenrat*, committed suicide, *Haboker* commented that the situation could not possibly be altogether desperate, for otherwise (it was argued) a revolt would surely break out.

When in later years people were looking for an explanation for the misinterpretation of the news from Europe – not to put it any stronger – one could point, of course, to various mitigating circumstances. The summer of 1942 saw Rommel's advance into Egypt; the Afrika Korps was poised to strike at the Nile valley; a German invasion of Palestine seemed at hand. It was only in the first week of September 1942 that Rommel was checked at Alam Halfa, and Montgomery's counter-offensive which broke German dreams in Africa began only on 23 October. Until that date the Jewish community in Palestine seemed in immediate danger. All other problems were bound to take second place. But this hardly explains the lack of interest and understanding before Rommel's advance during the summer. And it certainly does not explain the lack of understanding shown by American and British Jewry which did not face the danger of invasion and occupation.

It was not, in the final analysis, a matter of lack of information. As a labour leader put it: 'The news had reached Palestine, the newspapers had published them and also the [mandatory] radio service. The community read it and heard it but did not absorb it; and it did not raise its voice to alarm Jewish communities elsewhere.'[46] There were many voices of self-accusation after November 1942 and they included Prager and Hartglass. How had they been so blind not to believe the news? There was much recrimination against the leadership which had after all had more information at its disposal and yet had not sounded the tocsin.*

Y. Tabenkin, the veteran kibbutz leader, wrote that it was simply not true that the Jews in Palestine had not known about the fate of European Jewry: 'We knew everything. And now we

---

Hamashkif, 6, 11 December 1942 and many articles through 1943 and 1944 in the Hebrew press. But Prager in later years accused not only himself but even more strongly virtually everyone else (excepting only his friends of the ultra-orthodox *Agudat Israel*) and eventually reached the conclusion that the holocaust should not become the subject of historical research. (*Bet Ya'akov*, May 1974, 4–12) Prager (and others) refer mainly to the pessimism voiced by Y. Gruenbaum who in August 1942 expressed doubts whether the Jews of Poland could still be saved and whether any substantial help could be extended to them. (CZAS 26–1235, meeting between Gruenbaum and Rabbi Levin.) Gruenbaum thought that only the military victory of the Allies would save the remaining Jews and he believed that protest demonstrations and similar noisy actions were ineffective and pointless. (A. Morgenstern, 'Va'ad ha'hazala' etc. in *Yalkut Moreshet* June 1971, 71 *et seq*.) Many years later when Gruenbaum was interviewed about what he knew at the time he said that towards the end of 1942 'we got news from Geneva that something horrible happened in Poland – but we did not know what . . . – the confused account of an eighty-year-old man.' (*Etgar* 29 June 1961. Gruenbaum interview with Natan Yalin Mor.) For Dr N. Goldmann's *mea culpa* (written in the *pluralis majestatis*) see *Davar* 14 September 1966: 'Our generation did not do its duty, and I include myself too. . . . Most of the people did not understand the danger of Nazism. We did not warn of the possibility of death camps. Our imagination was too limited. . . . When the first news came on the murder of European Jewry American Jews did not react.'

look for the guilty ones among us. This is a manifestation of horrible helplessness. We know who is guilty but it is difficult to punish him, and therefore we look for them among us. Why should we accuse Gruenbaum?' Tabenkin said that if anyone reread the last six months of *Davar*, the daily organ of the left, he would find that everything had been reported, massacres, poison gas etc. 'But only when we met people who had come from the valley of the shadow of the death were we strongly impressed and felt the catastrophe in all its horror.'[47]

The senior officials of the Jewish Agency did, of course, read with attention the news from Europe. On 17 April 1942 Moshe Shertok, the head of the Political Department, addressed Sir Claude Auchinleck (Commander of the Eighth Army in North Africa and Montgomery's predecessor) as follows:

There can be little doubt that if Palestine were overrun by the Nazis nothing less than complete annihilation would be the lot of the Jews of this country. The destruction of the Jewish race is a fundamental tenet of the Nazi doctrine. The authoritative reports recently published show that that policy is being carried out with a ruthlessness which defies description. Hundreds of thousands of Jews have perished in Poland, the Balkan countries, Romania and the invaded provinces of Russia, as a result of mass executions, forced deportations, and the spread of famine and disease in ghettos and concentration camps. An even swifter destruction, it must be feared, would overtake the Jews of Palestine, were they to fall under Nazi sway. . . .*[48]

These were strong words and they were written moreover well before the Zygielbojm report and revelations of the Polish Government-in-exile. If so why did the Jewish Agency disbelieve Lichtheim? The answer is, in brief, that everything Shertok had said could also be found in the newspapers at the time. True, the 'institutions' had received some more details which is not to say that the information was fully believed.

*Shertok was not too successful with his plea to General Auchinleck. The Foreign Office was on the whole even more opposed to the idea of arming the Jews of Palestine. As Harry Eyes wrote commenting on a letter by Sir Lewis Namier on the very same subject: 'From the point of view of the Jews themselves it seems most dangerous to arm them if the Germans ever do reach Palestine. It seems inconceivable that even the Germans would set themselves in cold blood to massacre 400,000 Jews. But nothing is more likely to make them do that than the fact that the Jews were armed and might have in certain instances resisted the German advance or mopped up a party of parachutists.' (Minute dated 1 May 1941.)

Shertok's alarming words have to be read furthermore in the context in which they were written. The Jewish community of Palestine was in immediate danger, and in his letter Shertok pressed for specific demands for the defence of Palestine: the 'utmost mobilization' – more Jewish soldiers, more arms, a large-scale programme of military training, the expansion of the militia. To reinforce these demands Shertok invoked not only the military threat posed by Rommel (which was quite real) but also the news about large-scale persecutions in Europe which had been reported countless times but which were nevertheless more distant and probably only half believed.

Again, one example of the confusion then prevailing should suffice. When Shertok addressed his letter to Auchinleck, Meleh Neustadt (Noi) was on a mission to Istanbul. In May 1942 he returned to Palestine and in two long addresses, in closed session, he gave the most detailed and authoritative account available at the time to the Jewish leadership.* There was no one better informed at the time. Noi had established contact from Turkey with fifty Jewish communities in Poland and with virtually every other European country. He had discovered, much to his surprise, that with certain exceptions (the Baltic countries and eastern Poland) communication could easily be established. Air letters from occupied countries took ten to twelve days, cables were also sent and received, and one could even book long-distance telephone calls.† Noi noted that Jews in Eastern Europe did not like to use the telegraph so as not to attract attention. On the other hand, he said that inside Nazi-occupied Europe Jewish emissaries were frequently travelling from one place to another, that illegal newspapers were published and that there were regional and even nationwide meetings.

---

*On 25 May, at the *Mapai* (*Ihud*) World Secretariat, on 27 May at the *Histadrut* (Trade Union) Council. A stenogram was taken, and the speeches were, in early July, circulated ('restricted') among a limited number of people.

†It is known from various sources that Slovak Jewish leaders were in fairly frequent telephonic contact with the Jewish representatives in Switzerland. (Josef Kornianski, *Beshlichut Halutzim*, Bet Lohame Hagetaot, 1979, p. 93.) Dr Silbershein in Geneva had a phone call in May 1942 from an unknown representative of the German Red Cross in Kolomea, Eastern Galicia, in which he was told that a great many Jews there had died a violent death and that the remnants were living in conditions of abject poverty and needed urgent help. (Riegner to N. Goldmann, Geneva, 17 June 1942. World Jewish Congress, Institute of Jewish Affairs Archives, London.)

The bad news was the fate of Croatian and part of Romanian Jewry of which he was fully informed.* There had been victims in Eastern Galicia. Lodz was more or less cut off from the outside world. There was no direct contact but it had been learned that 'unproductive elements' had been deported from Lodz to Minsk, Kovno and Riga. Noi said that it was pointless to comment on the rumours concerning the fate of the Jews of eastern Poland (and the Baltic countries); one simply did not know. But he also said that nothing was more harmful than 'exaggerated information' which weakened and even put into doubt correct news about real atrocities. He expressed regret that neither the World Jewish Congress nor any other Jewish body had established so far an office in Istanbul, and that there were no journalists to sift and transmit the information from occupied Europe. For Istanbul was the best listening post.

The good news was that all over Europe Jewish life continued, that the Zionist youth movement was showing much activity in very difficult conditions and that it deserved the highest praise. Noi's information was in part amazingly detailed: he had exact figures about hospitals and orphanages in Warsaw, the price of bread in ghettos, the number of participants in sundry agricultural courses. In part, it was also very recent: he knew about the unsuccessful intervention of the Vatican in Slovakia. His prediction was that while the Nazis wanted physically to destroy the Jews, they also wanted to employ them for the war effort: 'And it is possible that this will save a great part of European Jewry.'

What was more striking in these reports: the measure of knowledge or of ignorance? The mass killings in the former Soviet territories had been reported in the press many months earlier and Polish sources had confirmed the destruction of most communities in Lithuania and Eastern Galicia. But seen from Istanbul these were still 'rumours'; silence did not necessarily mean death but perhaps isolation. Chelmno was not taken seriously and the beginning of 'evacuation' from most Polish ghettos was not reported.

It was argued in later years that certain Jewish leaders in the

---

*It was generally thought at the time that the fate of Croatian Jewry had been the worst. Thus Silbershein in a letter from Geneva dated 4 May 1942: 'What happened in Zagreb happened nowhere else. . . .'

United States as well as in Palestine delayed the publication of the full truth about the European tragedy because they feared that this would have a depressing, perhaps even paralyzing effect on the morale of the Jewish community in Palestine at a time of emergency. But explanations of this kind are more than doubtful. Internal evidence shows that most Jewish leaders were genuinely sceptical with regard to the extent of the catastrophe until 18 and 19 November when four of them went to interview a group of Jewish women and children of Palestinian nationality who had just arrived in Palestine from Europe.

They had been exchanged against a group of German nationals who had been detained at the beginning of the war on Allied territory. A first such exchange had taken place in December 1941, involving some forty-six women and children. But no one had paid much attention at the time, and the new arrivals had apparently not much of interest to tell. They had not come from the Baltic countries and western Russia where most of the massacres had taken place. Then, in November 1942 there came the second group about which more will be said presently: there was a third, much smaller contingent in February 1943 and some further exchanges in summer of 1944, mainly via Spain.

The attitude of the SS to such exchanges was, on the whole, negative; time and again, Eichmann and others argued that a certain person could not be released even if this was insisted upon by friends (such as the Italian Fascist party!) because 'she had seen too much' and would add fuel to the atrocity propaganda circulating outside Germany. But on occasion they were either overruled or did not persist in their opposition. Thus, the group of 137 was permitted to leave Poland on 28 October and Vienna (where they were kept for a few days prior to their departure) on 11 November. On 14 November their train arrived at the Syrian border. Among them were seventy-eight Jews (ten elderly men, thirty-nine women and twenty-nine children) and of these sixty-nine were Palestinian citizens. After a cursory interrogation by British military intelligence they were taken to Athlit, which had once been a British military camp (and also a detention centre) some miles south of Haifa, near the sea. It was there that two members of the executive of the Jewish Agency and two senior officials visited them (E. Dobkin,

M. Shapira, H. Barlas and Bahar). The new arrivals came from thirteen different cities in Poland (including Sosnowice, Kielce, Piotrkov, Cracow, Sandomir and Bialystok) from Berlin and Hamburg, from Belgium and Holland. They had also had the opportunity to meet in Vienna with the head of the Jewish community, Loewenherz, and his deputy, Gruen, who told them that 400 Jews were still left out of a community of 200,000. While most of the women had been held for some weeks in various prisons prior to their departure in Poland, they were able to move about more or less freely in Vienna. Thus they could provide a fairly comprehensive picture of the situation not only in Poland but also other parts of Europe.

But were they reliable? The visitors from Jerusalem seem to have been quite sceptical in the beginning. So often before simple-minded (and even not so simple-minded people) had simply repeated rumours, often baseless in character. But the new arrivals could not be so easily dismissed: among them was a scientific researcher employed at the Hebrew University, two members of Kibbutz Degania B – members of the Palestinian élite – a Zionist leader of long standing from Piotrkov and other such witnesses. ('People on whose judgment and discernment one could rely,' E. Dobkin was later to say.)

Dobkin summarized his findings in an address to the *Histadrut* Executive on 25 November 1942; similar reports were delivered to the leading bodies of the Jewish Agency and *Mapai* – the Labour Party. How to reply to the question asked by so many: was it true? Could it be believed?

As I was sitting in Athlit and listened to the stories of tens of women it became clear to me, that however great the sorrow, there remained no doubt and we have to accept it. Perhaps we sinned when we did not believe the first news which came via Geneva and Istanbul two months ago.[49]

What emerged from these accounts was firstly that a German government commission had been set up earlier that summer (*Sonder-* or *Vernichtungskommission*) under á certain commissar Feu or Foy to destroy Polish Jewry. (This information was, in fact, wrong or at the very least inaccurate. There was no 'special committee'; a regular department had been instituted in the Main State Security Office several years earlier.) 'Operation

Reinhard', in honour of the late Reinhard Heydrich who had been shot in Prague, was to exterminate Polish Jewry; it was under the command of Odilo Globocnik. Paradoxically, these inaccurate details had a greater impact on the Jewish leadership and public than the previous, more accurate reports. So far they had always thought in terms of pogroms rather than systematic destruction. But if a special commission had been appointed, this of course shed new light on the character and the purpose of the persecutions.

Furthermore, Dobkin continued, the majority of Polish Jewry had already been deported or was about to be deported. Among those who had arrived there was no one from Warsaw, the biggest ghetto, but they had met in (Polish) Upper Silesia some Jews who had escaped from Warsaw and who told them that only 40,000 Jews remained in the capital. (There were, in fact, still 60–70,000.) Of 40,000 Jews in Czestochova only 2,000 were still there; of 20,000 in Piotrkov only 2,600; of 30,000 in Kielce, 1,500. There was a general picture of murder and ruin. They had not been able to extract from those interviewed information about the fate of those who had been deported. They had been sent in an 'unknown direction' and there was no news from them, no letters, no personal regards conveyed.

What did it all mean? There were various rumours in Poland and they were apparently correct: some big concrete structures had been put up near the Russian–Polish border in which the victims were killed by poison gas and burned.(This referred apparently to Sobibor which was near the Russian border.) On the other hand, a woman from Oswiecim (Auschwitz) had told a story about three stoves for burning Jews which had been put up in a camp near that city.*

Above all, there was the systematic murder of children and elderly people. Dobkin said that he would never forget the story of an eight-year-old boy who had been hiding with his five-year-old sister in the house when the police came to collect them. He had warned the little girl not to cry, but overcome by fear, she

---

*There were no Jews in the city of Auschwitz; the witness was in fact from nearby Sosnowiec. She said that two more chimneys were now built. From time to time Jews from the neighbourhood were brought to the camps. *Tamzit Yediot* etc. Part one, 20 November 1942. The Information Department of the Jewish Agency circulated immediately after the Athlit visit fairly detailed summaries of the evidence given by individual witnesses. Other new arrivals mentioned Belzec and Treblinka.

had cried, was found and taken away – one story out of hundreds of thousands.

What also emerged from these accounts was that the campaign of destruction had equally affected other countries – Germany and Austria, Slovakia, Yugoslavia and Holland. No country under Nazi rule had been spared. In all of Germany only 28,000 Jews were now left (the actual number was nearer 50,000) and there were even less in Austria.

The representatives of Palestine Jewry who listened to the speech and who were reading the evidence that had been submitted to them were, of course, profoundly shocked. Cracow – no Jews left. Siedlec – no Jews left. Mislovice – a hundred Jews left. These had been major Jewish communities, how could they possibly have disappeared? They had read all this before but so far they had regarded it as mere rumours. But it was one thing to reject the impersonal news in the newspaper or radio based perhaps on doubtful informants. It was impossible not to accept the personal evidence of witness after witness: 'I left Palestine in June 1939 to visit my old parents in Cracow. . . .'

Witness after witness appeared: the resident of Tel Aviv who had lived through the destruction of the Piotrkov community, the woman born in Petah Tiqva who returned from Holland. It is more than likely that the information from Geneva would have had a cumulative effect sooner or later in any case. The fact that the news from Geneva was confirmed, albeit reluctantly and with some delay, by the Allied governments was of great importance. But as far as the consciousness of Palestinian Jewry was concerned the arrival of the group of the sixty-nine was the turning point.

Those listening to the reports and reading the evidence were asking themselves, as David Remes did: 'Is it possible that such authentic news did not reach America? I heard from Ben Gurion that they had heard the shocking news even before we did. . . .' Dobkin:

The news reached us and America via Geneva. But from the way people reacted here I can well imagine how they reacted over there. When we got the information many could not believe in its authenticity. Ben Gurion says that in America they thought that this was one of the methods of atrocity (*Greuel*) propaganda. We have now to make American Jewry understand that the information is indeed correct.[50]

There was great pressure for acting immediately: As one of the participants (M. Erem) said: 'Three days have already passed.' Three days!

On 22 November 1942 the Jewish Agency executive published an announcement according to which news had been received from 'authoritative and reliable sources' that the Nazis had started a systematic extermination campaign in Poland. During a two-day period from 30 November to 1 December expression was to be given to the feeling of the community and the conscience of the world was to be alarmed. There were demonstrations, meetings, speeches, and the newspapers appeared with a black frame all over the first page. Emergency and rescue committees were set up, emissaries were sent to Istanbul and other places trying to reach the Jews in occupied Europe; the idea of sending parachutists was first discussed.[51] But, as the US consul general in Jerusalem wrote in a cable to Washington, the feeling was one of tragic impotence – what could Palestinian Jewry possibly do to provide effective help?

From late November 1942 the subject of the holocaust was to preoccupy the Jewish communities in America, in Palestine and in Britain without interruption. But even now the full extent of the disaster had not altogether registered: Jewish organizations in America and elsewhere continued to publish declarations about Jewish life in the ghettos that was going on and about the continuing proud stand of the Jewish masses. Zionists, including leaders of the World Jewish Congress, were absorbed in 'post-war planning' and were paying little more than ceremonious attention to what was happening in Europe in stark contrast to the outcries from Geneva and Istanbul demanding immediate action to save the remnants.[52]

In later years Dr Riegner noted how much he and his colleagues in Geneva had been bewildered by the inability of the Jewish leadership abroad to understand both the extent and the speed of the destruction. They talked about two million victims when in fact four million had already died. The director of the Institute of Jewish Affairs in New York (J. Robinson) published a study with figures which were altogether inexact and which also appeared in the European press. The New York Rescue Committee (headed by Professor A. Tartakower) sent lists of thousands of Polish Jews to whom parcels should be dispatched;

they seemed not to accept that neither the people nor the addresses any longer existed.

We [in Geneva] had the impression that they no longer understood what happened. Their attitude can be explained by optimism and the incapacity to accept the worst. For us this was simply incomprehensible.[53]

CONCLUSION

THE evidence gathered so far shows that news of the 'final solution' had been received in 1942 all over Europe, even though all the details were not known. If so, why were the signals so frequently misunderstood and the message rejected?

1. The fact that Hitler had given an explicit order to kill all Jews was not known for a long time. His decision was taken soon after he had made up his mind to invade Russia. Victor Brack, who worked at the time in Hitler's Chancellery, said in evidence at Nuremberg that it was no secret in higher party circles by March 1941 that the Jews were to be exterminated. But 'higher party circles' may have meant at the time no more than a dozen people. In March 1941, even Eichmann did not know, for the preparations for the deportations and the camps had not yet been made. First instructions to this effect were given in Goering's letter to Heydrich of 31 July 1941. The fact that an order had been given by Hitler became known outside Germany only in July 1942 and even then in a distorted form: Hitler (it was then claimed) had ordered that no Jew should be left in Germany by the end of 1942. But there is no evidence that such a time limit had ever been set. It would not have been difficult, for instance, to deport all Jews from Berlin in 1942, but in fact the city was declared empty of Jews by Goebbels only in August 1943. Witnesses claimed to have seen the order, but it is doubtful whether there ever was a written order. This has given rise to endless speculation and inspired a whole 'revisionist' literature – quite needlessly, because Hitler, whatever his other vices, was not a bureaucrat. He was not in the habit of giving written orders on all occasions: there were no written orders for the murderous 'purge' of June 1934, for the killing of gypsies, the so-called euthanasia action (T4) and on other such occasions. The more abominable the crime, the less likely that there would be a written 'Führer order'. If Himmler, Heydrich or even

Eichmann said that there was such an order, no one would question or insist on seeing it.

2. The order had practical consequences, it affected the lives or, to be precise, the deaths of millions of people. For this reason details about the 'final solution' seeped out virtually as soon as the mass slaughter started.

The systematic massacres of the *Einsatzgruppen* in Eastern Galicia, White Russia, the Ukraine and the Baltic countries became known in Germany almost immediately. True, the scene of the slaughter was distant and it took place in territories in which at the time civilians and foreigners were not freely permitted to travel. But many thousands of German officers and soldiers witnessed these scenes and later reported them and the same is true of Italian, Hungarian and Romanian military personnel. The German Foreign Ministry was officially informed about the details of the massacres; there was much less secrecy about the *Einsatzgruppen* than later on about the extermination camps. The Soviet Government must have learned about the massacres within a few days; after several weeks the news became known in Western capitals too, well before the Wannsee Conference. The slaughter at Kiev (Babi Yar) took place on 29–30 September 1941. Foreign journalists knew about it within a few days; within less than two months it had been reported in the Western press. The massacres in Transniestria became known almost immediately. Chelmno, the first extermination camp, was opened on 8 December 1941; the news was received in Warsaw within less than four weeks and published soon afterwards in the underground press. The existence and the function of Belzec and Treblinka were known in Warsaw among Jews and non-Jews within two weeks after the gas chambers had started operating. The news about the suicide of Czerniakow, the head of the Warsaw *Judenrat*, reached the Jewish press abroad within a short time. The deportations from Warsaw were known in London after four days. There were some exceptions: the true character of Auschwitz did not become known among Jews and Poles alike for several months after the camp had been turned into an extermination centre. At the time in Poland it was believed that there were only two types of camps, labour camps and extermination camps, and the fact that Auschwitz was a 'mixed camp' seems to have baffled many.

3. If so much was known so quickly among the Jews of Eastern Europe and if the information was circulated through illegal newspapers and by other means – there were wireless sets in all major ghettos – why was it not believed? In the beginning Russian and Polish Jewry were genuinely unprepared, and the reasons have been stated: Soviet Jews had been kept uninformed about Nazi intentions and practices, Polish Jews believed that the massacres would be limited to the former Soviet territories. At first there was the tendency to interpret these events in the light of the past: persecution and pogroms. The Jewish leaders in Warsaw who learned about events in Lithuania and Latvia in early 1942 should have realized that these were not 'pogroms' in the traditional sense, spontaneous mob actions, nor excesses committed by local commanders. There are few arbitrary actions in a totalitarian regime. The *Einsatzgruppen* acted methodically and in cold blood. The majority of Jewish leaders in Eastern Europe did not yet realize that this was the beginning of a systematic campaign of destruction. The whole scheme was beyond human imagination; they thought the Nazis incapable of the murder of millions. Communication between some of the ghettos was irregular; Lodz ghetto, the second largest, was more or less isolated. But rumours, on the other hand, still travelled fast. If the information about the 'final solution' had been believed it would have reached every corner of Poland within a few days. But it was not believed and when the 'deportations' from Polish ghettos began in March 1942 it was still generally thought that the Jews would be transported to places further East.

The illegal newspapers and other sources conveyed disquieting news, and the possibility that many would perish was mentioned. But the information was contradictory. Most people did not read the underground press and there were no certainties. Perhaps the Nazis did after all need a large part of the Jewish population as a labour force for the war economy; perhaps the war would soon be over; perhaps a miracle of some sort or another would happen. Rumours are rife in desperate situations and so is the belief in miracles.

After July 1942 (the deportations from Warsaw) it is more

and more difficult to understand that there still was widespread confusion about the Nazi designs among Jews in Poland, and that the rumours were not recognized for what they were – certainties. Any rational analysis of the situation would have shown that the Nazi aim was the destruction of all Jews. But the psychological pressures militated against rational analysis and created an atmosphere in which wishful thinking seemed to offer the only antidote to utter despair.

4. Of all the other Jewish communities only the Slovaks seem to have realized at an early date some of the dangers facing them. (So did the Romanians but their position was altogether different.) But even they failed to understand until late 1943 that the Nazis aimed at killing all Jews. The other communities (including German, Dutch, Danish, French, Greek Jews, etc.) seem to have lived in near ignorance almost to the very end. These communities were isolated, the means of information at their disposal limited. But with all this, most Jews in Europe, and many non-Jews, had at the very least heard rumours about some horrible events in Eastern Europe and some had heard more than rumours. These rumours reached them in dozens of different ways. But they were either not believed or it was assumed that 'it cannot happen here'. Only a relatively small minority tried to hide or to escape, aware that deportation meant death. Nazi disinformation contributed to the confusion among the Jews. But the Nazi lies were usually quite threadbare and they cannot be considered the main source of the disorientation.

5. Jewish leaders and the public abroad (Britain, America and Palestine) found it exceedingly difficult in their great majority to accept the ample evidence about the 'final solution' and did so only with considerable delay. They too thought in categories of persecution and pogroms at a time when a clear pattern had already emerged which pointed in a different direction. It was a failure of intelligence and imagination caused on one hand by a misjudgment of the murderous nature of Nazism, and on the other hand by a false optimism. Other factors may have played a certain role: the feeling of impotence ('we can do very little, so let us hope for the best'), the military

dangers facing the Jewish community in Palestine in 1942. If the evidence was played down by many Jewish leaders and the Jewish press, it was not out of the desire to keep the community in a state of ignorance, but because there were genuine doubts. As the worst fears were confirmed, there was confusion among the leaders as to what course of action to choose. This was true especially in the US and caused further delay in making the news public. In Jerusalem the turning point came with the arrival of a group of Palestinian citizens who had been repatriated from Europe in November 1942. The leaders of the Jewish Agency, who had been unwilling to accept the written evidence gathered by experienced observers, were ready to believe the accounts delivered by chance arrivals in face-to-face meetings.

6. The Polish underground played a pivotal role in the transmission of the news to the West. It had a fairly good intelligence-gathering network and also the means to convey the information abroad through short-wave radio and couriers. Most of the information about the Nazi policy of extermination reached Jewish circles abroad through the Polish underground. The Poles had few illusions about the intentions of the Nazis and their reports gave an unvarnished picture of the situation. They have been accused of playing down the Jewish catastrophe in order not to distract world opinion from the suffering of the Polish people, and of having temporarily discontinued the transmission to the West of news about the killing of the Jews. The Polish underground, needless to say, was mainly pre-occupied with the fate of the Polish people, not with that of a minority. But it did not, on the whole, suppress the news about the mass killings in its bulletins and the information transmitted abroad. There was one exception – the period in late July, August and early September 1942 (the deportations from Warsaw), when the London Government-in-exile, either on its own initiative or following the advice of the British Foreign Office, did not immediately publicize the news received from Warsaw. The evidence is conflicting: the information was certainly played down for some time but there was no total blackout. There was delay in London but no more than the delay among the Jewish leaders who also disbelieved the

information when they first received it. It cannot be proved whether or not the London Polish Government-in-exile did show the members of the National Council all the material received. But Zygielbojm and Schwarzbart certainly had access to all essential information. The Polish Government was the first to alarm the Allied governments and world public opinion but it was accused of exaggeration, as were the Jews at a later date. From this time up to the end of the war the number of victims given in the official declarations of the Allied governments was consistently too low. Even after it had been accepted in London and Washington that the information about the mass slaughter was correct, the British and US governments showed much concern that it should not be given too much publicity.

7. Millions of Germans knew by late 1942 that the Jews had disappeared. Rumours about their fate reached Germany mainly through officers and soldiers returning from the eastern front but also through other channels. There were clear indications in the wartime speeches of the Nazi leaders that something more drastic than resettlement had happened. Knowledge about the exact manner in which they had been killed was restricted to a very few. It is, in fact, quite likely that while many Germans thought that the Jews were no longer alive, they did not necessarily believe that they were dead. Such belief, needless to say, is logically inconsistent, but a great many logical inconsistencies are accepted in wartime. Very few people had an interest in the fate of the Jews. Most individuals faced a great many more important problems. It was an unpleasant topic, speculations were unprofitable, discussions of the fate of the Jews were discouraged. Consideration of this question was pushed aside, blotted out for the duration.

8. Neutrals and international organizations such as the Vatican and the Red Cross knew the truth at an early stage. Not perhaps the whole truth, but enough to understand that few, if any, Jews would survive the war. The Vatican had an unrivalled net of informants all over Europe. It tried to intervene on some occasions on behalf of the Jews but had no wish to give publicity to the issue. For this would have exposed it to German attacks on one hand and pressure to do more from

the Jews and the Allies. Jews, after all, were not Catholics. In normal times their persecution would have evoked expressions of genuine regret. But these were not normal times and since the Holy See could do little – or thought it could do little – even for the faithful Poles, it thought it could do even less for the Jews. This fear of the consequences of helping the Jews influenced its whole policy. The position of the International Red Cross was, broadly speaking, similar. It had, of course, fewer sources of information than the Catholic Church and less influence. But it also magnified its own weakness. It was less exposed, in fact, to retaliatory action than it thought, and while its protests might well have been to no avail, it could have made known directly and indirectly the facts it knew. Some of its directors did so.

The neutral governments received much information about the 'final solution' through many channels. There was no censorship in Sweden (except self-censorship) and in 1942 Swiss press censorship did not prevent publication of news about the fate of the Jews. Not all Swiss newspapers showed an equal measure of understanding and compassion, and the Swedish press had instructions not to report 'atrocities', but their readers could have had few doubts about the true state of affairs by late 1942.

9. Neither the United States Government, nor Britain, nor Stalin showed any pronounced interest in the fate of the Jews. They were kept informed through Jewish organizations and through their own channels. From an early date the Soviet press published much general information about Nazi atrocities in the occupied areas but only rarely revealed that Jews were singled out for extermination. To this day the Soviet Communist Party line has not changed in this respect: it has not admitted that any mistakes were made, that the Jewish population was quite unprepared for the *Einsatzgruppen*. It is not conceded even now that if specific warnings had been given by the Soviet media in 1941 (which were informed about events behind the German lines) lives might have been saved. As far as the Soviet publications are concerned the Government and the Communist Party acted correctly – Soviet citizens of Jewish origin did not fare differently from the rest under Nazi rule, and if they did, it is thought inadvisable to mention this. The only

mildly critical voices that have been heard can be found in a few literary works describing the events of 1941–2. Some Western observers have argued that the (infrequent) early Soviet news about anti-Jewish massacres committed were sometimes dismissed as 'Communist propaganda' in the West and that for this reason the Soviet leaders decided no longer to emphasize the specific anti-Jewish character of the extermination campaign.* This explanation is not at all convincing because Soviet policy at home was hardly influenced by the *Catholic Times*, and it should be stressed that domestically even less publicity than abroad was given to the Jewish victims from the very beginning.

In London and Washington the facts about the 'final solution' were known from an early date and reached the chiefs of intelligence, the secretaries of foreign affairs and defence. But the facts were not considered to be of great interest or importance and at least some of the officials either did not believe them, or at least thought them exaggerated. There was no deliberate attempt to stop the flow of information on the mass killings (except for a while on the part of officials in the State Department), but mainly lack of interest and disbelief. This disbelief can be explained against the background of Anglo-American lack of knowledge of European affairs in general and Nazism in particular. Although it was generally accepted that the Nazis behaved in a less gentlemanly way than the German armies in 1914–18, the idea of genocide nevertheless seemed far fetched. Neither the *Luftwaffe* nor the German navy nor the Afrika Korps had committed such acts of atrocities, and these were the only sections of the German armed forces which Allied soldiers encountered prior to 1944. The Gestapo was known from not very credible B-grade movies. Barbaric fanaticism was unacceptable to people thinking on pragmatic lines, who believed that slave labour rather than annihilation was the fate of the Jews in Europe. The evil nature of Nazism was beyond their comprehension.

But even if the realities of the 'final solution' had been accepted in London and Washington the issue would still have

*Thus the (London) *Catholic Times* on 24 December 1942 – Christmas eve: 'It is no secret that the recent wave of propaganda about German atrocities against the Jews was Russian inspired.' But such comments were a fairly rare exception. The Roman Catholic Archbishop of Westminster, Cardinal Hinsley, was one of the first public figures in Britain to broadcast to Europe in July 1942 about the suffering of the Jews.

figured very low on the scale of Allied priorities. 1942 was a critical year in the course of the war, strategists and bureaucrats were not to be deflected in the pursuit of victory by considerations not directly connected with the war effort. Thus too much publicity about the mass murder seemed undesirable, for it was bound to generate demands to help the Jews and this was thought to be detrimental to the war effort.* Even in later years when victory was already assured there was little willingness to help. Churchill showed more interest in the Jewish tragedy than Roosevelt and also more compassion but even he was not willing to devote much thought to the subject. Public opinion in Britain, the United States and elsewhere was kept informed through the press from an early date about the progress of the 'final solution'. But the impact of the news was small or at most shortlived. The fact that millions were killed was more or less meaningless. People could identify perhaps with the fate of a single individual or a family but not with the fate of millions. The statistics of murder were either disbelieved or dismissed from consciousness. Hence the surprise and shock at the end of the war when the reports about a 'transit camp' such as Bergen-Belsen came in: 'No one had known, no one had been prepared for this.'

Thus the news about the murder of many millions of Jews was not accepted for a long time and even when it had been accepted the full implications were not understood. Among Jews this

*The Office of War Information in the United States and the Ministry of Information in Britain were inclined to soft pedal publicity about the mass murder in 1942–3 for a variety of reasons: because the public would not believe it, because it would stir up anti-semitism in the West, because it would not be unpopular in some European countries, because it would have a devastating effect on the morale of the European resistance, etc. It was not the only time that atrocities were played down. Thus, though British authorities were well informed about the fate of the British prisoners after the fall of Singapore, detailed information about Japanese behaviour was not provided at the time for fear that this would have a detrimental effect on morale on the British home front. It remains to be investigated in detail how much information was provided by the BBC and the American radio stations about the 'final solution' for listeners at home and abroad. Such quantitative analysis in conjunction with a survey of the instructions given to the radio programme directors by the PWE and the Department of State will probably show that publicity was given in December 1942 and January 1943 after the United Nations declaration about Nazi atrocities. But there was comparatively little throughout 1943; there may have been weeks, perhaps even months, during which the issue was not mentioned at all. Only in 1944 it became again a fairly frequent topic.

frequently caused a trauma in later years which in extreme cases led to the belief that every danger facing Jews, individually or as a group, had to be interpreted in terms of a new holocaust. Such a distortion of reality is psychologically understandable, which does not make it any less dangerous as a potentially disastrous political guideline. The impact among non-Jews has been small. There have been, after all, many intelligence failures throughout history. Optimists could still argue that one failure should not inspire pessimism and strengthen the argument for worst case analysis. As the long term (1910–50) British diplomat rightly said, his record as an inveterate optimist has been far more impressive than that of the professional Cassandras forever harping on the danger of war. He had been wrong only twice. . . .

It has been said that in wartime there are no 'strategic warnings', no unambiguous signals, no absolute certainties. Not only the signals have to be considered but also the background noise, the interference, the deception. If even Barbarossa and Pearl Harbor came as a surprise, despite the fact that the eyes of the whole world were scanning the horizons for such signals – and despite the fact that there was much evidence and many warnings to this effect – is it not natural that European Jewry was taken unaware?[1] But there was one fundamental difference: Barbarossa and Pearl Harbor were surprise attacks, whereas the 'final solution' proceeded in stages over a long period. Some have claimed in retrospect that *Mein Kampf* and Hitler's speeches should have dispelled any doubts about the Nazis' ultimate murderous intentions. But this is wrong. The 'solution of the Jewish question' could equally have meant ghettoization or expulsion to some far-away place such as Madagascar. It was only after the invasion of the Soviet Union that there was reason to believe that large parts of European Jewry would not survive the war. At first there were only isolated rumours, then the rumours thickened and eventually they became certainties. A moderately well informed Jewish resident of Warsaw should have drawn the correct conclusions by May 1942 and some of them did. But the time and the place were hardly conducive to detached, objective analysis; the disintegration of rational intelligence is one of the recurrent themes of all those who have written about that period on the basis of inside knowledge.

Democratic societies demonstrated on this occasion as on many others, before and after, that they are incapable of understanding political regimes of a different character. Not every modern dictatorship is Hitlerian in character and engages in genocide but every one has the potential to do so. Democratic societies are accustomed to think in liberal, pragmatic categories; conflicts are believed to be based on misunderstandings and can be solved with a minimum of good will; extremism is a temporary aberration, so is irrational behaviour in general, such as intolerance, cruelty, etc. The effort to overcome such basic psychological handicaps is immense. It will be undertaken only in the light of immediate (and painful) experience. Each new generation faces this challenge again for experience cannot be inherited.

The reaction of East European Jewry can only be understood out of their specific situation in 1942. But there are situations which cannot be recreated, however sophisticated the techniques of simulation, however great the capacity for empathy and imagination. Generalizations about human behaviour in the face of disaster are of limited value: each disaster is different. Some of those who lived through the catastrophe have tried in later years to find explanations. But while their accounts are of great interest, they are no longer *a priori* reliable witnesses. Their explanations are rooted in a different situation and this is bound to lead to a rationalization of irrational behaviour. The 'final solution' proceeded in stages, chronologically and geographically. This should have acted as a deterrent, but it did not, on the whole, have this effect. There were no certainties, only rumours, no full picture, only fragments. Was it a case of a 'people without understanding', which had eyes and ears but saw not and heard not? The people saw and heard but what it perceived was not always clear, and when at last the message was unambiguous it left no room for hope and was therefore unacceptable. It is a syndrome observed by biblical prophets and modern political leaders alike, that it is natural for man to indulge in the illusions of hope and to shut his eyes against a painful truth.

But it is not natural for man to submit passively to a horrible fate, not to try to escape, however great the odds against success, not to resist, even if there is no prospect of victory. True, there are explanations even for paralysis, but later generations can no longer accept them – hence the abiding mystery. Total hopelessness (the psychologists say) results in inaction; when there is no exit, such as in a mine or a submarine disaster, this leads to resignation.

The reaction of Dutch or Hungarian Jews can be compared to that of people facing a flood and who in contradiction of all experience believe that they will not be affected but are individually or as a group invulnerable. Some social psychologists will argue that such a denial of a threat betrays a fear of not being able to cope with it. But if such an explanation was true for some it certainly did not apply to others. They genuinely did not know what was in store for them. Danish Jews were perfectly able to escape to Sweden and if they did so only at the very last moment the reason was that they genuinely believed that they would not be deported. Equally, to give another example, the Jews living in Rhodes could have fled without difficulty to Turkey and would have done so had they known their fate in Auschwitz. But they did not know. Other Jewish communities were indeed trapped but their situation was still not identical with that of the victims of a mine disaster. Comparisons are only of limited help for understanding human behaviour in unique situations. In many cases the inactivity of Jews, individuals and groups, was not the result of paralysis but on the contrary of unwarranted optimism. As Isaac Schneersohn observed with regard to France: 'Les juifs étaient alors divisés en deux catégories: les pessimistes et les optimistes. Les premières cherchèrent à gagner les Etats Unis, la Suisse ou se camouflèrent comme ils purent. Les seconds, caressant de chimériques espoirs, devinrent par la suite les principaux candidats aux voyages à Auschwitz et Treblinka.'*

One of the questions initially asked was whether it would have made any difference if the information about the mass murder had been believed right from the beginning. It seems quite likely that relatively few people might have been saved as a result and even this is not absolutely certain. But this is hardly the right

*Monde Juif, 1963, 18. 'The Jews were thus divided into two categories: the pessimists and the optimists. The first tried to reach the United States or Switzerland or to hide themselves as best they could. The second, cherishing fanciful hopes, thus became the principal candidates for the journey to Auschwitz and Treblinka.'

way of posing the question, for the misjudgment of Hitler and Nazism did not begin in June 1941 nor did it end in December 1942. The ideal time to stop Hitler was not when he was at the height of his strength. If the democracies had shown greater foresight, solidarity and resolution, Nazism could have been stopped at the beginning of its campaign of aggression. No power could have saved the majority of the Jews of the Reich and of Eastern Europe in the summer of 1942. Some more would have tried to escape their fate if the information had been made widely known. Some could have been saved if Hitler's satellites had been threatened and if the peoples of Europe had been called to extend help to the Jews. After the winter of 1942 the situation rapidly changed: the satellite leaders and even some of the German officials were no longer eager to be accessories to mass murder. Some, at least, would have responded to Allied pressure, but such pressure was never exerted. Many Jews could certainly have been saved in 1944 by bombing the railway lines leading to the extermination centres, and of course, the centres themselves. This could have been done without deflecting any major resources from the general war effort. It has been argued that the Jews could not have escaped in any case but this is not correct: the Russians were no longer far away, the German forces in Poland were concentrated in some of the bigger towns, and even there their sway ran only in daytime – they no longer had the manpower to round up escaped Jews. In short, hundreds of thousands could have been saved. But this discussion belongs to a later period. The failure to read correctly the signs in 1941–2 was only one link in a chain of failures. There was not one reason for this overall failure but many different ones: paralyzing fear on one hand and, on the contrary, reckless optimism on the other; disbelief stemming from a lack of experience or imagination or genuine ignorance or a mixture of some or all of these things. In some cases the motives were creditable, in others damnable. In some instances moral categories are simply not applicable, and there were also cases which defy understanding to this day.

APPENDICES

APPENDIX 1. THE *ABWEHR* CONNECTION

Was information about the 'final solution' passed on by German military intelligence to Allied and Jewish circles during the war? Certain claims have been made that there were such signals but memories are fallible and many relevant *Abwehr* (military intelligence) records have been destroyed or are not in the West and are therefore inaccessible.

If Canaris was at all interested in the fate of the Jews, about which he was, of course, kept informed and informed others, he did not do much to help them. The case of the second-ranking man in the organization, Hans Oster, was different. Born in 1888, the son of a Protestant churchman, he fought in the First World War and later joined the *Reichswehr*. A staunch conservative, he was an early opponent of Hitler whom he regarded as the 'destroyer of Germany'. The war was 'madness'; on several occasions he passed on to the Allies warnings of impending Nazi attacks. He was head of Department 2 of the *Abwehr* which dealt with finance and administrative questions and kept the central list of agents. Together with a younger friend, von Dohnanyi (who also hailed from a leading Protestant family – Bonhoeffer was his cousin), Oster made it his business to deal with all kinds of operations unconnected with their immediate tasks. Hans von Dohnanyi, it should be noted in passing, was partly of Jewish descent. He was 'Aryanized' according to a special order issued by Hitler but while he could serve in key positions in various ministries and eventually in the *Abwehr* he was not permitted to join the Nazi Party.[1]

Oster's department should not have employed outside agents, but in fact it did and helped get individual Jews out of Germany (to Switzerland) and out of Holland (to Spain) during the war.*

*This refers to what became known as operation U7, the private rescue operation undertaken by Admiral Canaris to get two of his personal friends, Conzen and Rennefeld, out of Berlin to Switzerland together with their families. These seven non-Aryan Protestants (they were Jews only according to the Nuremberg laws) were joined by eight others who had been recommended by Protestant churchmen. It is not known

They were hired ostensibly to spy for the *Abwehr* in some minor capacity, but were told privately that they were not expected to engage in intelligence activities. One of the 'front organizations' founded under the protection of Oster by Colonel Marogna-Redwitz (another conservative opponent of Hitler) was a business enterprise called *Monopol* in Prague. Its main task was apparently to transfer money from frozen bank accounts in neutral countries to Germany in order to finance *Abwehr* activities. Several Jews were employed in this firm; they had served as officers in the German or Austrian army during the First World War and their erstwhile comrades tried to help them. According to the son of one of the employees of *Monopol*, Alfred Ziehrer, his father who was based in Prague used to visit Istanbul about once every three months – the last time apparently in 1943. Another Czech Jew, Dr Reimann, who joined him on his mission, did not return to Germany; Ziehrer did and met his death in Auschwitz. According to the son's evidence, his assignment was to transmit information to the British 'among other things about the fate of the Jews'.[2] Ziehrer, according to the son, was perfectly aware of the 'final solution'. Oster and von Dohnanyi were arrested in 1944 and executed in connection with their participation in the plot against Hitler. The fact that Oster did extend help to Jews and that he warned the Allies has been established beyond reasonable doubt. The discovery (by the SS) that Oster and von Dohnanyi had not only helped to smuggle Jews abroad but had also sent them money caused Oster's dismissal from the *Abwehr* in 1943. There is good reason to believe that these curious hostages of fate did meet Jewish emissaries in Istanbul. It cannot be demonstrated at present whether they did pass on credible information on the fate of the Jews and whether their stories were believed. Historians, for one reason or another, have not yet dealt with this episode and the survivors have not been eager to talk.

Even a *bona fide* German abroad trying to sound the alarm was bound to encounter at least some distrust and not without reason; for whose *bona fide* was certain? Again one illustration

---

whether members of this group passed on information about the fate of the Jews in Nazi-occupied Europe though it can be taken for granted that they did talk to the World Council of Churches in Geneva. An *Abwehr* officer in Holland also helped to save a few Jews by sending them as 'agents' to Switzerland.

will have to suffice: Ernst Lemmer had been one of the founder members of the liberal German Democratic Party in 1918 and represented it in the *Reichstag* from 1924–33. During the Hitler era he worked for foreign newspapers in Berlin. There is no reason to believe that deep down in his heart Lemmer ever accepted the Nazi ideology. But he certainly served his Nazi masters to the best of his abilities. As a former democrat he was eminently suited to stress in his many articles for publication abroad the moderate character and the positive achievements of Nazism. (Lemmer worked for the German-language Hungarian daily *Pester Lloyd* and the Brussels *Le Soir* after the occupation of Belgium, as well as temporarily for some Swiss newspapers.) His writings of these years make embarrassing reading and the East Germans were not slow to publish selections in the 1960s.[3] They have not so far published the articles of the great Richard Sorge, who represented Soviet intelligence in Japan under the cover of a German journalist.

Lemmer certainly played a double game. On one hand he would glorify German victories in Russia, on the other hand I have it on the authority of a travelling companion that during a tour conducted by the Ministry of Propaganda to the eastern front in late 1941, at an advanced hour and in a state of some drunkenness he would sit down at the piano and play the *Internationale* to the consternation of the Nazi dignitaries who were present. What matters in the present context is the fact that Lemmer was one of the first to convey information about the 'final solution' to journalists and political acquaintances abroad. He regularly spent his summer holiday in Switzerland during the war. In July 1942 he met several Swiss public figures in Zürich and told them about gas chambers, stationary and mobile, in which the Jews were killed. Lemmer repeatedly stressed that he found it incomprehensible that the Allies kept silent and that no attempt was made to alarm world public opinion. One of those whom Lemmer met that summer summarized his impressions many years later for my benefit as follows:

He doubtless had the intention to inform me, but he was also probably guided by other motives. There was an overall strategy behind these approaches: to provoke the Allies to become more strongly committed on behalf of the Jews, despite the fact that they were powerless to do anything about it. German propaganda would have exploited this to the maximum: British and American soldiers were fighting and dying to save the Jews! The Nazis had always believed that if only they used the Jewish question as a bone of contention, they would be able to undermine the fighting spirit of British and American soldiers. Some German circles wanted to keep the 'final solution' secret, others, on the contrary, were interested for a number of devious reasons to inform the Allies.

Whether this interpretation is correct or not, it is certainly understandable that in 1942 Lemmer was received in Switzerland with suspicion. As to his real motives there can only be speculation. Perhaps he acted without ulterior motives, perhaps he knew that he was 'used' but assumed that the calculation of those using him was wrong, and that it was essential to bring the 'final solution' to the notice of neutrals and Allies alike – whatever the consequences.

After the war Lemmer re-entered German politics and served as a minister in the Bonn Government, with short interruptions, from 1956 to 1965. He died in 1970. In his autobiography there is no reference to his warnings concerning the 'final solution' nor to his activities on behalf of the *Pester Lloyd*. He does say, however, that it was Nazi policy in the media to sow distrust and dissension among the Allies; Hitler's enemies behaved in the same way. But Lemmer does not think that neutral correspondents and those from satellite countries were taken in by such manipulations.[4]

Among the wartime visitors to Switzerland who were sponsored by the *Abwehr*, Dietrich Bonhoeffer and Adam Trott zu Soltz ought to be mentioned. Bonhoeffer was in touch with the World Council of Churches in Geneva (Visser't Hooft) and Trott had excellent contacts with various British and American diplomats. Bonhoeffer visited Switzerland twice in 1941 and again in 1942; among the information passed on were details about the persecution of the Jews. But it is doubtful whether they told the British and the Americans much they did not know already, and even the World Council of Churches was kept well informed by its Swedish co-director (Nils Ehrenström who could travel more or less freely in Germany), and by Hanns Schoenfeld, the German representative on the Council who had contacts with the German resistance, as had the German consul in Geneva, Albrecht von Kessel. If even top secret information could frequently be obtained in Switzerland it is not surprising that so much was known about a far less sensitive subject such as the fate of the Jews.

Lastly the case of Artur Sommer, scholar and spy, strange but in many ways not untypical in the troubled Germany of the 1930s. A large man with a powerful physique and a booming voice, Sommer (1889–1965) had served with distinction in the First World War. In the 1920s he began to study economics and was fascinated by the teachings of Friedrich List, one of the few original thinkers in this field in nineteenth-century Germany. List was largely ignored during his lifetime, but there was a List renaissance several decades after his death. Sommer became a leading figure in the List society, discovered some important List manuscripts in French archives and worked closely with Edgar Salin (1892–1974). Salin, who came from a Frankfurt Jewish family, had taught first in Heidelberg and in 1927 was appointed to a chair in Basel. They became close friends. One of the links in their friendship was their admiration for the poetry of Stefan George; they were members of the outer fringe of the George circle.

Sommer lived for years outside Germany, first in Switzerland, later in England. He joined the Nazi Party for reasons which are not entirely clear in 1932 while continuing his studies in London. It should be recalled that other younger members of the George circle were also initially very much attracted by Hitler – the most famous case is that of Colonel Stauffenberg who tried to kill Hitler in 1944. When, after his return to Germany, Sommer became more familiar with the rowdy character of the stormtroopers he was greatly shocked and said that much in a letter to a friend abroad, which, to his misfortune, was intercepted by the censor. Sommer was arrested and spent some months in a concentration camp. He did not suffer too much but with this blot on his curriculum an academic career was no longer possible. Sommer decided to rejoin the army, rapidly rose to lieutenant-colonel and became one of the liaison officers between the general staff and the *Abwehr*. In view of his economic expertise he was also appointed a member of the German delegation to review periodically trade relations with Switzerland. Beginning September 1940 this took him frequently to Switzerland and he re-established contact with his old friend and mentor, Salin.[5]

Salin reports that his friend told him in February 1941 about the growing strains in German-Soviet relations and later about the impending attack against Russia. Swiss political police seems to have been well informed about the identity of Salin's visitor and came to interrogate him. In September or October 1941 Sommer sent Salin pictures showing Nazi atrocities in Eastern Europe with the request to pass these on to the papal nuncio in Bern, which Salin did – without any success, however. In 1942 Salin found in his post box a letter to the effect that extermination camps were prepared in Eastern Europe to kill by poison gas all European Jews and also most Soviet prisoners of war. Sommer requested that this information should be directly transmitted to Churchill and Roosevelt and also suggested that the BBC should transmit daily warnings.

Salin relates that he did not know how to reach Churchill, but he got in touch with Thomas McKittrick, the American president of the Bank for International Settlement in Basel, who knew Leland Harrison, the American minister in Bern who in turn was in a position to convey messages directly to the White House. The information was allegedly passed on to Washington but again there was no response, and to quote Salin 'when the Allied troops uncovered some of the camps in 1945 it was pretended that no one had any inkling. . . .'

Sommer also tried to help to get a few Jewish acquaintances out of Germany in the middle of the war; among them was a relative of Ernst Kantorowicz, the well-known medievalist and also a member of the George circle. After the war Sommer resumed his academic career and this time with more success. He was offered a position at Heidelberg, his lectures were well attended, he was known as an excellent teacher and was requested to continue as a guest lecturer even after having reached retiring age. He died in 1965.

APPENDIX 2. PRESS COMMENTS ON THE HOLOCAUST IN NAZI-OCCUPIED EUROPE

How much was known in London and Geneva, in Washington and Stockholm, about the fate of European Jewry on the basis of newspaper reports? Details about the technique of extermination were not published in 1942–3 and there was relatively little about deportations in the German press inside the Reich, in France, Belgium and Holland.* Some of the truth would nevertheless emerge on occasion. Thus the German Official Gazette, the *Reichsanzeiger* announced on 12 April 1943 that Mr Kurt Teichmann of Beuthen, Bismarckstrasse 33, was divorcing his wife Ruth Sara Teichmann because she had been evacuated in June 1942 'and that she is not expected ever to return'. ('By order of the local court'.)

Some information came from neutral correspondents in Germany who, incidentally, did not have to submit their cables to the censor. They knew, of course, that they would be expelled if their coverage were hostile or if they dealt with 'sensitive topics'. But there was also a steady stream of information from newspapers published in the occupied countries. Many of these were available in Stockholm, Zürich or Lisbon; others – this refers mainly to small regional papers – should not have been sent abroad, but were received anyway and were read by the Allies and the Allied Governments-in-exile.

Slovak Jewry was the first to be deported to Poland in spring 1942; this was known almost immediately to the Swedish correspondents in Berlin, who noted that the Germans would continue to deport the Jews despite the fact that they badly needed the locomotives and rolling stock for the coming spring offensive.[6] From late March 1942 hardly a day passed without some news about the deportation in the German-language *Grenzbote* and the Slovak *Gardista*, both published in Bratislava. On 2 April 1942, *Gardista* said that foreign intervention on behalf of the Jews would be quite useless, and it engaged for a long time in polemics against certain circles wanting to protect the Jews 'by using false Christian arguments'. From these exchanges it appeared that both sides had a fairly accurate idea of the fate of the Jews in Poland. Thus *Evanjelicky Posol* (Bratislava) had written that what was done to the Jews was not in conformance with the principles of humanity let alone Christianity. The Catholic church papers (*Katolicke Noviny* and

---

*German editors received instructions in February 1942 not to report on the 'Jewish question' in Eastern Europe, not even to reprint official communiqués from newspapers published in the occupied territories (*Zeitschriftendienst*, 27 February 1942).

others) were ambiguous; sometimes they would argue that the Jews were, after all, human beings, at other times the impression would be created that the church was not in principle against deportation, provided that those who had been converted were not affected.[7] *Gardista* and other Slovak papers provided accurate figures fairly regularly about the number of Jews deported.

Another important source for the fate of Jews in south-east Europe was the *Donauzeitung* published in Belgrade which covered Hungary, Romania, Yugoslavia and Bulgaria. Readers of the *Donauzeitung*, accustomed to reading between the lines, would know what had happened to the Jews. Thus, on one occasion, commenting on a report that the Yugoslav Government-in-exile in London had revoked all pre-1941 anti-Jewish laws, *Donauzeitung* announced that certain *faits accomplis* had been created which no one could undo. The German-language paper in Prague (*Neue Tag*), as well as the Czech papers (such as *Ceske Slovo*), also contained frequent and detailed information about the disappearance of the Jews. In West European newspapers such information was much rarer but it could also be found. Thus, a Dutch newspaper announced that the deportation was proceeding so quickly that not a single Jew would be left in Holland by June 1943.[8] Among the German-language papers in Eastern Europe *Deutsche Zeitung in Ostland* (Riga) was the most informative both with regard to its denials and its information regarding the liquidation of certain ghettos.

In some of Germany's client states there were open or hardly-veiled discussions about Germany's Jewish policy. The Finns showed their disagreement in many ways. Thus the Finnish radio would announce that according to a report from Berlin (*sic*) Cardinal Hinsley had made a speech in London stating that 700,000 Jews had been executed. The Pope, according to this account, believed that this was a correct report, whereas the Germans emphatically denied it. But the Germans had not reported the Hinsley speech in the first place and had certainly not added that the Pope had endorsed it. There was open criticism of the Nazi treatment of the Jews not only by Finnish Social Democrats such as Fagerholm but even by pro-Germans such as Professor Eino Kalla, a philosopher, who wrote that the Nazis could not claim that they were defending European civilization if they committed actions which violated the very foundations of this assertion.[9]

A few more examples from a short period November–December 1942 show the extent of knowledge that could be gained from reading the press. A small Swedish paper, *Vestmansland Tidningen*, reported on 27 November 1942 that the whole General Government would be free of Jews by the end of the month. *Dagens Nyheter* on 21 December carried the impression of a Swedish businessman, who had been to Warsaw and Bialystok, according to whom the Jewish population had been decimated. *Volk en Vaderland* (Rotterdam) announced on 13 November 1942 that anti-Jewish demonstrations would soon no longer be possible because there would be no Jews. *Gardista* of Bratislava reported on 22 November that there had been a high level meeting in Slovakia on the 'final solution'; on 6 December the same paper announced that a local priest had been arrested who had forged certificates in order to save Jews. *Transocean* announced on 7 January 1943 that 77 per cent of all Slovak Jews had been deported. *Leipziger Nachrichten* of 14 November 1942 wrote that of the 60,000 Jews who had once lived in Cernauti, only 12,000 remained; the *Abend* (Prague) carried a news item according to which no Jews were left in the town of Nachod. Czech-language papers had similar reports about other cities. *Donauzeitung* (Belgrade, 10 December 1942) reported that in the Romanian city of Bacau the Jewish school had been closed and taken over by the authorities; *Kauener Zeitung* (Kovno, 16 December) said that all the former Jewish property in Lithuania was to be registered.

The pattern that emerges is unmistakable – the disappearance of the Jews.* True, there was also a certain amount of disinformation: the officially sponsored visit to Auschwitz by Fritz Fiala, a Nazi correspondent, is mentioned elsewhere in the present study (see pages 152–3). But there was misleading information also in quasi-scholarly journals. Thus *Ostland*, a periodical which came out twice monthly, featured in its issues of 15 November and 1 December 1942 articles on the

---

*Reference is made only to newspapers and periodicals which actually reached the Allies and were quoted in the daily *News Digest* of the Ministry of Information in London. This publication was made available to editors and commentators on foreign affairs: it included material not to be attributed to its source.

'conclusion of the resettlement of the Jews' which contained many figures, all of them quite wrong. According to the article which appeared on 15 November there were 480,000 Jews in the Warsaw ghetto, but in fact almost 90 per cent of them had been killed in the previous four months. The figure given for Warsaw and Lublin districts (800,000) was equally untrue. On 1 December there was a full list of fifty-five 'Jewish dwelling places', complete with the present number of inhabitants, most of which no longer existed. Was it a genuine mistake? This is hardly likely, for *Ostland* had on previous occasions commented on the 'extermination' and 'removal' of the Polish Jews and even of the 'extirpation of the Jewish ulcer' (1 August 1942). Readers of the German daily press were treated to explicit statements like: 'We have largely broken and destroyed the racial core of the Jewish power of darkness. For generations to come no stream of parasites will pour forth from the Jewish quarters of the East into Western Europe.'[10] Such a statement was open to only one interpretation.

When the joint declaration of the Allies on the murder of the Jews was published in December 1942, the German press following Goebbels' directives immediately counterattacked without, however, denying in any way the substance of the charges. *Transocean* (17 December) said that the Allied governments depended on the political wishes of Jewry to an exceptionally large extent and that there had been demonstrations against the Allies in Persia. The diplomatic correspondent of DNB, the official news agency, maintained that Eden's declaration was nothing but a bit of typical British-Jewish atrocity propaganda: 'People who could spare no word of pity and condemnation when in September 1939 over 60,000 Germans in Poland were slaughtered in the cruellest fashion – men, women and children – have no right to speak about humanity, for they are obviously strangers to it.' The European people knew that the declaration was a tendentious manoeuvre (18 December).

Only a few months later the German press reported that the Warsaw ghetto had been destroyed. *Donauzeitung* of 23 March 1943 announced that the 'dissolution' of the Jewish quarter in Warsaw had made 'extraordinary measures necessary in order to make the streets and houses again habitable, for their state defied all description'. Meanwhile the Scandinavian press reported the destruction of the ghettos of Riga and Minsk and the fact that they were disinfected to absorb 150,000 Germans evacuated from Germany. In Lwow, according to these sources, 7,000 Jews out of 160,000 had remained, the rest had been killed.[11] All of which tends to show that the basic facts about the destruction of European Jewry were reported by the press well before the end of the war.

APPENDIX 3. THE BRITISH FOREIGN OFFICE AND THE NEWS FROM POLAND: JULY–DECEMBER 1942

In August 1942 Dr Riegner's cable from Geneva was received in London reporting that Hitler had given the order to kill all European Jews. Foreign Office comment was sceptical. It was not doubted that Jews were brutally treated but the information on mass murder was on the whole disbelieved. The scepticism was particularly pronounced in the comments on the *Agudat Israel* cable (received in London on 11 September 1942) according to which soap and artificial fertilizers were produced from bodies.* The Foreign Office said that this information should be 'treated with the greatest reserve'; it reminded the officials of horror stories about the last war. But the comparisons with 1914 were not at all helpful for whereas the Belgian babies had not been bayonetted, the Jews had still been killed even though their corpses, as it later emerged, were not used for the German war effort. D. Allen said this much: 'As regards the mass murders we have no precise evidence although it seems likely that they have taken place on a large scale.'[12]

Foreign Office doubts concerning the news about the 'final solution' had by no means vanished when it was asked in September 1942 to provide information for a reply to a question which had been asked in Parliament by a Liberal member, G. Mander: had the Secretary of State any statement to make with reference to the employment by the German Government

---

*The Foreign Office received this dispatch on 11 September from Lord Halifax in Washington, who had obtained a copy from the Polish ambassador.

of gas to murder a large number of Jews in Poland in mobile gas chambers; and if steps would be taken to interview the three men forced to act as gravediggers who had escaped – with a view of collecting evidence against the perpetrators of this outrage?

This referred to the three Jews who had escaped from Chelmno in early January 1942. The three gravediggers saw a rabbi in a small nearby town and told him what they had been forced to do; they then made their way to Warsaw where the Ringelblum group (*Oneg Shabbat*) debriefed them. A detailed account of Chelmno was passed on to both the Jewish illegal press in Warsaw and the Polish underground. The information was brought to the West by courier. It was received in London some time in June and published in American newspapers in late July. The story also appeared in a small London local newspaper, the *City and East London Observer*, from which Mander or one of his friends had picked it up.

Following this D. Allen asked F. Savery of the British Embassy to Poland (i.e. the Polish Government-in-exile) to find out whether there was any truth in this story. Savery had lived in Poland for almost twenty years. He had been consul general in Warsaw, he was well known in Polish and Jewish circles, and his Polish was excellent. Savery reported back very quickly. He had discussed this with the Polish Ministry of Information. The story had been included in one of the periodical reports which the Polish Ministry of the Interior had received from its agents inside Poland. According to Savery the Polish official with whom he had talked had been 'frankly sceptical of the truth of the story although he had no real means of checking its authenticity'. In spite of his doubts which, according to Savery, may not have been shared by other members of the Polish Government, the story was released to the Polish Social Information Bureau, an unofficial organization largely run by Polish Socialists. Savery thought that the release was probably 'attributable to the pressure of Jewish interest in the Polish National Council'. As for the three gravediggers, Savery had ascertained that they were still in Poland and there was therefore no question of getting in touch with them.

The Poles had also told Savery that any reply in the House of Commons involved risks. The Polish Government's channel with Poland might be endangered; doubts might be cast on the veracity of the Polish Government's sources of information. Lastly 'undue publicity in the House might involve further suffering for the Poles, in particular for the three gravediggers and would only lead the Germans to be even more ruthless in order to ensure that on future occasions there should be no such survivors to tell the tale.' Some of the arguments were so illogical that it must be asked whether they were not misquoted in transmission: how could 'undue publicity' possibly harm the three gravediggers? They were on the run, and, on the other hand, the story had already been published in the press. If they had succeeded in escaping, it was not because the Germans had somehow facilitated their flight.

Savery then consulted Sir Cecil Dormer, the British ambassador to the Polish Government-in-exile, and they both decided that the best possible course would be to ask Mr Mander to withdraw his question on 'humanitarian grounds'. Otherwise the Government would have to give a 'very guarded reply': It had no means of confirming it.[13]

The reaction of the British Government raises a number of question marks. Nine months had passed since the escape of the three gravediggers. There had been many other reports from Polish and Jewish sources about mass extermination in all parts of Poland. The information about the use of poison gas had figured not only in clandestine reports from Poland and Russia, but also in the press. If some Polish officials had doubts about this, others, including the Prime Minister, did not. In fact, the reasons adduced in favour of persuading Mander to withdraw his story imply that the account was basically true: the gravediggers had escaped, many Jews had been killed and if there were any doubts they concerned the manner in which they had been murdered. There was, probably for psychological reasons, particularly strong resistance against accepting that people were killed by gas, a form of murder thought more reprehensible (and therefore more unlikely) than any other.

It took three more months to disperse Savery's doubts. On 3 December 1942 he sent Frank Roberts of the Central Department of the Foreign Office translations of reports just received by Mikolajczyk, the Minister of the Interior. This included very detailed descriptions of the liquidation of the

Warsaw ghetto, the report of a Polish policeman inside the ghetto, a report on the extermination camp at Belzec (based obviously on Karski's story, on which more below) as well as the protest against the mass murder of a group in Poland called *Front Odrozdenia Polski* (Front for the Regeneration of Poland).* Savery drew the attention of the Foreign Office to one sentence in the protest of the 'Front', concerning the 'stubborn silence of international Jewry' and the efforts of German propaganda to put the odium for the massacre on Lithuanians and even on Poles in which they discerned the 'outlines of an action hostile towards us'. This sentence did not appear in the *Polish Fortnightly* of 1 December 1942 but it was included in the official translation of the *Sprawozdanie* circulated as a manuscript among London editors and Members of Parliament. Savery added that he was impressed by the very sober (*sachlich*) tenor of the report: 'I feel we may accept pretty well everything which is said in the report about the happenings in Warsaw and the neighbouring towns.' But he was still uncertain exactly how to regard the three camps of Treblinka, Belzec and Sobibor (Chelmno and Auschwitz were not mentioned in the reports): 'On the whole, I think it is most likely that at least nine-tenths of the Jews sent away from Warsaw had met their deaths in those camps.' But he was not satisfied with the evidence about Belzec. He wrote that he did not put any cruelty beyond the Germans in Central Europe, and especially in Poland and towards the Jews but the evidence as evidence did not seem quite convincing.† D. Allen, another of those who had not been convinced about events in Poland, now commented on Savery's note: 'A horrible and impressive document'.[14]

Great publicity was given to these reports in the British press and the items were broadcast by the BBC in all languages. The weekly directive for the BBC Polish services 17–23 December stated that 'it is particularly important, however, to continue telling the Poles that we know about the suffering of the Jews. We do not necessarily need to inform them of details of these

---

*All these documents were published by the Polish Government-in-exile within a few days in both Polish and English. (*Polish Fortnightly*, 1 December 1942.)

†Savery was right on this point. The account on Belzec mentioned execution by electricity but not by means of poison gas.

sufferings. What we wish to impress on them is our knowledge.'*

Then the Polish department of the Political Warfare Executive suggested that Savery should broadcast in Polish about the German treatment of the Jews which he did on 17 December 1942 after checking with the Foreign Office, the censor and various other bodies. He had to make a number of changes. All figures had to become more vague. Not six thousand Jews were deported daily from Warsaw but 'several thousands'. Not 350,000 Jews (as he originally wrote) had disappeared from Warsaw but 'hundreds of thousands'. In the end Savery got somewhat annoyed and wrote to Frank Roberts:

After reading and re-reading it several times I do not see anything which the Germans could get hold of and use to start a polemic. My own impression is that the Germans themselves probably have no very accurate statistics of the deportations from Warsaw and the massacres of the last few months. I doubt whether they know for certain whom they have killed and whom they have left alive.

Savery was right, the Germans did not know, nor were they interested in polemics.[15]

APPENDIX 4. THE DEPARTMENT OF STATE AND THE UNITED NATIONS DECLARATION OF 17 DECEMBER 1942

Randolph Paul (who was the signatory), John Pehle and Josiah E. du Bois Jr, officials of the Department of the Treasury, were involved in the preparation in January 1944 of a memorandum 'On the Acquiescence of This Government of the Murder of the Jews'. It read, *inter alia*,

They [State Department officials] have not only failed to facilitate the obtaining of information concerning Hitler's plans to exterminate the

---

*These directives were issued by the Political Warfare Executive. The directives given during the previous weeks were in the same vein: 'The news about the conditions of Polish Jewry continues to grow worse . . . while there is no necessity to tell the Poles what they know already we should certainly show them that we know it as well. A careful scrutiny of the British press and radio on this point is advised.' (3–9 December 1942.) 'We should continue to seize hold of every opportunity of publicizing expression of British anger. Any declaration made by Great Britain and allied countries condemning this persecution will be based mainly on evidence produced by the Polish Government.' (10–16 December 1942.)

Jews of Europe but in their official capacity have gone so far as to surreptitiously attempt to stop the obtaining of information concerning the murder of the Jewish population of Europe.

Was this a fair statement of the facts? Wise had first written to Sumner Welles, Undersecretary of State, on 3 September 1942 concerning the Riegner cable; he received a first (telephonic) reply on 9 September. But even before, on 27 August, together with the leaders of the other major American Jewish organizations, Wise had written to Welles about the deportations from France. In this letter it was said that 'in accordance with the announced policy of the Nazis to exterminate the Jews of Europe, hundreds of thousands of these innocent men, women and children have been killed in brutal mass murders'.

Ray Atherton of the European Division of the Department of State suggested to Welles that in his reply to Wise he could safely state that it had never been confirmed that the deported Jews were actually 'exterminated'; 'rather it is our understanding that they are to be put to labor on behalf of the German machine as is the case with Polish, Soviet and other prisoners of war who are now working for their daily sustenance.'[16] It is impossible to say on what factual basis this information was provided. There was nothing in the dispatches from Europe reaching the State Department or in the newspapers from neutral countries which could have induced the belief that the Jews would work for the German war effort. It is possible that in August and early September 1942 Mr Atherton was not very well informed. It is more difficult to explain similar attitudes three months later after much additional information had been received and when preparations were made for the United Nations Declaration of 17 December 1942.

The initiative for the UN declaration condemning the 'bestial policy of cold-blooded extermination' came from the British Government which had been for some time under pressure from the Jewish community, the Polish Government-in-exile, some organs of the press, church dignitaries and others. On 7 December the diplomatic correspondent of the London *Times* reported that the American and Soviet ambassadors had met Mr Eden to discuss the fearful plight of the Jews throughout Europe and that Count Raczynski had laid before Eden some of the evidence out of Poland. He also reported that each occupied country had been given a date by Hitler by which it must have cleared out its Jewish people. It was only now that the German plans, long laid and carefully prepared, could be seen in practice for what they were. The Polish Government had urged the necessity not only of condemning the crimes and punishing the criminals but also of finding means offering the hope that Germany might be effectively restrained from continuing to apply her methods of mass extermination. Having seen this note, Churchill asked the Foreign Office for further information.[17] Ivan Maisky, the Soviet Ambassador in London, had expressed interest in a common declaration even earlier, on 2 December.

The main opposition came from the United States. This refers not to John Winant, US Ambassador in London, who on several occasions had intervened on behalf of the Jews with the British Government. In a cable on 7 December, Winant said that he supported a common declaration. On the next day he transmitted without comment a note on his meeting with Eden:

We discussed whether any steps could usefully be taken by the United Nations to make clear their condemnation of these horrors and possibly to exercise a deterrent effect on their perpetrators. We agreed that although little practical effect could be expected, it might be useful for the United States and the Soviet Government to join with His Majesty's Government in condemning these atrocities and in reminding their perpetrators that certain retribution awaits them.

The main opponent of giving undue publicity to the plight of the Jews was R. B. Reams, who was in charge of Jewish affairs in the European Division of the State Department. He had 'grave doubts in regard to the desirability or advisability of issuing a statement of this nature,' as he stated in a memorandum addressed to Hickerson and Atherton, his superiors.

In the first place these reports are unconfirmed and emanate to a great extent from the Riegner letter to Rabbi Wise. . . . While the statement does not mention the soap, glue, oil and fertilizer factories it will be taken as additional confirmation of these stories and will support Rabbi Wise's contention of official confirmation from State Department sources. The way will then be open for further pressure from interested groups for action which might affect the war effort. The plight of the unhappy peoples of Europe including the Jews can be alleviated only by winning the war. A statement of this kind can have no good effect and may in fact induce even harsher measures towards the population of Europe.[18]

On the next day in a meeting with Sir William Hayter, subsequently British Ambassador to Moscow and Principal of New College, Oxford, he complained that the statement proposed by the British Government was 'extremely strong and definite'. Its issuance would be accepted by the Jewish communities of the world as complete proof of the stories which were now being spread about.

These people would undoubtedly be pleased that the Governments of the United Nations were taking an active interest in the fate of their fellows in Europe but in fact their fears would be increased by such a statement. In addition the various Governments of the UN would expose themselves to increased pressure from all sides to do something more specific to help these people.[19]

Reams then said ('Speaking personally' and 'for Mr Hayter's private information') that he (Reams) believed that Riegner's cable to Wise was responsible for most of the present anxiety with regard to the situation. In other words, there would have been no trouble if the British had helped to suppress the Riegner cable. Reams tried to postpone as long as possible the confirmation of the 'stories'. Thus in an answer to Congressman Hamilton Fish in December 1942,

I replied that this whole matter was now under consideration and that it was difficult for me to give him any exact information. These reports to the best of my knowledge were as yet unconfirmed.[20]

This was the general line taken by the middle echelons in the State Department at the time. Thus Reams told an official of the Latin American Department, commenting on protests from Mexico on 15 December, that the information about the mass murder of the Jews was unconfirmed. A cable went out to San José, Costa Rica, two days after the United Nations declaration again claiming that 'there had been no confirmation of the reported order from other sources (except from a Jewish leader in Geneva)'. Answering a query by the *Christian Century* whether the Department would confirm or deny Rabbi Wise's statement mentioned by the Associated Press that Hitler had ordered the extermination of all Jews in Nazi-ruled Europe and that this had been confirmed by the State Department, M. J. McDermott, chief of the Division of Current Information, replied in a letter:

I today informed correspondents in confidence and am glad to give to you, not for publication, that Rabbi Wise was in the Department several months ago and again yesterday and he had consulted with the Department in connection with certain material in which he was interested and he now has this material. The State Department had only sought to facilitate the efforts of his Committee in getting at the truth and the correspondents should direct all questions concerning this material to Rabbi Wise.[21]

In short, the State Department wanted to have nothing to do with the content of the message.

The statement of 17 December was drafted in the Foreign Office in London. Maisky proposed one amendment, namely adding the sentence, 'The number of victims of these sanguinary punishments is taken to amount to many hundreds of thousands quite innocent men, women and children.' This was accepted and appeared in the final version as follows: 'The number of European victims of these bloody cruelties is reckoned in many hundreds of thousands of entirely innocent men, women and children.'

The United States made three amendments; two were accepted, the third came too late. Mr Reams, eager to weaken the statement, suggested the following: the original draft had said that 'the attention of the allied governments had been drawn to reports from Europe *which leave no room for doubt* that the Germans were carrying out their oft repeated intention to exterminate the Jewish people in Europe.' Reams wanted the italicized words deleted. Secondly, the original statement had that, 'From all the countries Jews are being transported *irrespective of age and sex* and in conditions of appalling horror and brutality to Eastern Europe.' Again Reams insisted that the italicized words be deleted. He argued that this had not been true up to the present time in France and might not be true in other occupied territories.[22] Reams was quite wrong: it was precisely this fact, the separation of children from their parents, which had provoked so many protests in France and Switzerland. The official bulletin of the Swiss churches wrote that the fact that children were brutally taken away from their parents reminded one of the murder of children at Bethlehem in the days of Jesus Christ. Cardinal Gerlier said in a protest declaration: 'Nous assistons à une dispersion cruelle des familles où rien n'est epargné' ('We are witnessing a cruel dispersal of families in which nothing is spared'). And Saliège, Archbishop of Toulon: 'Les membres d'une même famille soient séparés les uns des autres et embarqués pour une destination inconnue. . . .' ('Members of the same family are separated from each other and embarked for an unknown destination . . .').[23]

The last amendment came from the Secretary of State, and it had nothing to do with either Hitler or the Jews. According to the original version the first sentence of the statement listed the various members of the United Nations and then added 'and of the Fighting French Committee' (or 'French National Committee'). Cordell Hull sent a cable to London asking urgently for the insertion of the word 'also' in front of the 'French Committee'. It was the only cable concerning the whole affair which was sent with triple priority but it came too late. Lord Halifax, the British Ambassador in Washington, explained (and Winant from London supported him) that in view of the difference in time the telegram had reached Eden only when he was about to make his declaration in the House of Commons. The British Foreign Secretary had said moreover that it was too late to consult the other signatories. Consequently the statement was published in Washington with 'also' inserted before 'the Fighting French' whereas there was no 'also' in the London version or elsewhere.

Did Reams, McDermott, Breckinridge Long and the others genuinely doubt the available information? This is difficult to believe. It is more likely that their second line of argument was decisive: if the State Department confirmed the news it would 'come under pressure to do something'. But was the war effort really their overriding concern? This makes sense only if one also assumes that the American diplomats were more single-mindedly and relentlessly devoted to the war effort than Churchill, Stalin and all the others, a supposition which stretches the powers of even a vivid imagination.

APPENDIX 5. THE MISSIONS OF JAN KARSKI, JAN NOWAK AND TADEUSZ CHCIUK

The mission from Warsaw to London of Jan Karski (Kozielewski) has been repeatedly mentioned. Karski was neither the first nor the last courier to arrive from Warsaw, but as far as the information about the fate of the Jews in Poland was concerned, he was certainly the most important. Karski wrote a book about his mission which appeared in the United States in 1944 and became a bestseller; it was also published in Britain, Switzerland, and Norway. But the war was not yet over when the book was published and the author had to exert self-censorship.[24]

Who was Jan Karski, and what was the purpose of his mission? He was born in Lodz in 1914, studied at the Jan Kazimierz University in Lwow for a degree in law, served in the Polish army in 1935–6 and then for two years travelled in Central and Western Europe. In 1938 he entered the Polish Foreign Ministry as a trainee and graduated in January 1939 at the top of his class. When the war broke out he served as a lieutenant in the mounted artillery. With his unit he retreated to the East and was then taken prisoner by the advancing Soviet army. He disguised himself as a private. Polish officers were kept back by the Russians and most of them never returned. He was repatriated to Poland where the Germans put him on a train to a labour camp. He jumped from the train and made his way to Warsaw where he became an early member of the Underground. He acted as a courier between Angers (in France – where the exiled Polish National Council was located before the fall of France) and Warsaw. The usual route was Warsaw to Zakopane, by skis over the Carpathian mountains to Budapest–Italy–France. Professor Stanislaw Kot, the Polish Minister of the Interior at the time, asked him to return to Poland carrying with him the first blueprint for the creation of the various institutions which were to constitute the underground state. On another such mission in June 1940 he was caught by the Gestapo in Presov, Slovakia. Having undergone torture he tried to commit suicide by cutting his wrists, but failed. He was sent back to prison hospital where an underground cell succeeded in whisking him out. This operation was undertaken by a unit commanded by Jozef Cyrankiewicz, the future Prime Minister in Communist Poland, but at that time still a leading member of the PPS – the Socialists. Karski lived underground in Warsaw in 1941–2, engaged in 'black propaganda' among German soldiers, printing and distributing leaflets in German. In 1942 he was again asked to go to London as a courier on behalf of the *Delegat*. Various techniques were used at the time to get such couriers to Western Europe. The one chosen by those who arranged Karski's trip was simple. Thousands of French 'guest' workers were employed in Poland at the time. They had the right to go back to France twice yearly for their home leave. The Polish Underground offered them a two-week very well paid holiday on a Polish country estate in what were for wartime exceedingly luxurious conditions. French workers surrendered their passports; the pictures were removed and those of the couriers affixed. If the courier did not return in time they would have to report the passport's loss and had to pay a fine – which would be covered, needless to say, by the Underground.

Karski travelled through Germany in November 1942 to Paris where he stayed for twelve days in an apartment belonging to a priest. He spent his evenings in the cafés, restaurants, and gambling places in Montmartre and was struck by the spirit of fraternization between Frenchmen and Germans and the servile attitude frequently displayed. Equipped with new papers he made his way to Toulon where a Polish underground network took over. He was taken to Perpignan and crossed the Pyrenees with a Spanish Communist acting as a guide. In Barcelona he was fetched with a diplomatic limousine which seems to have belonged to the OSS rather than British intelligence. From there he went first to Algeciras and then to Gibraltar where he had dinner with the Governor. The following day he flew to London.

Karski's mission concerned, of course, predominantly Polish affairs. But prior to his departure he had several meetings with Jewish leaders, and he solemnly promised them to convey their message to the West. He did not know at the time the identity of those he met. Later he learned that one of them had been Leon Feiner; the identity of the other is not clear to this day. It was apparently Menahem Kirschenbaum or Adolf Berman. The two saw him by special permission of the *Delegatura*. Karski also visited the Warsaw ghetto in October 1942. This did not, in his words, present any special difficulty: the area of the ghetto had very much shrunk after the deportations of July–September 1942; the tramways crossed the ghetto to reach the streets which had been taken over by the 'Aryans'. Elsewhere one could enter or leave the ghetto through the cellars of houses which served as the ghetto wall.

Karski relates that he was taken to Belzec by a Jewish, but Aryan-looking, contact (who had told him that this was a transition rather than extermination camp) to a nearby shop. There he was approached by a man in civilian clothes who said he would provide both a uniform (of an Estonian guard) and a permit. Karski does not know whether this contact (who spoke perfect Polish) was a smuggler or a 'Racial German', perhaps even a low-level Gestapo agent who was in the pay of the Jewish underground. The two entered the camp through a side gate without attracting suspicion. There he saw 'bedlam' – the ground littered with weakened bodies, hundreds of Jews packed into railway cars covered with a layer of quicklime. The cars were closed and moved outside the camp; after some time they were opened, the corpses were burned and the cars returned to the camp to fetch new cargo. After watching the scene for some time he felt sick and began to lose his nerve. He wanted to escape and walked quickly towards the nearest gate. His companion who had kept some distance from him realized that something was amiss. He approached Karski and harshly shouted, 'Follow me at once!' They went through the same side gate they had entered and were not stopped. Karski says that he learned only in later years that Belzec was not a transit but a death camp and that most of the victims were killed in gas chambers. He had not actually seen the gas chambers during his visit, apparently because these were walled in and could be approached only with a special permit.

Karski arrived in London in November 1942. General Sikorski was in America at the time but he met him later; he participated however in two meetings of the Polish Government-in-exile. In the following weeks he met many British, American, and Jewish leaders and briefed them about the situation in Poland and the fate of the Jews. Among those he saw in London were Anthony Eden, the Foreign Secretary,

Lord Cranborne, Hugh Dalton, and Arthur Greenwood, members of the War Cabinet, Richard Law, Parliamentary Undersecretary for Foreign Affairs, Lord Selborne, who as Minister of Economic Warfare was in charge of SOE, Anthony D. Biddle and Owen O'Malley, the US and British Ambassadors to the Polish Government-in-exile, as well as various members of the House of Commons.

Among those he saw in the United States were President Roosevelt, Herbert Hoover, Cordell Hull, Henry Stimson, Francis Biddle, Adolph Berle, Archbishops Spelman, Mooney and Strich, Felix Frankfurter, Bill Donovan and John Wiley (both of the OSS), and the Apostolic Delegate.

Among Jewish leaders: Stephen Wise, N. Waldman, S. Margoshes, and M. Fertig. He also talked to many writers and newspapermen, among them: H.G. Wells, Victor Gollancz, Arthur Koestler, Kingsley Martin, Allen Lane, Walter Lippmann, Eugene Lyons, Dorothy Thompson, George Sokolsky, William Prescott, and Mrs Ogden Reed.

The message Karski transmitted to the West in November 1942 on behalf of the Polish Jewish leaders could not be published during the war. He wrote it down at my request in 1979:*

I. *My mission to the Polish and Allied Governments*
The unprecedented destruction of the entire Jewish population is *not* motivated by Germany's *military* requirements. Hitler and his subordinates aim at the total destruction of the Jews *before* the war ends and *regardless* of its outcome. The Allied governments cannot disregard this reality. The Jews in Poland are helpless. They have no country of their own. They have no independent voice in the Allied councils. They cannot rely on the Polish underground or population-at-large. They might save some individuals – they are unable to stop the extermination. Only the powerful Allied governments can help effectively.

The Polish Jews solemnly appeal to the Polish and Allied governments to undertake *extraordinary* measures in an attempt to stop the extermination.

They solemnly place historical responsibility on the Allied governments if they fail to undertake those extraordinary measures.

---

*I am grateful to Professor Jan Karski for having patiently submitted to detailed questioning. (Washington, 3 September 1979.)

This is what the Jews demand:

1) A public announcement that prevention of the physical extermination of the Jews became a part of the over-all Allied *war strategy*.

2) Informing the German nation through radio, air-dropped leaflets and other means about their government's crimes committed against the Jews. All names of the German officials directly involved in the crimes; statistics; facts; methods used should be spelled out.

3) *Public* and *formal* appeals (radio, leaflets, etc.) to the German people to exercise pressure on their government as to make it stop the extermination.

4) *Public* and *formal* demand for evidence that such a pressure had been exercised and Nazi practices directed against the Jews stopped.

5) Placing the responsibility on the German nation as a whole if they failed to respond and if the extermination continues.

6) *Public* and *formal* announcement that in view of the unprecedented Nazi crimes against the Jews and in hope that those crimes would stop, the Allied governments were to take unprecedented steps:

   a) certain areas and objects in Germany would be bombed in retaliation. German people would be informed before and after each action that the Nazi continued extermination of the Jews prompted the bombing.

   b) certain German war prisoners who, having been informed about their government's crimes, still profess solidarity with and allegiance to the Nazis would be held responsible for the crimes committed against the Jews as long as those crimes continue.

   c) certain German nationals living in the Allied countries who, having been informed about the crimes committed against the Jews, still profess solidarity with the Nazi government would be held responsible for those crimes.

   d) Jewish leaders in London, particularly Szmul *Zygielbojm* (BUND) and Dr Ignace *Szwarcbard* (Zionists), are solemnly charged to make all efforts so as to make the Polish government formally forward these demands at the Allied councils.

II. *For the President of the Polish Republic, Wladyslaw Raczkiewicz only:*

Many among those who directly or indirectly contribute to the Jewish tragedy profess their Catholic faith. The Polish and other European Jews sent to Poland feel entitled on humanitarian and spiritual grounds to expect protection of the Vatican. Religious sanctions, excommunication included, are within the Pope's jurisdiction. Such sanctions, publicly proclaimed, might have an impact on the German people. They might even make Hitler, a baptized Catholic, to reflect.

Because of the nature of this message and the source it came from as

well as because of diplomatic protocol's requirements, I was instructed
to deliver the message to the President of the Republic *only*. Let him use
his conscience and wisdom in approaching the Pope. I was explicitly
forbidden to discuss that subject with the Jewish leaders. Their possible
maladroit intervention might be counter-productive.

III. *For the Prime Minister and Commander-in-Chief* (General Wladyslaw
Sikorski), Minister of Interior (Stanislaw Mikolajczyk), *Zygielbojm and
Dr Szwarcbard.*

Although the Polish people-at-large sympathize with or try to help
the Jews, many Polish criminals blackmail, denounce or even murder
the Jews in hiding. The Underground authorities *must* apply punitive
sanctions against them, executions included. In the last case, the
identity of the guilty ones and the nature of their crimes should be
publicized in the Underground press.

Zygielbojm and Szwarcbard must use all their pressure, so that
pertinent orders would be issued.

In order to avoid any risk of anti-Polish propaganda, I was explicitly
forbidden to discuss that subject with any *non-Polish* Jewish leaders. I
was to inform Zygielbojm and Dr Szwarcbard about that part of my
instructions.

IV. *For the Commander-in-Chief of the Polish Armed Forces (General
Sikorski) and Zygielbojm and Dr Szwarcbard only.*

A Jewish military organization emerged. Its leaders as well as
younger elements of the Jewish ghettos, the Warsaw ghetto in
particular, contemplate some armed resistance against the Germans.
They speak about a 'Jewish war' against the Third Reich. They asked
the Home Army for weapons. Those weapons had been denied.

The Jews are Polish citizens. They are entitled to have weapons if
these weapons are in the possession of the Polish Underground. The
Jews cannot be denied the right to die fighting, whatever the outcome
of their fighting may be. Only General Sikorski, as commander-in-
chief, can change the attitude of the Commander of the Home Army
(General Stefan Rowecki). The Jewish leaders demand Gen. Sikorski's
intervention.

I *refused* to carry that message unless I was authorized to see Gen.
Rowecki in person, to inform him about the complaint and to ask for
his comments. Both Jewish leaders heartily agreed. I did see General
Rowecki. I did obtain his comments and I did refer the matter in
London as instructed.

In order not to feed any anti-Polish propaganda, I was explicitly
forbidden to discuss this subject with *any non-Polish* Jewish leaders. I
was to inform Zygielbojm and Dr Szwarcbard about this part of my
instructions.

V. *To the Allied individual government civic leaders as well as to the Polish and international Jewish leaders: request for financial and technical aid.*

There is a possibility to save some Jews if money were available. Gestapo is corrupted not only on the low level but also on the medium and even high level. They would cooperate for gold or hard currency. The Jewish leaders are able to make appropriate contacts.

a) Some Jews might be allowed to leave Poland semi-officially: in exchange for gold, dollars, or delivery of certain goods needed by the German authorities.

b) Some Jews would be allowed to leave Poland provided they have *original* foreign passports. Origins of those passports are unimportant. As large supply of such passports as possible should be sent. They must be *blank*. Forged names, identification data, etc. would be overlooked by the German authorities, for money, of course.

Provisions must be made that those Jews who do succeed in leaving Poland would be accepted in the Allied or neutral countries.

c) Some Jews of not Semitic appearance could leave the ghettos, obtain *false* German documents and live among other Poles under assumed names.

Money to bribe the ghetto's guards, various officials (*Arbeitsamt*) as well as subsistence funds is needed.

d) Many Christian families would agree to hide the Jews in their homes. But they risk instant executions if discovered by the Germans. All of them are in dire needs, themselves. Money is needed, at least for subsistence.

e) Money, medicines, food, clothing is most urgently needed by the survivors *in* the ghettos. Subsidies obtained from the Delegate of the Polish government-in-exile as well as other funds sent through various channels by the Jewish international organizations are *totally insufficient*. More hard currency, sent without delay, is a question of life or death for thousands of Jews.

VI. *Arousing the public opinion in the West on behalf of the Jews.*

In addition to all the messages I was to carry, both Jewish leaders solemnly committed me to do my utmost in arousing the public opinion in the free world on behalf of the Polish Jews. I solemnly swore that, should I arrive safely in London, I would not fail them.

Karski, it will be recalled, reached London in November 1942. The following month (on 7 December) the Polish National Council passed a resolution committing the Government to act without delay in connection with the extermination of the Jews. On 10 December, accordingly, the Polish Government issued a formal appeal to the Allied governments and on 17 December the Allied Council passed the resolution which has been quoted elsewhere. On 18 December the President of the Polish Republic sent a note to Pope Pius XII asking for his intervention. On 18 January 1943 Count Raczynski, the Polish Foreign Minister, presented the following demands at the Allied Council:

a)　The bombing of Germany as a reprisal for the continued extermination of the Polish Jews.
b)　To press Berlin to let the Jews out of the German-dominated countries, particularly Poland.
c)　To demand action so as to make the Allied as well as the neutral countries accept the Jews, who had succeeded or would succeed in leaving German-occupied countries.

Raczynski did not advance demands for reprisals against German war prisoners and German nationals living in the Allied countries, considering them contrary to the accepted practices of international law. Anthony Eden, acting on behalf of the British Government, rejected the Polish demands and offered instead some vague promises to intervene in certain neutral countries. The various diplomatic initiatives and the proclamations of December 1942 came as the result of the evidence which had accumulated over many months, but the Karski mission still played an important part in this respect.

What does Karski remember of his many meetings after his arrival in Britain? He assessed, quite accurately, the two Jewish members of the Polish National Council:* Zygielbojm met with him with suspicion and reacted 'irrationally' ('Why did they send you? Who are you? You are not a Jew. Let me see your wrists. . . .') and Schwarzbart ('A professional politician and a bit of a manipulator'). President Roosevelt listened to him for an hour and asked many questions; in the end he dismissed him with 'Tell your nation we shall win the war' and some more such ringing messages. There were no words of comfort for the Jews. Stephen Wise was the Jewish leader most interested in practical details: what kind of passports were needed? Any Latin American would do. . . . But would not the Gestapo see through this scheme? It probably would but low- and even middle-level Gestapo officials could be bribed. But those to be bribed needed

---

*There was a third, Leon Grossfeld (member of the PPS) who does not, however, figure prominently in this story.

at least a paper of some verisimilitude, even if it was not altogether genuine ... Rabbi Wise was fascinated by this scheme.[25]

Karski told Justice Frankfurter everything he knew about the Jews, and when he finished the Justice said some complimentary things and then, 'I can't believe you'. Ciechanowski, who was again with him, told Frankfurter that Karski had come under the authority of the Polish Government and that there was no possibility in the world that he was not telling the unadorned truth. Frankfurter: 'I did not say this young man is lying. I said I cannot believe him. There is a difference.' There is indeed a difference, and it is the main clue towards understanding why the news from Eastern Europe was not believed for so long. In England, H. G. Wells was actively hostile and Lord Selborne (the administrative chief of underground resistance) said that Karski was doing a magnificent job. But he also said that in the First World War there had been atrocity stories about Belgian babies; His Majesty's Government knew, of course, that they were false but had done nothing to stop them. The comparison between the Belgian babies who had not been killed and the Jewish who were dead was not reassuring. Selborne also said that the proposals to buy out some Jewish women and children by paying with gold and/or goods were totally unacceptable. Such a transaction could perhaps be kept secret in wartime, but it would have to be revealed after victory, and no prime minister or cabinet would accept this responsibility. It would surely be blamed for the killing of British soldiers as the result of prolonging the war. Eden's main concern was with the difficult question of where the Jews, if liberated, would go. Britain had already a hundred thousand refugees and could not accept more.*

Jan Nowak (Zdzislaw Jezioranski) also acted as an emissary to London in 1943 and 1944. His story has been told in fascinating detail but belongs to a later period.[26] It is of indirect interest, however, because Nowak fully confirms certain aspects of Karski's evidence, especially with regard to the reception in

---

*Eden sent two notes to the War Council after his meeting with Karski, but they concerned Polish affairs. The Poles would not be willing to accede to the Soviet demands for territorial change, and this was bad news.

London. He was the first emissary to arrive from Poland after the battle of the Warsaw ghetto. Nowak was debriefed by Frank Roberts, head of the Central Department of the Foreign Office, Brigadier Harvey Watt, Parliamentary Private Secretary to Churchill, Major Morton, Churchill's intelligence adviser, Osborn and Moray McLaren of PWI, representatives of MI9 and others. He dwelt at length on the fate of the Jews but there was no interest whatsoever in this topic, with the exception of one counter-intelligence officer who was personally deeply moved. The various minutes (by Frank Roberts, Lawford, Morton) which have been preserved, bear this out. Nowak also reports that in his meetings with Schwarzbart ('a tragic figure') and other Jewish leaders he was advised not to dwell too much on the number of the victims, for this would not be believed, but to refer instead to individual cases.[27]

Tadeusz Chciuk-Celt was sent twice by parachute from London to Poland during the war. The first time he stayed in Poland from 28 December 1941 to 16 June 1942. He stayed in Budapest from June to November 1942 and then had a somewhat troublesome journey via Switzerland, France and Spain back to England which he reached only on 16 June 1943. According to his account he sent a report from Budapest to London about the mass executions and mentioned specifically the efforts invested in enlarging Auschwitz's 'absorptive capacity'. He also mentioned the first signs of the liquidation of the Warsaw ghetto (the 'small ghetto') as well as the extermination of the Jewish communities in Radom, Lida, Minsk, Rovno etc.[28]

A NOTE ON SOURCES

I HAVE had access to most collections in which the material needed for the present study can be found. Three major exceptions were the Soviet and Vatican archives, and, less well known but of considerable importance, the collection of Nathan Schwalb, kept in the archives of the *Histadrut* in Tel Aviv. I would like to record my gratitude to the directors and staff of the following: National Archives, Washington DC; Yad Vashem, Jerusalem; the archives of the *Hagana*, the Labour Movement and the *Histadrut* executive, all in Tel Aviv; the Central Zionist Archives and the Israel State Archives in Jerusalem; Moreshet at Givat Haviva; Bet Lohame Hagetaot; Public Record Office, Wiener Library, World Jewish Congress, Sikorski Institute and Studium Polski Podziemnej, all in London; the YIVO Institute, the Franz Kurski Archives of the Jewish Labour *Bund* and the Leo Baeck Institute, all in New York; the Archives of the Royal Swedish Foreign Ministry in Stockholm; the Berlin Document Centre; the Swiss Federal Archives in Bern; the archives of the International Red Cross in Geneva; the German Federal Archives in Koblenz; the Institute für Zeitgeschichte in Munich and the military-historical archives in Freiburg. Unfortunately, I cannot say with any assurance that I had access to all the relevant material in all of these collections.

Special thanks go to those who have helped me with my research: Josef Algasy (who helped me greatly with research in Israeli archives), Mrs N. Pain and Mr Z. Ben Shlomo in London, Sophia Miskiewicz and Joseph Pilat in Washington, and Dr Svante Hansson in Stockholm.

The list of those whom I have consulted on specific aspects is long and this is also true with regard to others who have helped me to obtain material otherwise difficult to receive. I would like to thank in particular: in Britain – Peter Calvocoressi, Dr E. Eppler, Mrs Elna Ernest, Professor M.R.D. Foot, Dr J. Garlinski, Dr F. Hajek, Professor F. Hinsley, Baroness Hornsby-Smith DBE, Professor L. Labedz, Ronald Lewin,

Professor M. Marrus, Sir Cecil Parrott, Dr S. Roth, Professor Sir Hugh Trevor-Roper, Mrs S. Wichmann, Professor Z. Zeman; in Israel – Dr Y. Arad, Professor Y. Bauer, Dr W. Eitan, Dr I. Fleischauer, Dr M. Gilbert, Dr I. Gutman, Dr M. Heiman, Dr S. Krakowski, Dr O. Kulka, Shlomit Laqueur, Mr Philip, Ambassador Gideon Rafael, Professor Y. Reinharz, Dr L. Rotkirchen, Dr M. Sompolinski, Professor B. Vago, Dr Reuben Hecht; in Switzerland – Dr H. Boeschenstein, Kurt Emmenegger, Dr O. Gauye, Dr Graf, Dr W. Guggenheim, M. J. Moreillon, A. Müller, Dr G. Riegner, Madame C. Rey Schirr, Dr E. Streiff, Dr L. Stucki; in Sweden – Professor W. Carlgren, Ambassador M. R. Kidron, Dr Jozef Lewandowski, Dr H. Lindberg, Baron G. von Otter, Professor M. Peterson, Ake Thulstrup; in Germany – Dr H. Abs, Dr Auerbach, Dr H. Boberach, T. Chciuk-Celt, Professor J. Rohwer; in the Netherlands – Dr Louis de Jong; in the United States – Ambassador J. Beam, Professor H. Deutsch, Dr L. Dobroszycki, Howard Elting Jr, A. Gellert, Ambassador A. Goldberg, Dr R. Graham sj, Professor Feliks Gross, Dr F. Grubel, David Kahn, Professor J. Karski, Hillel Kempinski, Professor G. Kennan, S. Korbonski, Dr David Kranzler, Dr J. Kuhl, Dr F. Lessing, Professor G. Lerski, Jan Nowak, A. Pomian, Ambassador H. Probst, Dr B. Rubin, A. Szegedi Maszak, John E. Taylor, Dr H. Tütsch, Dr Robert Wolfe, Norbert Wollheim.

I shall be forgiven for not providing a bibliography. All the major books on the final solution include bibliographies and there are, furthermore, specialized guides on unpublished materials prepared by Yad Vashem.

CHAPTER NOTES

I. GERMANY: A WALL OF SILENCE?

1. The many bureaucratic ramifications are described in great detail in H. G. Adler, *Der Verwaltete Mensch* (Tübingen, 1974).

2. See also the Ferris, Longden and Davison affidavits, Nuremberg Documents, N1–11693, N1–11703, N1–11694.

3. Nuremberg war crimes trial, 20 October 1947, N1–11984.

4. Nuremberg Documents, N1–6645.

5. Dr L. de Jong, *Het Koninkrijk der Nederlanden in de tweede Wereldoorlog* ('s Gravenhage, 1976), VII, part I, p. 333.

6. Affidavit Schulhof, 21 June 1947, NL–7967. Quoted in R. Hilberg, *The Destruction of the European Jews* (New York, 1961), p. 596.

7. Nuremberg Documents, NG–1535.

8. 10 December 1941, T/120/465/226345–60 (Inland 11g 431), quoted in Christopher Browning, *The Final Solution and the German Foreign Office* (New York, 1978), p. 74.

9. Montevideo to D111, 2 September 1941 (PA, Inland 11A/B54/1), quoted in Browning, *German Foreign Office*, p. 54

10. The case of Klingenfuss, an official of *Abteilung Deutschland,* is of particular interest in this respect. Browning, *German Foreign Office*, pp. 147–8.

11. Browning, *German Foreign Office*, p. 152.

12. Evidence Tippelskirch, Nuremberg Documents, NG–2429.

13. *The Secret Conferences of Dr Goebbels* (New York, 1970), p. 309.

14. W. Schwipps, *Wortschlacht im Aether, der deutsche Auslandrundfunk in zweiten Weltkreig* (Deutsche Welle, 1971), p. 20; 'BBC Europe Audience Survey', *Germany-European Intelligence Papers*, Series 5, 28 June 1943; *US Strategic Bombing Survey* (Washington, 1946).

15. Willi A. Boelcke, 'Das Seehaus in Berlin-Wannsee. Zur Geschichte des deutschen Monitoring Service während des zweiten Weltkrieges' in *Jahrbuch für die Geschichte Mittel-und Ostdeutschlands,* 23 (Berlin, 1974), pp. 231ff.

16. *Wollt ihr den totalen Krieg? Die geheimen Goebbels Konferenzen 1939–1943* (Stuttgart, 1967), p. 212.

17. The only exception known to me is R. Hilberg, 'The Reichsbahn and its part in the killing of the Jews', *Yalkut Moreshet* (October 1977), pp. 27ff.

18. Hilberg, 'The Reichsbahn', p. 48.

19. Bormann was head of Hitler's Chancellery. He mentioned that the measures were discussed (*Erörterungen angestellt*) among the population. The circular letter said that the news about these discussions had come from various parts of Germany (VI 66/881 of 9 October 1942. Reprinted in *Aus Verfügungen . . . von der Parteikanzlei,* 11 (1944), p. 131. This is an internal

top secret Nazi publication, printed but not for sale). Another circular letter sent out by Bormann from Hitler's headquarters after the assassination of Heydrich on 8 June 1942 tends to show that the fate of the Jews was discussed even earlier (R 28/42 g). This communication, which went to all senior Nazi regional leaders, refers to suggestions allegedly made by the population that after the completion of the evacuation of the Jews it should be the turn of the Czechs.

20. *Hitler's Table Talk,* ed. H.R. Trevor-Roper (London, 1973), p. 162.

21. About the 1943 rumours see O.D. Kulka, 'Public opinion in National Socialist Germany and the Jewish Problem' (in Hebrew), in *Zion,* 1975, p. 242ff. The activities of the SD were directed by the RSHA, the Main State Security Office. Department IV of this office was the Gestapo, Department VI dealt with foreign intelligence.

22. This correspondence is in the archive of the Leo Baeck Institute, New York.

23. Quoted here from *Strassburger Neueste Nachrichten,* 20 May 1942.

24. *Das Reich,* 14 June 1942.

25. Conversations with Andor Gellert (11 October 1979) and Aladar Szegedy-Maszak (18 October 1979). Szegedy-Maszak was the second-highest ranking official in the Political Department at the time. The two accounts agree on all essential points. Szegedy-Maszak was arrested by the Germans after the invasion and spent the last part of the war in Dachau. Gellert was dispatched to Stockholm in late 1942 and became involved in the peace feelers with the Allies.

26. The memorandum appears in Elek Karsai, *A budai varto a gyepuig* (Budapest, 1966), pp. 202–5.

27. N. M. Nagy Talavera, *The Green Shirts and Others* (Stanford, 1970), p. 184.

28. Milan S. Durica, *Dr Joseph Tiso and the Jewish problem in Slovakia* (Padua, 1964), p. 12. The evidence is discussed in Y. Jelinek's essay in B. Vago and G. L. Mosse, *Jews and Non-Jews in Eastern Europe* (New York, 1974), pp. 221–56.

29. General Pieche revealed in an interview in 1961 that his help had been enlisted by Gaddo Glass, a Jewish citizen from Trieste. The document appears in *Relazione sull'opera svolta dal Ministerio degli Affari Esteri per la tutela della Comunità ebraiche (1918–43)* (Rome, n.d.). See also Giuseppe Mayda, *Ebrei sotto Salo* (Milan, 1978), p. 21ff.

30. The Viherluoto report is reprinted in Elina Suominen, *Kuoleman laiva SS Hohenhörn. Juutalaispakolastainen kohtalo Suomessa* (Provoo-Helsinki, 1979), p. 56.

31. Report to Pilet-Golaz, 22 December 1942.

32. Report to Pilet-Golaz, 31 May 1943.

33. A. Szegedy-Maszak.

34. *Zror Reshimot,* 3, Vaad Ha'hazala, p. 5. These are the typewritten circular letters sponsored by the Palestinian Rescue Committee in Istanbul.

35. In the following I am drawing on chapter 6 of Professor Michael Marrus's hitherto unpublished study on Vichy and the Jews.

36. *Les églises protestantes pendant la guerre el l'occupation* (Paris, 1946), p. 32.

2. THE NEUTRALS: 'UNANIMOUS AND RELIABLE REPORTS'

1. *Bericht der Polizeiabteilung zum Flüchtlingsproblem.* Jezler report. Annexe to letter dated 4 August 1942, Swiss Federal Archives.

2. Willi Gautsch, *Geschichte des Kanton Aargau* (Baden, 1978), pp. 450–8.

3. Rudolf Bucher, *Zwischen Verrat und Menschlichkeit* (Frauenfeld, 1967), pp. 187–8, and Benjamin Sagalowitz, *Was wusste man in der Schweiz vom Schicksal der Juden* (Zürich, 1955), privately published.

4. *Angelegenheit über die Vorträge von Dr Bucher über die Ärztemission an der Ostfront*, Bundesarchiv, Bestand 27–12707.

5. *Warschau 1942* (Zürich, 1945). Censorship prevented the publication of the book during the war.

6. Stucki to Pilet-Golaz, 2 October 1942.

7. *Thurgauer Zeitung*, 2 October 1942.

8. *Deutsche Hörer,* 55 Radiosendungen (Stockholm, 1945), p. 44.

9. *Berner Tagwacht*, 3 August 1942.

10. *Thurgauer Arbeiterzeitung*, 25 August 1942, and *Basler Nationalzeitung*, 20 August 1942, *Die Tat*, 29 August 1942, and many others.

11. Letter dated 20 November 1942.

12. Georg Kreis, *Zensur und Selbstzensur* (Frauenfeld, 1973), p. 194.

13. See for instance *Schweizer Armeekommando*, 20 November 1943, and letter to *Nation*, Bern, 17 December 1943, in Swiss Federal Archives.

14. *Basler Nationalzeitung*, 18 December 1942.

15. C. Ludwig, *Die Flüchtlingspolitik der Schweiz in den Jahren 1933 bis 1955*, p. 242.

16. Personal communication from Baron von Otter and interview in *Aftonbladet*, 7 and 8 March 1979. There was an earlier interview in *Rheinischer Merkur*, 14 July 1963.

17. The letter is dated 23 July 1945. I would like to express my gratitude to Professor W. Carlgren and Dr Svante Hansson in this connection.

18. For instance, Olle Nystedt, Göteborg, 29 November 1942, quoted in *Nordiska Röster mot judeförföljelse och vald* (Stockholm, 1943), p. 14.

19. *Svenska Dagbladet*, 6 December 1942; *Nya Daglight Allehanda*, 27 November 1942; 'It is not difficult to imagine the fate awaiting them,' *Social Democraten*, 29 November 1942.

20. *Smalands Folksblad*, 27 November 1942; *Falkuriren*, 25 November 1942; *Barometern*, Kalmar, 28 November 1942; *Göteborgs Tidningen*, 29 November 1942; *Eskilstunakuriren*, 30 November 1942.

21. *Göteborgs Handelstidning*, 18 December 1942; *Arbetet*, Malmö, 19 December 1942.

22. 24 July 1943. Nuremberg Documents, NG–5050.

23. Quoted in B. Wasserstein, *Britain and the Jews of Europe 1939–1945* (London, 1979), p. 237.

24. *Le Figaro*, 14 December 1963.

25. Hans Gmelin, Nuremberg Documents, NG–5291; *Actes et Documents du Saint Siège relatifs à la Seconde Guerre Mondiale*, VII (Vatican, 1974), p. 453.

26. *Saint Siège*, VII, p. 608.

27. Casaroli to Archbishop Jadot, letter dated 25 September 1979.
28. *Report of the IRC on its activities during the second world war* . . . (Geneva, 1948), I, p. 11.
29. *Report of the IRC* . . . , I, p. 21.
30. *Inter Arma Caritas* (Geneva, 1947), p. 85.
31. These quotations, unless otherwise indicated, are from the files of the IRC archives in Geneva. I am indebted to the executive of the IRC for having given me permission to consult these materials. I was, I believe, the first historian who had access to these files except for the author of an official general history of the Red Cross between 1914 and 1954 published a few years ago. The files are, however, far from complete. Dr Burckhardt, the foreign minister of the IRC and a professional student of classical diplomacy, left no correspondence at all.
32. Squire's memorandum was in the form of a personal letter to Harrison, sent on 9 November 1942. National Archives.
33. Riegner, *Aktennotiz*, Geneva, 17 November 1942, in Lichtheim Correspondence, Central Zionist Archives (CZA).

3. THE ALLIES: 'WILD RUMOURS INSPIRED BY JEWISH FEARS'

1. Glasberg, *A recherche d'une patrie* (Paris, 1946), p. 64.
2. The structure of British intelligence is described authoritatively in F. H. Hinsley *et al., British Intelligence in the Second World War* (London, 1979), I, *passim.*
3. *Die Zeitung*, London, 25 October 1941. The Swedish account was also carried in the *Sunday Times* of 24 October and other newspapers. Eichmann's name had figured in Swedish diplomatic reports much earlier—in November 1939. This refers to a report made by two members of the Swedish Embassy in Berlin, Einar von Post and Karl Damgren, about transports of Jews from Moravia. I owe this information to Hans Lindberg's study on Swedish refugee policy 1936–41. Dr Lindberg believes that it is unlikely that the Swedish authorities knew about the mass murder prior to von Otter's report. This is based on an interview with Ambassador Gösta Engzell who was then in a key position in the Swedish Foreign Ministry. Hans Lindberg, *Svensk flyktingpolitik under internationellt tryck 1936–41* (Stockholm, 1973).
4. *Stockholm Tidningen*, 22 July and 10 August 1941; *Aftonbladet*, 18 August 1941.
5. *Pravda*, 7 January 1942. Occasionally there were Soviet reports for publication abroad only. This refers, for instance, to the report of the Jewish Anti-Fascist Committee in Kuybishev on the murder of 72,000 Jews in Minsk between November 1941 and April 1942. This appeared in British and American newspapers (cf. *Daily Telegraph*, 15 August 1942) but not in the central Soviet newspapers.
6. *Pravada* and *Izvestia*, 19 December 1942.
7. *Front bez liniya fronta* (Moscow, 1975), p. 63. This is a collection of essays written by or about NKVD agents left behind in the Nazi-occupied areas. Vasili Ardamatski's novel *Granat calling Moscow* also deals with this topic. The

official three-volume history of the Ukraine during the war mentions the fact that the German authorities gave orders on 28 September 1941 to the Jewish population to assemble at 8.00 the next morning, but from this point on the nationality of the victims is no longer mentioned. *Ukrainskaia SSR v velikoi otechestvennoi voini Sovetskovo Soyuza 1941–45* (Moscow, 1978), I, p. 351.

8. *JTA Bulletin*, 15–16 May 1942.

9. See Y. Gelber's excellent monograph 'Haitonut ha'ivrit be' Erez Israel al Hashmadat Yehudei Europa' in *Dapim le'heker hashoa ve'hamered* (Tel Aviv, 1969), p. 46.

10. 'Benjamin Sagalowitz' – a brochure privately published by his friends after his death in 1970 – p. 31.

11. Hinsley, *British Intelligence*, p. 58.

12. *Commentary,* March 1980.

13. Comments on the Riegner cable by F. Roberts, D. Allen, E. A. Walker, Miss Scofield and draft prepared for Sir Brograve Beauchamp in PRO FO 371 30917 XK 6759.

14. Dr Riegner wrote a seven-page 'Report concerning the Jews in Latvia' on the basis of the Zivian interrogation. World Jewish Congress, Institute of Jewish Affairs Archives, London.

15. 23 November 1942. National Archives 740.0016 EW 1939/726.

16. Wasserstein, *Britain and the Jews,* p. 169.

17. See, for instance, Hilberg, *The Destruction,* p. 470 (Slovakia), p. 331 (Poland).

18. PRO FO 371/34551. Mr Cavendish-Bentinck later explained that his pre-war experience of Germany had been limited and that he therefore disbelieved the atrocity stories in 1942–3. He added that when he visited Auschwitz in late 1945 and reported to the Foreign Office that millions of people had been killed there, it was still not believed.

19. D. Allen, PRO FO 371/30917, dated 14 August 1942.

20. Kelly to Roberts, PRO FO 371/26515.

21. Hinsely, *British Intelligence,* pp. 357–8. Documents pertaining to Ultra railway intelligence are not yet accessible at the Public Record Office.

22. Lahusen report on trip to Russia, NOKW 3147, 23 October 1941.

23. *Neue Zürcher Zeitung,* 5 May 1979.

24. PRO FO 371/30898. Censorship reports will not be declassified in Britain for another fifty years. The one quoted reached the present writer by accident. It shows that these reports were a source of great importance.

25. MOI memorandum, 25 July 1941, INF 1/251. The PWE suggested that Nazi atrocities against the Jews should be featured in the media but this was only in December 1942 (10, 24, 31 December) and there was only sporadic follow-up. See Michael Balfour, *Propaganda in War* (London, 1979), *passim.*

26. MOI memorandum, R. Frazer, 10 February 1942, INF 1/251.

27. Ian McLaine, *Ministry of Morale* (London, 1979), pp. 164–6.

28. *Ibid.*

29. *New York Herald Tribune,* 25 November 1942.

30. Henry L. Feingold, *The Politics of Rescue* (New Brunswick, 1970), p. 180.

31. National Archive Records of oss, 26896. This report is identical with the information received by Lichtheim in Geneva and forwarded by him to Jerusalem (see below).

32. Stephen S. Wise papers, Frankfurter to Wise, 16 September 1942.

33. Sikorski's letter is dated 22 June 1942, the Roosevelt answer 3 July. These documents, as well as the cables emanating from Biddle, can be found in the National Archives, record group 84. Warsaw 1942, file 711 – Jewish atrocities.

34. RG 226; OSS 27275.

35. OSS, Research and Analysis, No. 605; *New York Herald Tribune*, 29 October 1941 (Oechsner dispatch). Richard Helms had worked for Oechsner at the Berlin UP bureau; when Oechsner joined the oss he enlisted Helms for the organization.

36. OSS 88254. The Research and Analysis department of the oss concluded as early as March 1942 that 'the pattern of German violence includes the systematic liquidation of Jews'. (Report 605, 14 March 1942.)

37. OSS 24736.

38. OSS 24728.

39. H. Johnson to Secretary of State, Stockholm, 5 April 1943.

40. Werner Rings, *Advokaten des Feindes* (Düsseldorf, 1966).

41. *New York Times*, 4 December 1942. Two days earlier it had been said in an editorial in the same paper that 'to sum up this horrible story, it is believed that two million European Jews have perished and that five millions are in danger of extermination.'

42. W. A. Visser't Hooft, *Memoirs* (London, 1973), pp. 165–6.

4. THE NEWS FROM POLAND

1. On the AK see *Polskie Siły Zbrojne . . .* (London, 1950), III (*Armia Krajowa*); T. Rawski, A. Stapor, J. Zamojski, *Wojna wyzwolencza narodu polskiego . . .* (Warsaw, 1966), I; the important autobiographical books by Bor Komorowski, Korbonski, Zaremba, Jan Karski, Jan Nowak, Stefan Dolega-Modrzewski and others. W. Jacobmeyer, *Heimat und Exil* (Hamburg, 1973) deals with the beginnings of the Polish underground up to June 1941.

2. J. Garlinski, *Poland, SOE and the Allies* (London, 1969).

3. The full story of the Swedish connection has only recently been described in an interesting monograph by Jozef Lewandowski, *Swedish Contribution to the Polish Resistance Movement during World War II 1939–42* (Uppsala, 1979). Some of those involved, such as Herslow (*Moskva-Berlin-Warsawa* (Stockholm, 1947)) and the singer Elna Gisted (*Fran operett till tragedi* (Stockholm, 1946)) subsequently published their memoirs which, however, leave many questions open – such as for instance whether the Swedish diplomatic pouch was used to carry their mail. The Swedish connection was rediscovered inside Poland in 1968–9 with the publication in the Warsaw journal *Stolica* of a series of articles by the historian Bohdan Kroll, as well as by Roman Papay and Tadeusz Radzinski, who had participated in the events they described.

4. The Himmler report, dated 31 December 1942, is reproduced in Lewandowski, *Swedish Contribution,* pp. 86–99. The arrest was front-page news in the Swedish press at the time. Cf. *Dagens Nyheter,* 31 July 1942.

5. W. Bartoszewski and Zofia Lewin, *Righteous among Nations* (London, 1969), xxiv and *passim.*

6. Vladka Meed, *On both sides of the Wall* (New York, n.d.), p. 108.

7. Jan Karski, *Story of a Secret State* (Boston, 1944), p. 321.

8. K. Iranek-Osmecki, *He Who Saves One Life* (New York, 1971), p. 186.

9. Bartoszewski and Lewin, *Righteous,* p. 654. The date given is Warsaw, 30 November 1940, but this is surely a misprint.

10. *Sprawozdanie,* 16–30 November 1941; file 14–30 *Studium Polski Podziemnej* (SPP).

11. SPP 15–13. 'Zalacznik do aneksu Nr. 28', 'Masowe ekzekucje Zydow w powiecie kilskim'. In English–*The Ghetto,* 5 August 1942, and *The Black Book of Polish Jewry* (New York, 1945).

12. Meldunki, 10 July 1942, SPP 15–81.

13. SPP 14–102.

14. SPP 14–57.

15. See also 'Relacja Policjanta'—SPP 15–84, dated 11 August 1942, about the police station in the Warsaw ghetto. This and other reports quoted here ultimately found their way in English translation into OSS offices—but only in 1943.

16. Natalia Zarembina, *Oboz smierci* ('Death Camp'), Zofia Kossak, *W piekle* ('In Hell'), Halina Krahelska, *Oswiecim, pomietnik wieznia* ('Auschwitz, Diary of a Prisoner').

17. *Informacja Biezaca* 33, 8 September 1942, quoted in *Zeszyty Oswiecimskie,* Special Number, Warsaw 1968.

18. T. Bor Komorowski, *The Secret Army* (London, 1950), p. 99. Other sections of the underground must have received this information even earlier for the news had already reached London on 26 July. See below.

19. Bor Komorowski, *Secret Army,* p. 101.

20. Stefan Korbonski, *W Imieniu Rzecypospolitej* (Paris, 1954).

21. SPP, *Armia Krajowa W Dokumentacje* (London, 1973), II, p. 210.

22. Quoted in Y. Gutman, 'Polish attitudes towards mass deportations from Warsaw', in *Rescue Attempts,* p. 406.

23. The speech appeared later in a brochure, *Stop Them Now* (London, 1942).

24. Personal communication, September 1979.

25. Personal communication, September 1979.

26. Hershel V. Johnson to Secretary of State, 21 July 1942, FW 862 4016/2237.

27. OSS 88254; 862.4016/2242.

28. European War 1939/597^ PS/SF.

29. SPP 74/221.

30. SPP 74/252.

31. SPP 15/107.

32. Karski, *Secret State,* p. 321.

33. Karski, *Secret State,* p. 327–8. The killing in Belzec was not usually by

quicklime (calcium oxide) put on the floor of railway cars, but in gas chambers. See Appendix 5, 'The Mission of Jan Karski'.

34. Karski, *Secret State,* p. 336.

45. Karski, *Secret State,* p. 336.

5. THE JEWS IN NAZI-OCCUPIED EUROPE: DENIAL AND ACCEPTANCE

1. Dvorzhetski evidence quoted in G. Hausner, *Justice in Jerusalem* (London, 1967), p. 195.

2. The manifesto was apparently published only in a few copies and read out at meetings. But the text has been preserved. The author was Abba Kowner, the poet and partisan leader. The text is given in several books such as Rozka Korczak, *Lehavot Be'efar* (Merhavia, 1965), pp. 56–7; Yizhak Arad, *Vilna hayehudit* (Tel Aviv, 1966), pp. 160–1.

3. Nina Tennenbaum-Becker, *He'adam Ha'lochem* (Tel Aviv, 1964), *passim.*

4. I. Tabakblat, *Churben Lodz* (Buenos Aires, 1946), p. 124.

5. N. Blumental and Y. Karmish, *Hameri vehamered begetto Warsha* (Jerusalem, 1965), p. 75.

6. Joseph Kermish in his introduction to Ringelblum's *Polish-Jewish relations during the second world war* (Jerusalem, 1974), p. xvi.

7. I. Trunk, 'Letters from the Years of the Holocaust' (in Hebrew), *Yediot Bet Lohame Hagettaot,* April 1957, pp. 22–3.

8. I. Trunk, 'Letters'.

9. *Dokumenty i Materialy,* Part One: *Obozy,* ed. N. Blumental (Lodz, 1946), pp. 232–3.

10. *Dokumenty,* I.

11. Parts of the diary were damaged. See J. Kermish, 'E. Ringelblum's notes hitherto unpublished' in *Yad Vashem Studies,* VII, 1968, p. 173.

12. Julian Leszczynski in *Biuletyn Zydowskiego Instytutu Historycznego,* I, 1979, p. 100.

13. 'Powstanie i rozwoj z.o.b.' report on the Jewish military organization, written in March 1944. Quoted from L. S. Dawidowicz, *A Holocaust Reader* (New York, 1976), p. 363.

14. *Scroll of Agony* (New York, 1965), *passim.*

15. Kermish, 'Ringelblum's notes', pp. 180–1.

16. SPP file 15, 26. Translation based on Y. Bauer, 'When did they know?', *Midstream,* April 1968, p. 57.

17. SPP file 15, 107.

18. *Slowo Mlodych,* quoted in *Etonui Gordonia be'machteret ghetto Warsaw* (Tel Aviv, 1966).

19. Randolph L. Braham, 'The Kamenets Podolsk Massacres', *Yad Vashem Studies,* IX, 1973, p. 141.

20. P. Gosztoni, *Hitlers Fremde Heere* (Düsseldorf, 1976), p. 161.

21. Julius S. Fischer, *Transnistria* (South Brunswick, 1969), p. 71.

22. *Saint Siège,* VII, p. 453.

23. *Min Hamezar* (New York, 1960), p. 13. An informative book written in rabbinical Hebrew. Weismandl also reports that Kametka, the local arch-

bishop, told Jewish representatives in March or April 1942 that all Jews would be slaughtered in Poland. Pp. 34–5.

24. *Der Kastner Bericht* (Munich, 1961), p. 37.

25. Alex Weisberg, *Advocate for the Dead* (London, 1958), p. 31.

26. J. Kornianski, *Beshlichut, op cit. passim.*

27. This is reproduced as document 76 in Livia Rotkirchen, *The Destruction of Slovak Jewry. A Documentary History* (in Hebrew), (Jerusalem, 1961), pp. 166–204.

28. Oscar Neumann, *Im Schatten des Todes* (Tel Aviv, 1956), pp. 119–20.

29. Karmasin, leader of the Volksdeutsche in Slovakia, to Himmler, 29 July 1942. NO-1660.

30. Chief of German Security Police, Operations Situation Report USSR 151, dated 5 January 1942. NO-3257.

31. Norbert Wollheim, New York, 24 September 1979.

32. Collection of letters in the Wiener Library, London.

33. Eric H. Boehm, *We Survived* (New Haven, 1949), p. 293.

34. Billig, *Solution finale* (Paris, n.d.), p. 176.

35. Quoted in Louis de Jong, 'The Netherlands and Auschwitz', *Yad Vashem Studies*, VII, p. 44. Dr de Jong has again dealt with this subject in his massive study, *Het Koninkrijk der Nederlanden* etc., VII, part I, 'Wat weest man van Auschwitz an Sobibor?' pp. 320–62.

36. De Jong, *Koninkrijk*, VII, p. 340.

37. Quoted by Leni Yahil, *The Rescue of Danish Jewry* (Philadelphia, 1969), pp. 214–15.

38. Quoted from *Pariser Zeitung*, 353, 23 December 1942.

39. Alfred Wetzler in 1946 in a Slovak court in Bratislava, in Rotkirchen, *Slovak Jewry*, p. 158.

40. De Jong, 'The Netherlands and Auschwitz', p. 47.

41. John Hinton, *Dying* (London, 1967), p. 102.

42. De Jong, 'The Netherlands and Auschwitz', p. 54.

6. WORLD JEWRY: FROM GENEVA TO ATHLIT

1. *Congress Bulletin,* 16 February 1940.

2. 2 December 1942. Stephen S. Wise papers. Brandeis University.

3. World Jewish Congress, Institute of Jewish Affairs Archives, London. The reactions of the Anglo-Jewish leadership are discussed in M. Sompolinski, 'Ha'hanhaga ha'anglo-yehudit . . .', doctoral dissertation, Bar Ilan University, Tel Aviv, 1977.

4. Maria Syrkin, *Midstream,* May 1968.

5. Greenberg's article first appeared in *Yiddisher Kemfer* in February 1943; it first appeared in English in *Midstream,* March 1964.

6. M. Kwapiszewski, Polish Minister Plenipotentiary in Washington, in a letter dated 4 September 1942. Quoted in *Polish Review,* I, 1979, p. 47.

7. Cables dated 19 September, 1 October and 10 October.

8. He was one of many sources for the news about the German build-up against the Soviet Union. See *Master of Spies, The Memoirs of General Moravec*

(London, 1975), and Hinsley, *British Intelligence.* See also L. Otahalova and M. Cervinkova, *Dokumenty z histoire ceskoslovenski politiky* (Prague, 1966) which includes the diaries of Smutny, who was Benes' chief assistant during the period.

9. Benes to A. Easterman, 11 November 1942. World Jewish Congress, London Archives.

10. Antonin Tichy, *Nas zive nedostanou* (Liberec, 1969).

11. Thümmel, unlike many other *Abwehr* officers, was an old Nazi Party member and had been at one time close to Himmler. R. Strobinger, *Spion mit drei Gesichtern* (Munich, 1966); Amort and Jedlicka, *Tajemstvi vyzvedace A-54* (Prague, 1965); V. Kural, 'Vyhravaji spioni valky?' in *Ceskolovensky Vojak,* 7, 1967.

12. Nichols, British Legation to the Czechoslovak Republic, to Eden, 13 June 1942, FO 371/30837; Benes Report XIX, 'Political Situation in the Protectorate', 23 May to 5 June 1942, *ibid.*

13. '48,000 Jews from Prague deported to East', 29 October 1941. See also *Nova Dobe,* 16 January 1942, about the deportation of all Jews from Pilsen and many other such reports.

14. *New York Herald Tribune,* 25 November 1942.

15. This refers for instance to such papers as *Grenzbote* (Bratislava), *Donauzeitung* (Belgrade), *Krakauer Zeitung, Warschauer Zeitung, Minsker Zeitung, Ukraine Zeitung, Der Neue Tag* (Prague).

16. The original files of the ISLD in London seem to have disappeared, or were destroyed. But copies are available in the CZA. British intelligence considered systematic interviewing in Lisbon (by Ridley Prentice) of Jewish refugees from Germany in October 1941 on the basis of departure schedules given in the *Jüdisches Nachrichtenblatt,* the only remaining German-Jewish bulletin. (Adams to Lord Gage, FO 898/19).

17. De Jong, 'The Netherlands and Auschwitz', p. 78.

18. *Peulot Hazala be Kushta* (n.p., 1969), p. 41.

19. *Bericht über die jüdische Lage in Europa,* 15 September 1940, CZA.

20. Report from Geneva dated 11 December 1940, CZA.

21. 27 August 1941 (letter 461 via Istanbul), CZA. The letters exchanged between Geneva and Jerusalem during the war were numbered.

22. 20 October 1941 (letter 506 via Istanbul), CZA.

23. 13 November 1941, CZA.

24. 10 November 1941, CZA.

25. *Ibid.*

26. *Ibid.*

27. 22 December 1941, CZA.

28. Thus in a letter dated 29 May 1942: 'It is certainly no exaggeration to predict that at the end of this war two to three million Jews in Europe will be physically destroyed.' CZA.

29. 19 March and 13 May 1942, CZA.

30. 30 March 1942, private letter to L. Lauterbach, CZA.

31. 22 July 1942, CZA.

32. *Ibid.*

33. Lichtheim to Linton (London), 27 August 1942, CZA.

34. Lauterbach to Lichtheim, 28 September 1942, CZA.
35. Dvorzhetski interview with Riegner, Geneva, 13 July 1972.
36. 8 October 1942 (letter 845 via Istanbul), CZA.
37. 20 October 1942 (letter 858 via Istanbul), CZA.
38. Protocols of the meeting of the executive of the General Federation of Jewish Labour, p. 2.
39. Moshe Prager, *Yaven Mezula Hehadash* (Tel Aviv, September, 1941), p. 7. I have been reading the Palestinian Hebrew press for the period (1941–2) but mainly I have been drawing on Y. Gelber's pioneering study, *Ha'etonut ha'ivrit* . . .
40. *Davar*, 12 July 1942; *Hatzofe*, 8 February 1942; quoted in Gelber *Ha'etonut ha'ivrit*, p. 43.
41. *Ha'olam*, 27 August 1942.
42. *Hatzofe*, 24 April 1942; *Hamashkif*, 29 May 1942; quoted in Gelber *Ha'etonut ha'ivrit*, pp. 44–5.
43. *Hatzofe*, 18 March 1942; *Davar*, 16 March 1942.
44. 'Daf' in *Davar*, 17 March, the initials apparently of Dan Pines, one of the editors.
45. Davar, 8 October 1942. It had been published in August in 'The Ghetto Speaks', in the New York *Forward* (31 July) and elsewhere.
46. Y. Gothelf, *Davar*, 10 December 1942, quoted in Gelber, *Ha'etonut ha'ivrit*, pp. 50–1.
47. Y. Tabenkin in *Zror Mikhtavim*, 22 January 1943. Quoted in Y. Gelber, 'Tguvat ha'yishuv ha'ivri . . .', seminar paper, Hebrew University, 1969.
48. s 25/6005 CZA.
49. Protocols of *Histadrut* executive.
50. Protocols, p. 8.
51. The first reactions are discussed in detail in Chava Wagman-Eshkoli's study 'Emdat hamanhigut . . .' in *Yalkut Moreshet*, October 1977, pp. 87ff.
52. Y. Bauer, *The Holocaust in Historical Perspective* (Seattle, 1978), p. 28.
53. Riegner, Dvorzhetski interview, p. 11.

CONCLUSION

1. Roberta Wohlstetter, *Pearl Harbor, Warning and Decision* (Stanford, 1962), *passim;* Burton Whaley, *Codeword Barbarossa* (Cambridge, Mass., 1973), *passim.*

APPENDICES

1. Letter signed by Martin Bormann, dated 17 January 1939, in Nazi Central Archives (Berlin Document Centre).
2. Yaakov Zur, in *Peulat Hazalah be' Kushta* (Jerusalem, 1969), pp. 54ff.
3. Ernst Lemmer, *Goebbels Journalist, Nazi Spitzel, Revanche Minister* (East Berlin, 1964).
4. Ernst Lemmer, *Manches war doch anders* (Frankfurt, 1968), p. 208.
5. The following is based on Edgar Salin, 'Über Artur Sommer den Menschen und List Forscher', *Mitteilungen der List Gesellschaft*, Fasc 6, 30 November 1967, pp. 81ff. According to Sommer's personal file in the Nazi Central

Archives (Berlin Document Centre) he joined the party in May 1933. Curiously enough he was not excluded from the party depsite his arrest. On the other hand the file notes that his permission to teach was revoked in 1935 and that he had Jewish relations by marriage (*jüdisch versippt*).

6. *Social Demokraten,* 31 March 1942; *idem,* 2 April 1942; *Stockholm Tidningen,* 21 April 1942.

7. *Grenzbote,* quoting *Gardista,* 11 April 1942; *Gardista,* 29 April; *National Zeitung,* Essen, quoting *Gardista,* 30 April.

8. *De Storm,* 17 July 1942; this was the organ of the Dutch ss.

9. Lahti, 10 July 1942; Fagerholm in *Arbeterbladet,* 6 October 1943; *Hufvudstadsbladet,* 5 October 1943; Radio Motala, 5 October 1943.

10. *Das Hakenkreuzbanner,* Mannheim, 24 December 1943.

11. *Aftontidningen,* Stockholm, 24 August and 5 December 1943.

12. FO 371/31097, X/PO 3703.

13. *Ibid.* It is only fair to add that when the Chelmno story was first published in the Palestinian press it also met with some disbelief.

14. FO 311/31093.

15. FO 371/31097, X/PO 3703.

16. 840. 48 Refugees, 3 September 1942, National Archives, Washington.

17. Wasserstein, *Britain and the Jews,* p. 172.

18. 740.00 116 European War 1939/694 PS/DG 5 December.

19. *Ibid.* 10 December.

20. *Ibid.* 674 10 December.

21. *Ibid.* 625 25 November 1942.

22. *Ibid.* 664.

23. *Schweizerische Kirchenzeitung,* 27 August 1942; *Tribune de Genéve,* 26 September 1942.

24. Karski, *Story of a Secret State* (Boston, 1944).

25. The conversation with Roosevelt was described in some detail in the recollections of the Polish ambassador, Jan Ciechanowski (*Defeat in Victory,* New York, 1948), who was present.

26. *Kurier z Warszawy* (London, 1978).

27. Conversation with Jan Nowak, Washington, 7 September 1979.

28. Personal communication, October 1979. T. Chciuk-Celt described his peregrinations in Poland and abroad in a number of articles published soon after the war (*Nowa-Polska,* London 1945; *Proza Polska,* part II, Paris; *Tygodnik Powszechny,* Krakow 1947; *Nasz Znak,* Stockholm 1951).

INDEX